9/23

42

Third Edition

Introducing Religion
From Inside and Outside

Robert S. Ellwood
University of Southern California

D0368269

PRENTICE HALL
Englewood Cliffs, New Jersey 07632

Library of Congress Cataloging-in-Publication Data

Ellwood, Robert S., 1933-
    Introducing religion : from inside and outside / Robert S.
Ellwood.—3rd ed.
        p. cm.
    Includes bibliographical references and index.
    ISBN 0-13-503566-X
    1. Religion. I. Title.
BL48.E43   1993
200—dc20   92-19824
                                            CIP

My feet were set upon a narrow pathway
Crossing worlds of worlds to find Love's Center;
I shall not return as I.

                                        G.F.E.

For Fay Elanor Ellwood
May she find that path.

Acquisitions editor: *Ted Bolen*
Editorial/production supervision
    and interior design: *Maureen Richardson*
Cover designer: *Maureen Eide*
Prepress buyer: *Herb Klein*
Manufacturing buyer: *Robert Anderson*
Photo Research: *Fran Antman*
Photo Editor: *Lorinda Morris-Nantz*

Cover art: Josef Albers, Homage to the Square Ritardando 1958.
Oil on board, 30 × 30 inches. Collection of Neuberger Museum State University of New
York at Purchase, gift of Roy R. Neuberger. Photograph by Jim Frank.

Collection Neuberger Museum of Art State University of New York
at Purchase. Gift of Roy R. Neuberger.
Photo credit: Jim Frank 8/92

© 1993 by Prentice-Hall, Inc.
A Paramount Communications Company
Englewood Cliffs, New Jersey 07632

All rights reserved. No part of this book may be
reproduced, in any form or by any means,
without permission in writing from the publisher.

Printed in the United States of America

10 9 8 7 6 5 4 3

ISBN 0-13-503566-X

Prentice-Hall International (UK) Limited, *London*
Prentice-Hall of Australia Pty. Limited, *Sydney*
Prentice-Hall Canada Inc., *Toronto*
Prentice-Hall Hispanoamericana, S.A., *Mexico*
Prentice-Hall of India Private Limited, *New Delhi*
Prentice-Hall of Japan, Inc., *Tokyo*
Simon & Schuster Asia Pte. Ltd., *Singapore*
Editora Prentice-Hall do Brasil, Ltda., *Rio de Janeiro*

Contents

Foreword

Gratified by the response which this introduction to the academic study of religion has received, I have prepared a third edition of *Introducing Religion from Inside and Outside* in the hope of making it still more useful to college and university students and to all who are interested in exploring different ways of looking at religion.

The overall scope and organization of the book has remained unchanged, although some of it has been rewritten. Study aids, in the form of statements of chapter objectives, summaries, and a glossary were added to the second edition. Entirely new chapters on religion, art, and ethics have been put into this edition, together with a new appendix giving students suggestions for ways of writing and studying in religious studies classes.

This book continues to represent a *way of thinking* about religion in which understanding of oneself goes hand in hand with understanding this human phenomenon. From the initial definitions of religion to the concluding reflections of how changes in the way we live and think might affect the future of religion, the relation between religion as an outward, visible activity and the inward, invisible matter of how we humans think and experience our lives is an ongoing theme of this book. As the title suggests, religion, like life in general, can be both felt subjectively and looked at objectively. It is hoped that the book will help many readers, each in his or her own way, to do both, and in the process to know themselves better too.

Giraudon/Art Resource

Traditional portrayal of Mecca, the Muslim city of pilgrimage.

Scenarios
for the Real Self

Chapter Objectives

- Formulate and defend the *descriptive* definition of religion that seems best to you. (This means a definition *not* based on what you believe is the right or true religion but one which simply describes what religion is in human life.) Compare the definition you formulate now with what you would have said before reading the chapter.

- Discuss the idea that religion expresses, or intends to express, one's real self—that its acts are "scenarios for the real self."

- Explain why, at least from the religious point of view, the ideas of real self and ultimate reality are inseparable, so that to talk about one you must also talk about the other. Give an example from a religion you know something about.

- Discuss the idea that religion presents another "reality" from the ordinary and is not just concerned with "practical" ends and means.

- Explain the meaning of transcendence, the supernatural, and the sacred in religious studies.

- Discuss sacred space and time.

- Consider how the approach of modern religious studies, especially when allied with social science and psychology, differs from that of most people in the past in understanding religion.

As you read the chapter, also look for important words. The key words defined in the glossary at the end of the book are in boldface type at their first use in the text.

PICTURES OF RELIGION

What is **religion?** Nearly everyone has some idea, perhaps some mental picture, to go with the word. If one tries to turn that idea or picture into a clear, comprehensive definition, however, the task may be surprisingly difficult. Time and again, one may feel one has pushed and pulled one's words until they neatly package the picture and wrap up what in human experience ought to be labeled religion. But wait! Here is an odd corner still sticking out; there something has slipped and a whole side is bare to the sun. The definer has failed to deal with the tribal rain dance, which surely looks like religion but seemingly has nothing to do with ultimate salvation, or with the Buddhist sutra chanting of robed monks in incense-laden temples, which also looks like religion but seemingly has nothing to do with God, at least as God was known amid the mountains of Sinai, where Moses received the Ten Commandments.

In the pages that follow, we will pursue some lines of thought that, if they do not settle the definition of religion once and for all, may at least lead to some fresh perceptions of what religion is and how it works. They may also lay the groundwork for further study of human religion past, present, and future.

Our basic idea will be that religious thought and activity represents one's acting out, or **actualizing**, who one thinks one really is deep within. Religion simultaneously includes a corresponding relationship to our ultimate environment, infinite reality itself. (Of course, who one thinks one really is may not coincide with reality, for there are various kinds of self-deception that can be practiced in these matters. Moreover, not everyone would make the assumption that his or her inner nature has a relation to ultimate and infinite reality. Religion must assume, however, that one can come to know one's true nature, and that it is meaningful and dwells within a universe of meaning with which it can have a relationship.)

First let us look at some of the phenomena that suggest both the diversity and unity of the entity called religion.

Picture the great shrine at Ise (pronounced Ee-say) in Japan on the eve of the Harvest Festival. Ise is the preeminent place of worship of Shinto, the religion of the ancient gods of the island nation. Here at Ise are worshipped Amaterasu, the solar goddess said to be ancestress of the imperial family, and Toyouke, goddess of food and bestower of plenty. Each of these high goddesses has her own shrine, the two nearly identical temples being about five miles apart. Each shrine is a simple, rustic house of unpainted but gold-tipped wood set in a rectangular field spread with white gravel. The field, which holds three or four auxiliary buildings, is surrounded by four wooden palisades. Every twenty years, the entire shrine complex is rebuilt with new wood in exact imitation of the old on an adjacent alternative site, also spread with white gravel.

On the night of the Harvest Festival, torches flare in the crisp October air as a procession of white-robed priests bearing boxes of food offerings, their black wooden shoes crackling like snare drums on the white gravel, approaches the shrine. The priests enter behind the fences and are lost to the observer's view as they carefully spread the plates of rice, water, salt, rice wine, vegetables, and seafood before the encased mirror that represents the presence of Amaterasu. One can, however, hear the shrill, mysterious music of the reed flutes, so suggestive of uncanny divine activity. A prayer is read, and then the offerings are slowly and solemnly removed. The priests next proceed to a smaller shrine on higher ground above the principal temple. This is a shrine to the *aramitama*, the "rough spirit" or aggressive side of the divine Amaterasu. Here offerings are also presented. Later, in early morning while it is still dark, the whole **ritual** is repeated. The following night it is repeated—again, twice—at the shrine of Toyouke. Why it is done twice and why it is done at night are matters lost in centuries of tradition at the Ise shrines (if there ever existed an explicit reason). The very sense of mystery evoked by the feeling of something lingering from a half-forgotten past, and the atmosphere of mystic wonder in which actions seem weighted with meanings the human mind does not quite grasp, give Shinto rites their particular kind of religious aura.

Now turn to another scene. It suggests not only one kind of self-finding religious experience but also one major type of religious personality, the founder of a great religious movement lasting many centuries. Although based on real experiences, the following retelling is a stylized and idealized account of a self-transformative religious experience in a Christian context. It is not presented as being representative of all Christian experience. It offers, however, a subjective counterpart to the preceding religious expression in **rite**, and **subjective** experiences vary, to some extent, from individual to individual. The account shows three common characteristics of such experiences: the rise to a high pitch of feeling followed by joyful calm, the pivotal role of key symbols such as scripture and the internalized image of the founder or savior, and the tendency of such transformative experiences to fall into stylized, paradigmatic patterns as they are remembered or retold. Here is the scene:

An American girl was in her room reading the New Testament and praying. As she read, a vivid image came before her mind's eye. The land rose somewhat, becoming a small hill. He was near the top of the hill, and a crowd was around him. The hill was crawling with them—short, sick, hungry human bodies, bundled in patches of rough handwoven material. She saw Jesus on that hill with all those short, tremulous bodies in homespun around him. He stood out because he was taller, was dressed in

The Grand Shrines of Ise, consisting of the Kotai-jingu, or Naiku (Inner Shrine, pictured here), and the Toyouke-daijingu or Geku (Outer Shrine).

Japan Information Center; Consulate General of Japan, NY.

something a bit fuller and whiter, and was on higher ground. Above all, he had an air of power and calm amidst the suffering, and his hands were raised in healing. His face had in it a simple majesty, and his eyes made you want to keep looking at them. Then he seemed to step out of the gospel scene to look directly at her. He beckoned.

She prayed on, and deep and warm feelings about the image sang through her, rising and falling like cresting surfs of molten light. She saw other scenes from the story—the manger, the cross with the bleeding flesh on it, and the garden where the ecstatic women saw the figure in calm white outside the empty tomb. These tableaux grew brighter and brighter. In contrast, her life, as it came into view beside the mind-painted images, was gray, lacking all sparkle or color. Indeed, much in it was worse than gray, things she wished could be washed out or made to belong to another life. She thought of people she liked and even envied who talked of accepting Christ and of being forgiven or being saved. She saw the beckoning hand wanting to make her a part of his story.

She felt herself entering the vision and prayed still more deeply. She then sensed clear and distinct words being spoken in her, almost as though by a new person coming into being within her mind and body, words of accepting Jesus Christ as the center of her personal faith. She arose, tingling, feeling full of light, and almost floating, with a queer but beautiful sort of quiet deep-seated joy. She sat down, with little sense of time or place, just bathing in the new marvelous experience.

ANOTHER REALITY

You have just read two very different vignettes that have one thing in common. Both would be accepted by most people as expressions of human religion, primarily because they are thoughts, feelings, or actions that do not meet ordinary, practical needs in ordinary, practical ways. They do not directly spin cloth or pick grain. Even if they were directed toward a practical end, such as a better harvest, they do not go about it through a practical course of planting and cultivating. They add to what is practical by implying another point of reference and another level of activity. Even if a religious act is a dance or prayer for rain, it does not set about meeting the practical need by using ordinary deduction about cause and effect. Contrary to what some have believed, primitive peoples are nearly as aware as moderns of the distinction between the practical and the nonpractical. Certainly modern Shinto priests at a Harvest Festival are as aware of the facts of meteorology and agricultural science as are Americans expressing gratitude to God on Thanksgiving Day.

Religion, however, adds other dimensions full of color, stylized acts, and symbols that outsiders sometimes see as bizarre and totally nonsensical. In this they are akin to such human practices as wearing clothes even in hot weather, writing poetry, or flying to the moon. These are also impractical things that like religion must be profoundly human, for they are only dimly foreshadowed in the behavior of our animal kin. Something in these gestures must be making a statement about a side of being human that is not just concerned with practicality. They must be trying to tell us—emphatically—that there is another side to being human. Apart from speech and fire, in fact, what most obviously separates even very primitive human societies from animals are things such as haunting masks, paintings on stones of spirit ancestors, and the magic rocks or tufts of grass of sorcerers. They tell us across great gulfs of cultural development that here were creatures who did not just deal in practicalities but who feared pictures in the mind; thought about who they were and where they came from; told stories; sensed the working of indirect invisible currents of force in the cosmos as well as the obvious; and doubtless knew wonder, humor, joy, and dread.

Even more puzzling, if the only point of life were to know in a practical way how to eat, drink, reproduce, and fend off death as long as possible, is that side of religion that does not relate to practical means or ends. It is hard to see any practical point to experiences of salvation or mystical rapture or any practical value to such means toward them as are usually urged—reading scriptures, praying, accepting a saving doctrine or figure (as did the girl caught up in the New Testament), chanting, yogic postures, and so forth. Yet such things are far from uncommon. Indeed, it can be observed that often those people whose lives seem to be focused primarily on meeting practical needs and solving practical problems are the ones most likely to keep some counterbalancing area of life secure for its opposite. They are careful to hold sacred one day a week, to read the scriptures a bit after a hard day's labor in the fields, or to put an offering at the household shrine before going out to work.

Religion is made up of gestures that make no sense at all if ordinary practical reality is all there is; if the universe is only matter and space; if humans are only organisms that feed, mate, and die. If such were the case, religion might still be explained as a widespread psychological quirk, but it would not have grounding in any reality, inner or outer. Religion always presupposes a reality other than the visible. This other reality can hardly be weighed or measured and is usually seen and heard only with the eyes and ears of the soul. Yet, religion affirms, it is the true undergirding of the visible and tangible universe and is somehow also submerged in the depths of consciousness. Religion declares that, compared to that reality, what we think about most of the time is like sound and foam on the surface of a deep lake or the hopping about of grasshoppers beneath the infinite sky.

TRANSCENDENCE

The added dimension implied by religion is often called **transcendence**, which means "climbing across" or "going beyond." Students of religion have often made the existence of transcendence a central point in any definition of religion. Thomas Luckmann, for example, has argued that the essence of religion lies in the ability of humans to transcend or go beyond their biological nature by means of the cultural construction of universes of meaning—music in place of noise, art in place of the haphazard coloration of nature, societies and political systems in place of herd instincts. These cultural constructions are objective and condition moral and social behavior and even one's inner, subjective experience.[1] **Supernaturalism**— concepts of God or gods—expresses transcendence in the language of a society. By this definition, social and political structures and scientific worldviews that construct universes of meaning in which human life is lived as more than strictly biological would be included along with symbol systems involving gods. Thus everything really human is religious.

Peter Berger, although accepting the basic type of argument pursued by Luckmann, feels that his understanding of religion is so broad as to lose usefulness. Berger argues that it is necessary to distinguish between, for

[1] Thomas Luckmann, *The Invisible Religion* (New York: The Macmillan Company, 1967).

example, a scientific and a strictly religious view of the cosmos even though there is value also in showing that the two can function in parallel ways. Berger would say that the term *religion* should be used only for systems that establish a *sacred* cosmos.[2]

The term **sacred**, as it has been used by such historians of religion as Rudolf Otto and Mircea Eliade (to be discussed in Chapter Two), indicates a reality not only transcendent over biology but also transcendent over the ordinary human in a way that implies another order of reality. Indeed, as Otto would have said, it suggests something "wholly other."[3] It creates in humans a special kind of reaction not induced by mere scientific or social transcendences—a sense we are dealing with reality that is in some way alive, tremendously alive, that outcrops in our world in specific times and places (examples: festivals, visions) and to which we can relate.

The sacred is not only conceptual but is also a power and presence with definite demarcations—within one's mind and probably outwardly by such signs as the gates of a shrine or the doors of a church and the special, different atmosphere behind them. Otto spoke of the sacred as the **numinous**, as "mysterium tremendens et fascinans," a tremendous yet fascinating mystery, which evokes in those brought near it deep responses that combine wonder, fear, awe, attraction, dread, and love.

The sacred, according to Otto, can seem uncanny, weird, even terrible. It is always a breaking through of "otherness," yet people, despite a wholesome timidity, are drawn toward it, for it possesses a fullness of reality beside which all else is gray and empty. It has the feel of the Ise shrine on the night of the Harvest Festival or of Jesus amidst the sick or in the believer's heart. Religion, Berger claims, is the enterprise by which a "sacred cosmos" is established—a universe of meaning that ratifies the social order and moral values and above all gives individuals what sense of meaning and relation to the cosmos they have. It is centered on some form of the power and presence of the numinous, sacred realities that are transcendent above the human order as the human order is above the biological.[4] It is a three-story universe instead of a two-story structure.

Robert Bellah has emphasized this point by speaking of religion as "transcendent experience"—as a level of consciousness rather than a particular kind of concept that transcends both the biological and the human.[5] He also stresses, however, that this level of consciousness and experience is necessarily expressed in **symbols**, verbal, visual, or whatever. "The

[2] Peter L. Berger, *The Sacred Canopy* (Garden City, N.Y.: Doubleday & Company, Inc., 1969). For the discussion of Luckmann, see especially pp. 176–77. See also their joint work, Berger and Luckmann, *The Social Construction of Reality* (Garden City, N.Y.: Doubleday & Company, Inc., 1966).

[3] See Rudolf Otto, *The Idea of the Holy* (London: Oxford University Press, 1950).

[4] Berger, *The Sacred Canopy*, p. 25.

[5] Robert Bellah, "Transcendence in Contemporary Piety," in *The Religious Situation*, ed. D. Cutler (Boston: Beacon Press, 1969).

experience must be symbolized in order to be completed as experience."[6] Yet the particular symbol used, although of great meaning within the context of a culture and an individual life, is ultimately less important than the way that a symbol successfully establishes the existence of transcendent experience and enables others to move into its orbit, as did the symbol of Jesus for the girl living nearly two thousand years after him.

The philosopher Alfred North Whitehead has spoken of symbolism in this way: "The human mind is functioning symbolically when some components of its experience elicit consciousness, beliefs, emotions, and usages, respecting other components of its experience. The former set of components are the 'symbols,' and the latter set constitute the 'meaning' of the symbols."[7] Symbols, in other words, are like bridges. They enable us to link, to relate, to cross between one experience and another. They show how one experience has meaning for another and can even form the ordering nucleus of others. A symbol can be polyvalent—it can have different, but related, meanings in different contexts.

The cross in itself is a symbol of the death of Jesus Christ. The cross in a church builds a bridge between that event and today by indicating that one can today find self-transcending meaning in that event and that an important institution can be built around the meaning. The cross on the crown of a European king shows that the event and its meaning can also legitimate the general social order that gives people their place in communities and repels chaos.

Conceptualizations of what the sacred reality *is* are like symbols of the sacred within the mind. (They may, of course, correspond to what the sacred really is.) These conceptualizations are our ideas of the divine. As we shall see later, they may take the form of a personal God, an impersonal absolute; of a universe of many gods; of a human figure like the Buddha; or of spirits and ancestors. These conceptualizations function as sacred symbols *within* the mind, building bridges from one area of its experience to another, just as do crosses or Muslim minarets *outside* the self in the fabric of man-made culture, or those sacred trees and mountains where religion has seemed to break through in the midst of nature.

BRIDGES FROM THERE TO HERE

Returning to Bellah's thought, we note that for him symbols are essential just because there is a need for bridges, since two points of reference are

---

[6] Personal communication by Robert Bellah to Morris Augustine and Richard Kalish. Cited in Morris J. Augustine and Richard A. Kalish, "Religion, Transcendence, and Appropriate Death," *The Journal of Transpersonal Psychology*, 7, 1 (1975), p. 7.

[7] Alfred North Whitehead, *Symbolism: Its Meaning and Effect* (New York: Capricorn Books, 1959), pp. 7–8.

involved—transcendent experience and human experience.[8] Symbols complete the experience itself because only they can bring these two together; even the one having the experience is human and needs symbols to relate the experience to oneself and to communicate it to others or enable others to participate in a similar experience. We need symbols, as Whitehead's definition shows, even to relate different parts of our own minds.

Words are such symbols, and it could be argued that their function in enabling us to think things through to ourselves is even more important than their function in communicating to others. (Try thinking through a fairly complicated idea totally without employing words, without "talking to yourself.") Certain gestures, mental pictures, feelings, and acts by which we signify to ourselves the relation of one experience to another are also symbols we use to talk to ourselves—to relate one part of our experience meaningfully to another.

Symbols are necessary to complete the transcendent experience that underlies religion because religion, above all other human affairs, implies two realms that need to be bridged and related. (The chief priest of the ancient Romans, like the modern pope, was called *pontifex*, which means "bridge-builder.") The other, invisible reality implied by religion can only be communicated to others or even to oneself by symbols having their being in this side, the visible and audible side, of reality. Yet symbols must point toward and participate in the other side in such a special way as to make them stand out amidst all else on this side that is visible or audible. That is what affords them, from our perspective, those qualities of numinousness, uncanniness, mystery, and fascination that entitle them to be called sacred.

Such religious symbols are much the same as what the historian of religion Joachim Wach has called "forms of **religious expression**."[9] Religious symbols are not only such discrete artifacts as crosses or images of a Buddha but also religious concepts, persons, services, groups, institutions, or practices—whatever is like a bridge, signpost, sentence, or activity set up between the religious reality and this side. The forms of expression really comprise together the whole of what can be called the phenomena of religion—the things that appear around numinous or transcendent experience, from art to ethics.

According to Wach, there are three basic forms of religious expression: the **theoretical**, which covers what is thought and said, the stories, rhetoric, doctrines, and ideologies of religion; the **practical**, which includes what is done, the rites, worship, spiritual techniques, and customary practices; and the **sociological**, referring to the types of groups, leadership,

---

[8] Robert Bellah, *Beyond Belief* (New York: Harper & Row, Publishers, Inc., 1970).
[9] Joachim Wach, *Sociology of Religion* (Chicago, Ill.: University of Chicago Press, 1944), pp. 17–34.

Tea Garden in Golden Gate Park.

Peter Menzel/Stock, Boston

an interpersonal relations that appear. All these are best understood if they are seen as ways in which one component of experience—the transcendent experience—is eliciting a response in the form of consciousness, belief, gesture, action, or interpersonal interaction in another and so becomes an interpretative bridge between the two. (Later in this book, we look in more detail at these three forms. Chapter Four deals in large part with the practical form of rite and related practices. Chapter Six treats the sociological side of religion, showing how a religious group or institution is in itself a symbol of transcendent reality. Chapter Seven discusses the theoretical form of religious expression and endeavors to demonstrate how religious words, sentences, stories, and concepts are symbols in several different ways at the same time.)

Think again of the notion of an inner reality, an invisible but more real reality than the outer, concealed like bones beneath the flesh, which religious expression presupposes. Religion wants both to perceive it and to call it into perceivable and participatory reality. Religion is both an X-ray and a drum calling dancers to the floor. On its contemplative side, religion wants to see and know what the inner reality is, to perceive it with awe and wonder and even love. On its active side, it wants to create rituals, dances, words, books, and moods in which the inner comes to life. In the Ise Harvest Festival, as in any church service or even in looking at a piece of sacred art, one *sees* and, if one fully participates, enters the other side. That is why in religious rites people may wear garments, say words, play music, and even walk and gesture in ways different from someone on the street, in ways that make no sense on any other grounds than religious reality. It is as though one had crossed an invisible boundary to a very different country, as Dorothy crossed the Great Sandy Desert from Kansas to Oz.

Nevertheless, the other worlds of religion—the world of the Harvest Festival when humans become co-workers and exchangers of gifts with the life-giving deities, the fresh new inner world of becoming a new person in Christ, the world of spiritual reality evoked by Mass, Yom Kippur, or dancing before Krishna—are not just fantasy alternative worlds like Oz. For the religionist, they are *more real* than the outer universe. To call them into being is to *see things as they really are* or to *act in accordance with the way things really are*, regardless of appearances.

People may differ about which proffered religious reality is the way things really are and may think that others than their own are no more real than Oz. It is, however, important to realize that to every real believer, at the moment of transcendent experience, the religious world is the real world—a reality greater, more profound, and older than the deepest sea or the oldest mountain on this side.

This brings us to perhaps the profoundest thing about religion's self-understanding that can be put into words: in religion one is one's real self. (We mean, of course, that this is how a believer experiences himself or herself in religious participation.) In religion one acts out who one really is; the real self is the one who participates in transcendent experience and through it enters the other side. Religion may be called *scenarios* for the real self. Its theme is "I am a somebody," and in it, if not in the outer world, one becomes that somebody. In the outer world one may be just another face on the street, another hand in a factory or field, or another presence bobbing up and down in the circle of family and friends, sometimes in and sometimes out in the lotteries of kinship and love. When one's religious world takes form around one, in rite or prayer or meditation, one becomes what one really and always is, a beloved child of God, a flame of the eternal fire, or a member of the great dance of gods and wheeling seasons.

BECOMING A SOMEBODY

What is the difference between a somebody and a nobody? First, a somebody has a sense of place. He or she belongs—to family, to community, to the universe. Second, a somebody has an inner place—an inner identity he or she can really accept—and even if one does not always exemplify it or even recall it consciously, somehow on a deeper level one knows it is there. A nobody, on the other hand, feels like a wallflower in the dance of life and like wastepaper instead of an identity card inside. Religion old and new has tried to meet these two needs for place in manifold and often dramatic ways. In rites like the Shinto Harvest Festival, in sanctifying family life, or in making church or temple a center of community life, it has made the biological and social units to which one belongs important enough—and closely enough related to the transcendent level—to afford one a sense of absolute place in them.

Religion draws maps of the invisible world—the real, bones-of-the-universe world—in the architecture and location of temples and shrines and in their art and symbols. When one is around them one can feel near the way things are, which is the same as being near place and home. The realities so represented step out of the shrine for the believer to be interiorized as guarantees of his or her own inner place.

Religion may even offer a place to ostensible outsiders, such as holy men, monks, wanderers, widows, orphans, and the insane, who are often given residences and special places to pray and accept alms in or around temples and churches. Religion often suggests that though people like these seem at disjuncture with ordinary society, they are actually closer to God or the religious reality than the ordinary, and so require special veneration as living signs on the map of the invisible world.

Whatever the identity, however, the devout religious participant feels that the other religious identity is the real one; in religion he or she is an actor in a play that is true and not just made up. The true identity can be thought of as the quality that comes through in those snapshots of friends and loved ones that cause us to say "This is *really* so-and-so." Sometimes a picture catches a particular smile or crinkling of the eyes to provoke that reaction. Even if it is a look the person pictured has only once a week or so, in some unfathomable way it shows who that person really is. Similarly, there are times when we *feel* as though we are now being who we really are, even if it is only on rare occasions. Ideally, religion facilitates those occasions.

Not all religious experience, of course, provides this feeling for everyone. A lot of religious participation is not right in that sense for many participants. For some, religion indeed seems more like acting out a false and made-up role than almost anything else they do. Some people have experiences that give them a sense of who they really are mostly outside of formal religion—in exploring nature, in sports, in love, even in their work. Our purpose now, however, is to understand religion, and the first realization to be grasped in the quest for this understanding is that what is implicitly *intended* in the acts and attitudes of religion is to make one who one really is in the largest frame of reference.

Religions may have any number of practices, teachings, and names that assure one that the real self afforded by the faith is oneself as seen from the highest perspective, from a mountaintop where the view is unlimited. This is the one thing all religion does and is what separates it from that which meets only biological or limited psychological needs. In studying religion, one must realize that in any significant religion many people have found that sort of identify, and for some that is doubtless the most important fact in life.

Who one *thinks* one really is and who one really is may be two different things. A self is a bewildering and complex thing whose riddle is not necessarily solved just by one religious adjustment. The theologian Paul Tillich has spoken of "pseudo," "crypto," and "quasi" religion, and no doubt there are many religious conceptions, as well as nonreligious conceptions, of the self that are partial or evasive ways of dealing with the problem of who one is rather than actually helping toward becoming one's real self. To understand the meaning and power of religion, we must understand its intention and the fact that it does work as a real self-identity for many, many people. Although to be a real self may be an ideal, it is striving after such ideals that leaves cultures and societies in the wake; the forms of religious expression are the waves and surf above the underlying current toward the real self. Despite qualifications, then, it seems that to think of religion as scenarios for the real self, as ways of acting out and so becoming who one really is, provides an understanding of religion that is most conducive in an inner empathy with what it means to religionists themselves.

SACRED AND PROFANE

The distinction between one's real self—the clear, genuine, authentic identity—and a false, empty self without place is a manifestation (perhaps the most fundamental manifestation) of something very basic to human thought, making distinctions. For religion, though, this distinction is not only within oneself but is also reflected or observed in the outer world as well. Some outer times, places, people, or modes of behavior are most compatible with the real self and others with the false self.

Scholars of religion in the tradition of Emile Durkheim and Mircea Eliade (to be discussed in the next chapter) have talked about this distinction as one religion makes between the *sacred* and the *profane*. Eliade rightly tells us that for religious persons, the world is "nonhomogeneous."[10] Certain times and places have a special quality about them. The sacred is touched by the numinous; it inspires awe, wonder, and dread because it

[10] Mircea Eliade, *The Sacred and the Profane* (New York: Harcourt Brace Jovanovich, Inc., 1959).

has a feel of transcendent presence, of pristine power, and of being itself unmatched by the circles of the profane. The profane is not cursing but just plain, drab, ordinary reality as we live it in the context of empty and meaningless workaday lives. The nonhomogeneous quality of religious life, though, indicates that some times and places have for the religious person more of a sense of the sacred about them than do others. They are times and places when one can best act out a scenario for the real self. It may be that an ordinary, secularized, modern individual feels nothing different in a cathedral or temple than in a factory or city park. That would be far from the case for one for whom the cathedral or temple actualizes the real self and provides access to the farther ranges of one's infinite environment. It is in this perspective that *sacred space* and *sacred time* must be appreciated.

Sacred space is the precincts of temples or churches, holy shrines, or sacred hills—any place that has a special, different, awesome feel about it as a spot where the transcendent power breaks through. When you are in a church or temple, even if nothing is happening, you may feel something special that makes you want to walk quietly and talk in hushed tones. It is a different aura from walking down the street or going to school or the store. You may, however, get a similar feeling in the midst of a lovely grove or on a mountaintop—and these places have also been made sacred down through the ages. The difference is that a real sacred space is seen as a place where gods descended to earth, visions (as at Fatima in Portugal in this century) were experienced, the creation of the world began, the central pillar of the earth stands, or access to the transcendent world above is particularly easy (as at Mecca for Muslims or Mount Zion in Palestine for medieval Christians.)

Sacred time is the different time of festivals, rites, sacred stories, or holidays—any block of time in which the flow of ordinary, one-thing-after-another time stops and the transcendent, where time goes at a different rate or ceases altogether, takes over. The time of Mardi Gras or Carnival in Latin countries is an example. At Carnival, one can wander through the streets, seeing brilliant costumes, hearing lively music, dancing, laughing, without thought of past or future, just being there full of joy. This is close to the way a real self feels, and the festive atmosphere makes it possible. Sacred time can also be a solemn rite, such as the Roman Catholic High Mass, the Greek Orthodox Liturgy, or a formal Buddhist rite with offerings and chanting of scriptures accompanied by drums and bells. In a different way, these can lift one into a place where ordinary time stops and one feels united to what really is, beyond all change or dimension.

Sacred space and time are felt by the religious to be sources of power and especially of rejuvenation or renewal. Eliade tells us that is because they are felt to be like continuing islands of the beginning, the time when the gods were strong or God was vigorously active and the world was made. Ordinary time and space seem to run down, becoming thin and gray, but in sacred time and space it is as though the clock were wound back up, the first sunrise had ventured back to the east again, and what had become unraveled were reknitted. To participate in sacred space and time is to bathe again in the power of the beginning or its restitution. To the Shintoist, to worship in the sacred space of Ise at the sacred time of the Harvest Festival is to return to the primal "Divine Age." For the Christian,

United Nations

Worshippers preparing for a Hindu religious festival in Nepal. The special marks they are applying to their faces will help establish the festival as a sacred time and place involving persons symbolically identified with their gods.

receiving baptism or holy communion, probably in a sacred place full of signs and symbols of faith, is a trip back to the New Testament power and presence of Jesus Christ.

A SIMPLE AWARENESS
AND A COMPLEX HISTORY

In the first chapter of this book, we have centered an understanding of religion around the idea of being a real self—that is, one who has a full sense of unity within oneself and with all that is, and so feels what we call meaning and fulfillment.

How did this simple real self-awareness come to have such a complicated grip on human life and such an elaborate set of ways of working itself out? At least part of the answer, as one might suspect, lies in an equally complex history. Tracing its outline is the task of the next chapter. First, a preliminary word or two about that chapter. Because it is the pivotal point relative to a general study of religion, the matter of the emergence of human religion at the dawn of human history (speculative as it is) is given preeminent attention. The major periods of religious history, each of which has responded to new experiences of what it means to be a real self and has shown that response through new symbols and new networks throughout the world, are outlined in very cursory form.

We pause a bit longer, though, at the end of the next chapter to take up some nineteenth- and twentieth-century interpreters of religion as an aspect of human life. They are introduced here because one of the most significant of all events in religious history has been the profound change in the way people view themselves and their society that has come with modernization in these last two centuries, and especially with the appearance of such disciplines as social science and psychology.

Not accidentally, it was also only in the nineteenth century that accurate information about all religions began to be circulated worldwide and that people began, often painfully, to reflect in a modern way on the fact that we live in a **pluralistic** world. The hermetically sealed circle of culture and faith in which many premodern people lived, and the abysmal ignorance of others that went with it, is (even though it sometimes still exists) not easy for educated modern people to comprehend fully. That change is, in itself, one of the most important events in religious history.

We shall then conclude the history of religion with a notice of some of the thinkers who have been articulators of that change. (The change itself, of course, was grounded not only in modern intellectual currents but also in modern technology and Western expansion.) Some of these interpreters of religion have been describers, and others have sought to interpret religion in terms of other perspectives, such as psychology, economics, historical forces. It is important to know about them; it is equally important to know what they collectively represent in the history of religion. They mark a new discovery about what it means to be a real self. Let us turn from the real self to the story of discoveries about it and the way it has manifested itself through the language of the sacred.

SUMMARY

Ideally, the attitudes and actions of religion spell out who one is in one's real self, that is, who one is in relation to ultimate reality. Religion presupposes another reality from the ordinary and another side of the human from that merely concerned with practical goals. Its attitudes, symbols, and rites make this side evident and allow one to participate in it, thereby becoming one's real self rightly related to ultimate reality. This ultimate reality may be called the transcendent or supernatural, and in religion it has the qualities of being sacred and numinous, full of mystery and power. It is communicated to humankind through symbols, concepts, objects, or acts which tell something of the nature of the transcendent and evoke feelings proper to it.

The expressions of religion, of the sacred in this world, are diverse and make any religion a collection or network of many different things, not just one thing. Religion has theoretical, practical, and sociological expression, that is, expression in ideas and words, in worship and acts, and in groups and social relations. Religion does, however, tend to polarize the world and human experience into sacred and profane—that which is, however remotely, aligned with the real self and ultimate reality and that which is at odds with it. In particular, traditional religions are likely to set apart sacred places, such as temples, and sacred times, such as festivals and holy days.

Religion offers both joys, such as those of sacred space and time, and strictures enjoining people to uphold the society's values and avoid **taboos**. These work together to keep society on an even keel, but if the two become unbalanced religious change may result.

Religion has a long and complicated history. In modern times the objective study of religious history and patterns has grown.

NASA

This view of the Earth from the Moon reminds us that our world is a planet, with a tumultuous history millions upon millions of years long.

Chapter

2

History of Religion on Planet Earth

Chapter Objectives

- Ask yourself what was the most important step for the beginning of human religion.

- Describe some basic features of the religion of prehistoric hunters, such as initiations, shamanism, and the sacred meaning of the animal and the hunt.

- Discuss new developments that came to religion with the emergence of agriculture: the new importance of mother goddesses, seasonal festivals, and sacrifice, including human. What is the relation of all these to archaic agriculture?

- Interpret the religion of the ancient empires, with their sacred kingship and elaborate polytheism.

- Present very briefly the names and basic characteristics of the world's great religions: Hinduism, Buddhism, the faiths of China and Japan, Judaism, Christianity, and Islam.

- Discuss the significance of the emergence of the great religions in the "axial age" and the time of the ancient empires, when writing was becoming widespread, society was becoming more and more complex, and trade and political units were expanding.

- Present and discuss the stages of development of the great religions as suggested by this book: apostolic, consolidation, devotional, reform, modern. Discuss some different ways religion has responded to modernity around the world.

- Talk about what you think the future of religion will be.

- Describe the positions of some major modern interpreters of religion, such as Schleiermacher, Hegel, Dilthey, Marx, Durkheim, Troeltsch, Eliade, Weber, Kierkegaard, Otto, and Barth.

HUMAN RELIGIOUS BEGINNINGS

How did religion begin? This question has not been definitively answered and is probably unanswerable because it is put the wrong way. The words *religion* and *begin* are misleading in this question. It was a long time before those elements of human culture and thought we now call religion could meaningfully be separated from acquiring speech, concepts, social order, and awareness of selfhood. **Myth, magic**, ritual, sacred art, and **spiritism** were not just a chapter in the process of becoming human, but in a real sense they *were* the process because fundamentally they were not beliefs but tools with which to think, talk, and know about self and world. They were (and are) a kind of language. Learning the secrets of hunting meant talking about it and acting it out; this meant telling stories about it and doing ritual-like hunting plays in which the souls of the animals and controlling forces in the forest come alive as spirits and gods. Other aspects of life, such as toolmaking and fire, were also important for the emergence of the earliest humans. These advances were probably *inseparable* in their discovery and continuation from the parallel discovery and use of concept and memory, and the formation of human thought was *inseparable* from the use of mythic "pictures in the head" and ritual gestures as pegs on which to put thoughts and memories. Thoughts about birth, feelings, and death arose also; these too needed symbolic pegs in thinking and doing.

The idea of a beginning of human religion is equally misleading. There certainly was no single dramatic moment when it all started. Humankind brought over from the animal world raw material with which to make human religion, including instinctive capacities for ritual, hierarchy, and social morality; for territoriality; for play as a means of setting apart separate time and space for learning and creating paradigmatic situations; and for sensing depth and meaning in certain events. It remained, as the human mind undertook that strange and unprecedented expansion that endowed it with capacity for concepts and choices, to get all these things together in a way that would help humans to think about and handle their world and above all themselves, their own turbulent subjectivity, now alive with memories, moods, and awareness of birth and death.

The most important, distinctively human inputs into religion were the discovery of death and articulation of memory, both dependent on language. Both were reinforced by association with the sacred and the numinous. Most likely both were first thought out through stories, as were all other complex ideas; we first think in stories because we learn sequence of action from the memory that makes one's past a story.

Stories themselves are a kind of language. When the development of language along with a mind powerful enough to use it opened up past and future as well as present, people began to query where all things had come from and what their destiny was. At first the answers were in terms of stories, just as our own memories come out as stories that help to tell us who we are today. We put word symbols around birth, life, and death; talk and chatter about them; tell stories about them; feel their glory or horror in new and different ways; and sometimes forget about them in the fascination of a tale. These stories were (at least the most significant of them) what is called in religious studies **myth**. Myth does not here mean a story that is not true. Rather, myth means a story that presents in the form of a narrative the basic worldview of the society. Whether it tells of the world being made by the gods from the body of a monster or emerging from a cosmic egg or of the first men and women rising out of the ground, it tells a great deal about how the society views itself and about the relation of people to the universe.

Memory is a rough instrument in humans. We do not remember everything that ever happened to us with equal clarity but only certain things, generally those that have a major symbolic or actual bearing on who we think we are today. They are what has gone into making you or me real selves. In the same way, myth and religion do not remember everything just as it was in the sacred past but concentrate on moments from the past that, clothed in symbolic significance, illuminate the present. Not every society has stories about the beginning of the world or even of humanity, and far fewer have any idea of the ultimate end of the world. Nearly all, however, have narratives about gods, animals, divine ancestors, or heroes that help to explain who the people of today are. Most have some concrete idea expressed in myth and burial cultus about what happens to a person after death—for all humans have confronted death, and few are prepared to accept it.

THE RELIGION OF EARLY HUNTERS

The earliest humans were hunters and gatherers. The hunt was very important to them and was a ritual affair. It was typically undertaken after fasting, dancing, and magic. After an animal was taken its spirit might be propitiated, for the archaic hunter saw himself as part of a web of life through which all souls, animals and human, circulated.

Another characteristic feature of primitive religion is **initiation**. Typically all young men, and often young women, experienced an initiation into adulthood that involved isolation and pain, in effect a symbolic death and rebirth. It was a way of acquiring the society's knowledge of memory and death. Indeed, initiation was really a way of learning the symbolic language of the society, for initiates would be taught the myths in the context of experiences to reinforce them.

The most striking representative of early religion is the **shaman**. That is the title, derived from Siberia, given to a figure common in primitive religion (though not universal) who foreshadowed much of what religion was to become. The shaman is much the same as the person more popularly called "witch doctor" or "medicine man." The shaman, through a process usually involving an altered state of consciousness, is able to contact spirits, find lost or strayed souls, heal, and ascertain the will of the gods, all the while providing a dramatic performance that in itself is a religious experience for his public.

According to commentators like Mircea Eliade, the most important fact about shamans is the means by which they come to their office.[1] Theirs is not an easy accession through heredity or professional schooling. Rather, the shaman has felt called out by the gods or spirits and has then acquired mastery over them through an intense initiatory ordeal. He or she has, in the process, felt torn apart, nearly killed, by invisible entities. One has then gone through an arduous training to control them—perhaps given by a senior shaman, perhaps in dreams or visions, perhaps alone deep in the woods or mountains. As one Eskimo shaman put it, "All true wisdom is only found far from men, out in the great solitude, and it can be acquired only through suffering. Privation and sufferings are the only things that can open a man's mind to that which is hidden from others."[2]

As a result, shamans are reborn new persons able to use the spirits as supernatural allies. They are subsequently able to divine and heal; often they enact dramatic scenarios in which, entranced by the beat of their drum or the throb of their chanting, they fly invisibly to the lands of the gods and the dead to intercede or seek out lost and stolen souls. The Altaic shaman in Siberia, for example, sacrifices a horse and transfers its spirit into a wooden mount. For his public performance, he seats himself astride it and beats his drum as he enters a light trance. When fully in the spirit, he moves to a tree trunk, representing the axis of the world, to which platforms have been attached—each of these stands for one of the nine heavens. He climbs them, calling down to the assembled tribespeople his

---

[1] Mircea Eliade, *Shamanism: Archaic Techniques of Ecstasy* (New York: Pantheon Books, Inc., 1964).

[2] Andreas Lommel, *Shamanism: The Beginnings of Art* (New York: McGraw-Hill Book Company, 1967), p. 151.

Arthur Tress/Photo Researchers

Eskimo shaman in Point Hope, Alaska, chanting a whaling song. The arches are made of whale bone.

dialogue with the gods at each level. This shaman also has a scenario in which he rides his wooden steed to the underworld, bearing messages to and from the departed souls of his people.

Shamans are key figures in human religion and culture because they early made the transition from the parareligious behavior of animals to that of beings for whom religion is a quest for the real self. Their call and trances are individual and are given in their ecstatic chants and mutterings a verbalized or artistic meaning. In many archaic societies the shaman is the principal custodian and creator, out of visions, of what art and poetry there is. Their vocabulary is often much larger than that of ordinary people, and they are said to speak the language of birds.

The shaman's vocation is perhaps the first example of division of labor in which an individual is set apart, and supported by the rest, on the grounds of a subjective experience he has had and for the sake of his contribution to the spiritual, psychological, and cultural good of the whole. However bizarre the shaman's behavior may seem (though the psychotherapeutic value of much of what shamans do is being increasingly appreciated), the paleolithic shaman advanced human society far along the road toward the kind of community it now is. He healed mind and body, saw visions, told the future, spoke to the gods, made costumes and artwork rich with symbols from out of his supernatural encounters, and chanted the lore of the gods and the tribe. In his craft lay the seeds of those cultural growths that would lead to the physician, the psychiatrist, the scientist, the priest, the mystic, the magus, the poet, the artist, and the spirit medium. These callings are now quite diverse and not always temperamentally sympathetic to each other, but they have in common a creative use of human inner life and spirit.

Perhaps more than anyone else in earliest times, shamans articulated the most distinctive and striking idea in religion: the existence of gods, supernatural beings, or a supreme God. Shamans, in their vision flights, were not bound by ordinary perception but met and even married spirits and gods who transformed them, or they encountered a high God who had made the world.

For a million years or more, human societies subsisted by hunting and gathering. As is always the case, the forms of religious expression were deeply interwoven with the economic sources of life. The animal, the source of economic life, was a symbol of the ultimate sources. Beasts were bridges from here to there and there to here. As sacrifices they were messengers from one world to another; as totem of a tribe they represented its life.

When looking into the animal's shining eyes, early humans saw an ambivalent spiritual power with which they had to establish a harmonious working relationship, learning the skills and magic that would enable sufficient animals to be taken and the propitiations that would satisfy the spirits of the killed animals and their divine protectors, thus allowing them to return and be taken again. Over the years, as good a spiritual balance as one could hope for in this uncertain world was achieved by the hunting society. Human population was sparse and could not grow beyond what could be supported by a fairly mobile life of following game. Although certain species, such as the giant ground sloth of North America, may have been driven to extinction by paleolithic hunting, archaic hunters learned their ecological niche in the world and generally took no more than was needed. Also, men and women, leaders and followers, were often more equal in the small bands and tribes of archaic hunters than they have been in the later more complex, male-dominated societies of kings and slaves.

ARCHAIC AGRICULTURE

The next development shattered forever this equilibrium. It set humankind off on a course of meteoric growth and change that was very sudden from the perspective of geological or biological timetables. Population grew phenomenally, as it still sometimes grows, when fertile areas were suddenly able to support many times the people they could from hunting. Towns and finally cities appeared where once there had been only wandering bands, and empires where before had dwelt only tribes. Humanity was off on its careening ride in history as we know it, with its incredible misery and splendor and above all the rapid rate of change in the world—a world in its horrors and glories alike so different from that of animals or even primeval hunters.

The catalyst of all this change was, of course, agriculture. Planting and harvesting crops and keeping domestic animals meant a change in the way most people spent most of their time and in the relationship between them and the earth on which they lived. All of which was enough to cause the dramas in which people enacted their real selves to be revised.

Agriculture emphasized the idea (although the thought was not new) that the earth was like a mother; in the religion of archaic agricultural societies appeared a new emphasis on the mother goddess. The turning of the seasons and the sacredness of place understandably became newly important, for agricultural people were nonmigratory and bound to the cycle of seeding and harvest, expressed in anxious planting and protective rites and joyful harvest festivals such as that of Ise.

At the same time a darker side of spiritual experience also appeared. This was the relationship of death to life, the experience that blood and death were necessary for life to flourish, analogous to the seed that seemed to die and be buried in the soil or the animal whose slaughtered body gave life to many. Archaic agriculture was the milieu in which animal and human sacrifice, cannibalism, and headhunting most prospered.

As indicated, however, archaic agriculture also made possible a great increase in population. A given amount of land, if fertile, could support far more farmers than hunters. Furthermore, farmers were bound to one place and often dependent on organized systems of trade, irrigation, and defense against raiders. For this reason agriculture led to the creation of larger political units, particularly along the banks of great rivers where commerce and massive hydraulic works were feasible—the Nile, the Two Rivers of Mesopotamia, the Indus, the Yellow River in China.

ANCIENT EMPIRES

Let us imagine one of those ancient riverside empires, so important as transitions between prehistoric and semimodern culture. In their bosoms appeared writing, philosophy, and the great religions that still flourish.

Here, along the banks of a wide watercourse, a procession of singing priests is moving with the slowness of ancient ritual. Behind them, surrounded by courtiers, comes the king, resplendent in gold cloth and green jade. He is making progress toward the vast burnished temple of the young god who returns to these riverbanks every spring and then grows old with the year. The sacred king opens the planting time by ritually plowing three furrows in the temple courtyard, while incense burns and trumpets blare.

The ancient empires above all idealized order, both human and cosmic, and the two were thoroughly integrated. For them, a real self—usually symbolically personified for all in the king—dwelt as harmoniously as well-tempered ritual or music with the seasons and the gods. Order was far from consistently achieved, but it was the ideal toward which religion, politics, and philosophy strove. That was understandable, for order was the apotheosis of agrarianism; what the farmer even today desires above all else of the universe is security and reliable seasons. The ancient empires, profoundly attuned to agriculture, wished a universe as regular as planting and harvest in a good year. Generally they held a concept of a universal law or regulating principle: Maat in Egypt, Rita or Dharma in India, T'ien or Heaven in China. It embodied the order, and gods above, like kings below, were themselves servants of order and its exemplars and upholders.

One common institution of the ancient empire was sacred kingship. The sovereign would ritually fight and defeat the forces of chaos to create anew the world every year, as in ancient Babylon, or begin the new planting season by wearing colors appropriate to the force of growth and creativity and by plowing the first furrows, as in China. The ruler, like the pharaoh or the Chinese emperor, was no mere political figure. He was a part of the divine order. He represented heaven—the sacred law and primal power—to his people, even as he represented them to heaven. His ritual actions, which occupied a large part of his time, were deemed crucial to society because they mystically harmonized human life with the power of the turning of the seasons and the life-producing work of the gods. It was usually felt that if the king performed his ritual and moral obligations wrongly, nature itself would respond with flood or drought, and society with war or revolution.

The ancient empires also represented the beginning of widespread religious networks, for priests or scholars allied with the court were the king's representatives in far-flung provinces and incorporated the common people (and their gods) into the religious system centering on the king. The religion of the ancient empires exhibited a rich polytheism. Primitives had, to be sure, accepted a plurality of gods and spirits, even as they also often venerated a high god who represented the steady, creative, and regulative force. The ancient empires brought together many tribes, each contributing its own deities to a common pool. Furthermore, the increasing complexity and variety of the new imperial and urban ways of life suggested divine functions unthought of before. The pantheon tended to become a heavenly court that was a celestial model of the earthly, as in China, or a set of options for spiritual experience to match the many temperaments and ways of life of humankind, as in Egypt or India.

Polytheism came to full flower in the ancient empires. It meant not only that there were a great quantity of gods but also that spiritual life had a special quality. For the polytheist, the universe was a rich spiritual complexity with every time, place, and occasion having its own sacred meaning, being in a deep but finite sense its own spiritual center. It was in every grove, mountain, and hearth and in every hour whether of war or love, dread or rapture.

The old heritage of the shaman was perpetuated too. Teachers brought client or disciple through private initiations into a new sacred consciousness. The gurus of India and the mystagogues of the ancient Mediterranean were popular within ancient imperial societies, as they have been before and since. The related mystery religions of the Greek and Roman world spoke of the same quest; they offered elaborate rites, such as those of Eleusis or the Egyptian goddess Isis, to give recipients an assurance of salvation in the life to come.

That increasingly individualized quest for salvation points up a basic religious problem affecting the ancient world; the cosmic and social order it so deeply craved never seemed quite attainable. Things kept changing and would not change back. Try as one would, the old gods would not meet the needs of new generations, and even sacred kings fell as warlords marched back and forth across the earth. Old rituals of familiar tribes and groves faded before a new individualism. In this situation, many a person felt that seeking personal salvation in a better world and adhering only to a deity who could provide it was the best one could do; let society and nature crumble away if they must.

Fundamentally, of course, what was happening was that a new image of what it meant to be a real self was emerging as experience taught new meanings for life and time. A person was not just a part of nature or of a sacred order ruled over by a sacred king but an individual who had to find salvation amid change and even chaos in a hard world. This was not fully understood consciously by everyone, to be sure, but it was what seemed to be suggested by the next great religious development and the new forms of religious expression it brought—new kinds of religious thought, worship, and sociology that often had foci other than harmonizing with nature, the seasons, and the organic society presided over by a sacred king—even though much of the old world was incorporated into the new forms. The next stage was the work of the great religious founders and the great religions started by them, which persist into the world of today.

RELIGIOUS FOUNDERS
AND THE GREAT RELIGIONS

We cannot here discuss in any detail the history and teachings of the major world religions, and other books are devoted wholly to that task.[3] What we shall do is name and identify the most important faiths and discuss briefly the significance of their appearance in history around the time of the ancient empires and the principal stages of their development.

Hinduism is perhaps the most difficult to encompass in a few words, for it includes the vast complex of ideas and practices associated with the culture of India, from yoga to village shrines. Although it has no single founder, its chief philosophical and devotional traditions first emerged in roughly the same period as the founding of the other major faiths. Especially on an intellectual level, its main emphasis is on knowing the divine in all things and oneself and realizing this divinity through meditation or devotion to the gods.

Buddhism started in India with the teaching of Gautama, called the Buddha or Enlightened One (563–483 B.C.E.), but is now established mostly outside of India in Southeast and East Asia. Centering around the *sangha*, or order of monks who are successors of the Buddha's disciples, Buddhism teaches that one attains liberation through meditation and related methods that counteract attachment to partial realities.

Chinese religion should be considered as a whole, even though it is comprised of several strands. Confucianism is based on the teaching of Confucius (551–479 B.C.E.), which emphasizes the good society based on virtue, family loyalty, and a respect for tradition and ancestors affirmed by solemn rites. Daoism, according to tradition ascribed to an older contemporary of Confucius called Laozi, inculcates a more romantic and mystical path aimed at oneness with the Dao, nature or the cosmos. Buddhism and folk religion were also very important in China. Most prerevolutionary Chinese had some relation to all these faiths.

Japanese religion is a comparable matter. Here Buddhism and Shinto, the veneration in lovely shrines of the polytheistic gods of ancient Japan, both have a place in the worship of most people. Confucianism has been very influential too, and more recently a number of new religions have flourished.

In the West, three great monotheistic religions have dominated the spiritual scene for centuries. All three worship a single personal God, and all are rooted in the spiritual experience of Jews in Ancient Israel.

The faith that most directly continues this heritage is Judaism, found in the state of Israel and as a minority around the world. Believing that God

---

[3] See, for example, Robert S. Ellwood, *Many Peoples, Many Faiths* 4th ed. (Englewood Cliffs, N.J.: Prentice-Hall, Inc., 1992).

United Nations

Children worship and learn about religion in a modern Hindu temple in India.

has a special calling for them in world history, serious Jews have kept their identity intact by being faithful to the moral and ceremonial norms of the Law and the passion for righteousness of the prophets.

Christianity traces its origin to the ministry of Jesus, called the Christ or Anointed One (about 4 B.C.E–30 C.E.) Traditional Christianity is based not only on following the moral teachings of Jesus but also on the belief that in Jesus, God worked in a special way for the salvation of humankind. Christianity has taken many forms throughout history, but all have been seen as ways of identifying oneself with God's work in Jesus.

Islam (the name means "submission," submission to the will of God) derives from the ministry of Muhammad (570–632 C.E.) in Arabia. Believing that the Koran, the Islamic scripture, is the final revelation of God given through Muhammad, Islam is concerned with applying the teachings of God in all areas of life, from the Muslim's devout life of prayer to the organization of society. Islam is a simple, deep faith with both legal and mystical aspects.

These great faiths and the five or six human beings who have been founders of major religions have influenced human history far more than countless kings and kingdoms. On the other hand, kings and kingdoms have been deeply intertwined with their histories. Faith has provided integration for large and complex cultures, such as those of India, Japan, and medieval Europe. Religions sweeping across many diverse lands (such as Buddhism, Christianity, and Islam) have carried innumerable cultural gifts with them and have helped missionized lands awaken into the mainstream of history. Sometimes, as in Western Europe, the great religion arose to power only toward the end of the ancient empire stage. Sometimes the great religion aligned itself with an empire (Buddhism in India) or even helped create one (Islam and the Damascus-Baghdad caliphate). In retrospect, though, we can see religion as gestating in the world of the ancient empires but finally helping people to transcend their perspective of sacred king and agrarian/cosmic cycles and to facilitate a sense of internationalism and history. This was particularly true of the three most intercultural faiths, Buddhism, Christianity, and Islam, together with Judaism.

It is significant that all these great religions center on a set of sacred writings or scriptures. They also center on a symbolic pivotal person—the Buddha, Confucius, Jesus, Muhammad—or a pivotal period of history. Even if one quibbles about how important the founder and the scriptures actually were in relation to other factors in the development of the religion, the religious meaning of the emergence of these two new symbolic centers of the sacred was of immeasurably great significance.

If earlier religions found the sacred in the animal, the plant, or the shaman's scenario, as sources of communal life, or in kings and gods, as sources of order, the new great religions found the sacred in a person and in a product of a cultural development, writing. In a symbolic individual, a particular point in the stream of history, and permanently recorded words, the transcendent appeared to put a grid of meaning over the chaos of human life. This change of symbols clearly reflected changes in human life and society and finally in the intuited meaning of what a real self was. The person and the word now transcend nature, plants, ecstasy, and sociopolitical units. The new sacred person and words about him or her go beyond all that, even as did the figure of Jesus for the girl at the beginning of our last chapter.

This period of transition when the founders and great religions emerged has been called by philosopher Karl Jaspers the "axial age." It was a time of transition from prehistoric and ancient empires. People were barely aware of the movement of history and thought (or hoped) either that things had always been and always would be about the same, or that time moved in great cycles. Now some came to understand that time moved forward in an irreversible line (or else in cycles as immense as those of Hindu and Buddhist thought). This was expressed religiously in the idea of a teacher who appeared at one particular point, like Jesus or Muhammad, making time after him in history profoundly different from life before him.

The beginnings of the great religions all have that kind of meaning and impact. In this way they were different from those religions that seemingly had always been. This axial age when the great religions began, lasting roughly from 500 B.C.E. to C.E. 500, was really only a short period in the long history of humanity. Yet only in it (or as far back as 1300 B.C.E., counting Moses in the same category) did the major religious founders appear and great world religions originate. They have spread and changed on a large scale, but no new religions of comparable dimensions have arisen since the birth of Islam some fifteen centuries ago.

Let us now trace, roughly and in outline, the stages of development through which the great religions have passed. Each stage can best be understood as presenting a novel sort of drama that interprets the meaning of one's real self.

The first period may be called the apostolic. It is the first few generations after the founder in founder religions. It is a time of expansion within a culture ostensibly devoted to other values. There is tension and perhaps persecution. It is a time of rapid change in the new religion and of deep-seated personality conflicts and doctrinal debates. Indeed, the forms the religion takes in all the forms of expression are in flux. For a religion that is to survive, enthusiasm is even greater than these difficulties and prevails.

The next period is one of doctrinal and institutional consolidation, of stylization, after a measure of success has been gained within the socio-political order. This period is Buddhism in the empire of Ashoka, Confucianism in Han China, and Christianity in the Roman and Byzantine empires after Constantine. There emerge councils presenting dogmatic definitions, forms of worship meeting the needs of both peasants and converted intellectuals, and institutional structure appropriate to the dominant imperial faith that parallels the state. The doctrinal forms are probably made to tie in with existing traditions of wisdom but are deepened by new symbols from the erstwhile underground faith. One thinks of Han Confucianism, Christianity, and Islam in this stage appropriating forms from Neoplatonism and of Buddhism relating to Vedanta philosophy. The theological emphasis is likely to be a reaction against the radical discovery of history implied by the life and work of the original founder, and movement toward putting his message in terms of external truths that are behind all changes in history and behind the existing forms of worship and structures of society adopted by his religion.

This religious structure is then apt to form the basis to a great civilization, perhaps of new empires but more likely of smaller kingdoms linked by a common international religion. Within them, however, grow the seeds and then the flower of the next religious form, what may be called devotionalism. It is characteristic of high medieval religion in the Christian, Jewish, Muslim, Hindu, and Buddhist spiritual worlds alike. In bhakti in India, Pure Land in Chinese and Japanese Buddhism, or the Franciscan style of devotion in medieval Europe, the emphasis is on the ability of even the simplest to achieve the highest liberation through devotional fervor, faith, and love for God, saints, or Buddhas and bodhisattvas—a goal that might take the wise infinitely longer because of their insistence on proper technique or theological wisdom. In a subtle way, medieval devotion undercuts the hierarchical structure of the medieval type of society by saying it does not matter what class or caste a person is or how wise, as long as the person loves the Lord in his or her heart.

In the next stage, reform, there is an intensification of the devotional mood within a major segment of the religion to the point of a radical break with the tradition, ostensibly in favor of return to its original or pure essence. This generally occurs after about fifteen hundred years of development. One thinks of Kamakura Buddhism in Japan and its Pure Land and Ch'an equivalents in China between C.E. 1000 and C.E. 1500; the kind of radical Hindu bhakti represented by Chaitanya, spiritual father of the modern Krishna Consciousness movement; and the Reformation of Luther and Calvin in Europe. Perhaps Islam, only some fifteen hundred years old now, is now moving into this stage, expressed in the current resurgence of Islamic "fundamentalism."

The last stage we shall here consider may be called the modern. Unlike the previous stages, it does not occur because of the internal dynamics of the history of the particular religion but is necessitated by developments in the world as a whole. For the last hundred and fifty years or so, all the world religions have had to adjust to the whole panoply of developments we call modernization: the Industrial Revolution; Western expansion (and then retreat); a rapid pace of change; new scientific ideas; population growth; educational growth; the worldwide spread of consumerism, nationalism, and Marxism. They have reacted to all this in many ways. Different parties in each religion have, in fact, taken diverse tacks: rigid conservatism, reformism, nationalism, thorough-going adjustment to the new. None, however, are what they were before.

One event of especial interest to us in the last stage of the history of religion (to date) is the emergence of the *study* of religion. The academic study of the history and comparative forms of religion as a phenomenon within human life, in contrast to its study from the point of view of one religion or another, is (with a few ancient exceptions) a new departure and one that owes much to the modern mentality and the pluralism (experience of many religions and lifestyles coexisting side by side) it has facilitated. We shall close this chapter with a review of some of the persons whose ideas have affected the modern study of religion as a general human experience.

MODERN INTERPRETERS OF RELIGION

Friedrich D. E. Schleiermacher (1768–1834), especially in his earlier writings, presented a view of religion that has been quite influential in the development of its general study. He saw religion as starting from a special feeling of wonder toward and dependence on the whole cosmos. This high feeling can become clouded by sensuous feelings, or it can be enhanced by communication of it through powerful symbols and through persons filled with it, such as Jesus Christ. The feeling itself does not necessarily have anything to do with morality, rational knowledge, or any particular concept of God. These may come later, as ways of symbolizing and passing on the experience. Schleiermacher's teaching provided a way of objectively understanding the great religions and their symbols while maintaining empathy with them. These religions, he thought, had grown up around figures who have preeminently radiated the religious feeling. As symbol systems, they retain the aura of that feeling and so serve as a means to turn it on again.[4]

The German philosopher Georg W. F. Hegel (1770–1831) viewed religion as a way in which the human spirit becomes aware of itself as *spirit*, that is, as a manifestation of the One. Hegel's spirit (*Geist*) can also be rendered "mind." Consciousness, the searchlight of spirit or mind within humanity trying to know itself, cannot find a permanent object for its concentration outside itself and so finally must turn back upon itself and discover itself as the One. Until spirit finally achieves this, however, it creates images, forms, symbols, and ideas (in a word, religion) outside of itself as guideposts and reflections of this quest. History, for Hegel, is a process by which spirit drives on to reach the stage of absolute knowledge, "spirit knowing itself as spirit." When this comes, religion, as a reflexive mediator of spirit's self-knowledge, is no longer needed. Whether or not one accepted the full Hegelian system, the ideas that the origin of religion lay in the mind's trying to know itself and that the history of religion was a history of the evolution of consciousness had profound consequences.[5]

Wilhelm Dilthey (1833–1911), in his work on the history of ideas, stressed that the metaphysical systems of each age are symbols of the way the world was experienced by that age, just as are its art and literature. One can see that this kind of approach induces a mood of relativism that defuses the intense, anguished confrontation with decision others would feel ought to be a part of our traffic with ultimate things. But it also makes possible a more or less open appreciation of ways of faith and culture in all times and places.[6]

---

[4] See Friedrich D. E. Schleiermacher, *The Christian Faith*, 2nd ed., trans. Hugh Ross Mackintosh and J. S. Steward (Edinburgh: T. & T. Clark, 1928); and *On Religion: Speeches to Its Cultural Despisers*, trans. John Oman (New York: Harper & Row, Publishers, Inc., 1958).

[5] See Georg W. F. Hegel, *The Phenomenology of Mind*, trans. J. B. Baillie (London: George Allen & Unwin, 1931); and *The Philosophy of History*, trans. J. Sibree (New York: Dover Publications, Inc., 1956).

[6] See H. A. Hodges, *The Philosophy of Wilhelm Dilthey* (London: Routledge and Kegan Paul, 1952).

Karl Marx (1818–1883), seeing Hegel's evolution of spirit to be manifest in social and economic history, combined that insight with Ludwig Feuerbach's (1804–1872) theory of religion as a projection of human nature. Marx viewed religion as a product of a stage in human development in which inner contradictions are not yet completely resolved. It is basically alienation between classes of society that produces those psychological aberrations that result in religious projection. For the exploiting classes, religion is a means of controlling the masses and also of justifying their own role. For the exploited, ideas such as heaven and hell and God's love are desperately desired compensations for a hard lot. As in Hegel's final era of absolute spirit, however, when there are no more contradictions, no more exploitation, the need and desire for religion vanishes.[7]

Emile Durkheim (1858–1917) expounded the cultural basis of religion in another way. Holding that religion is essentially grounded in communal life, he taught that religious feelings stem from the *social effervescence* of primitive tribal societies—from the sense of timeless joy and coherence created by the festival. Religious objects, persons, and practices—the sacred—were ways of creating and perpetuating the community that realizes itself in festival. For Durkheim religion is essentially a social feeling that can be created in any number of external settings. Thus, there is no religion that is false.[8]

The German Protestant theologian Ernst Troeltsch (1865–1923) believed, following Kant, that a religious *a priori*, or absolute, exists that cannot simply be explained away by sociology or psychology. Its expression, however, takes many forms in different cultures and personalities, none of which are in themselves absolute. His work in describing types of religious groups has been of great importance in the study of religion.[9]

Several of these strands of the social and cultural approach have been brought together in the work of Mircea Eliade. The title of one of his books, *The Sacred and the Profane*, is a key to his thought. Like Troeltsch, Eliade accepted that there is a religious absolute that is *sui generis*, of its own type and not reducible to anything else. At its core is humankind's yearning for transcendence of the ordinary, profane world of space and time, to share in the mythic and absolute world of origins, the other time when the gods made the world or heroes walked the earth. Times of religious festival and rite are sacred times that try to recapture that strong time; temples, holy mountains, and sacred trees represent sacred space, places set apart as ways of access to the other world. Sacred space and time may also be

---

[7] See Karl Marx and Friedrich Engels, *On Religion* (New York: Schocken Books, Inc., 1964); and John C. Bennett, *Christianity and Communism* (New York: Association Press, 1951).

[8] See Emile Durkheim, *The Elementary Forms of the Religious Life*, trans. Joseph Ward Swain (New York: Collier Books, 1961).

[9] See Ernst Troeltsch, *Social Teachings of the Christian Churches*, trans. Olive Wyon (New York: The Macmillan Company, 1931).

interiorized, as by yogis and mystics; a charismatic individual may himself or herself be a sacred object.[10]

For the German sociologist of religion Max Weber (1864–1920), religion was best understood as a means toward knowledge and power. It provides knowledge of the supernatural and ways of managing and manipulating it. For Weber this knowledge and power were primarily transmitted to and through individuals who possessed charisma or special divine gifts—magicians and priests—rather than, as for Durkheim, residing in society as a whole. But he believed that the social impact of religion and such religious specialists was very great.[11]

Another style of interpretation of religion that has been immensely influential in modern thought has been the psychological or psychoanalytic represented by such thinkers as William James, Sigmund Freud, and Carl Jung. It is discussed in the next chapter. One kind of interpretation that must be presented here, however, as a counterbalance to the social and cultural is the existential and orthodox (better, neo-orthodox), which starts with religion not as a cultural phenomenon but as an absolute reality impinging on the subjective consciousness of an individual and forcing him or her to react and choose.

Soren Kierkegaard (1813–1855), a Danish theologian, vigorously opposed Hegel. He said that religion is a *choice*, not just the way a spirit knows itself through the process of a long historical unfolding in which the ordinary individual might seem to count for little. The point is emphasized by the title of one of his books, *Either/Or*. One cannot know what the plan of God in history is because one cannot know the mind of God. Religious faith is simply choosing God when the arguments for or against God seem more or less equally likely. The alternatives to choosing God are a life of merely seeking aesthetic satisfaction or of fulfilling ethical duty; both options carry with them the seeds of inner despair. Kierkegaard made possible for the history of religions, as well as for philosophy, a new way of understanding religion, not according to its social, cultural, or symbolic expression but according to the nature of the personal subjectivity—the way one is inside—of the one who makes the *choice* it demands. Subjectivity, he and the **existentialist** thinkers who followed him said, is a world of its own and can never be reduced to rationalized categories.[12]

The German theologian and historian of religion Rudolf Otto (1869–1937) perceived religion as experience of the holy, or the numinous, that is

---

[10] See Mircea Eliade, *The Sacred and the Profane* (New York: Harper & Row, Publishers, Inc., 1961); *Cosmos and History* (New York: Harper & Row, Publishers, Inc., 1959); and *Patterns in Comparative Religion* (New York: Sheed & Ward, Inc. 1958).

[11] See Max Weber, *The Sociology of Religion,* trans. Ephraim Fishoff (Boston: The Beacon Press, 1963).

[12] See Robert Bretall, ed., *A Kierkegaard Anthology* (Princeton, N.J.: Princeton University Press, 1951).

always mysterious, strange, tremendous, and fascinating. It draws men by its uncanny power, yet also fills them with dread. It has a weird, intrusive feeling and may be grisly and uncomfortable, yet men run from it in vain. In a person like Martin Luther, and likewise in the temples and taboos of religious people through the ages, Otto saw the marks of this kind of encounter with divine Otherness. Religion was, for Otto, a kind of feeling, but its difference from mere aesthetics or moral feeling was heavily stressed. One can study the manifestations of this feeling in psychology and symbol and in myth and idea, but only if one first recognizes its unique, autonomous nature.[13]

For the Swiss Protestant theologian Karl Barth (1886–1968) and his followers, the uniqueness of the vertical experience with God was the central spiritual event. Only God can initiate it by revelation. All religions of human origin, whether in the non-Christian world or in the Christian church when it is not founded solely on God's revelation, are attempts by humans to anticipate God and reveal only their alienation from God. Religion, then, is really a human attempt to fill the void left by the absence of God due to human rebellion. Religious phenomena, insofar as they are not based on direct revelation by the Holy One, are of a quite different and lesser nature, though they may serve as reminders of the possibility of true spirituality and of human need.[14]

These are a few figures representative of thought in the latest stages of the history of human religion. Many other thinkers are of equal, or almost equal, importance. Indeed, the day in the sun of some of them is already passing, but they are so monumental in recent history—and so important are their ideas beyond the passing fads and fashions of thought—that they must have a place in even the most haphazard history of religion. At the same time, let the reader, reflecting on this story and these ideas, begins to think out his or her own interpretation of the history of human religion.

SUMMARY

The roots of the planet earth go deep into geological time, and so do the roots of religion, for there are parallels or apparent parallels between certain forms of animal behavior—such as territoriality, ranking, ritual, and play—which remind one of religious behavior or behavior sanctified by religion in human society. However, religion does not emerge until the human awareness of time and death, the use of language and story,

---

[13] See Rudolf Otto, *The Idea of the Holy*, trans. John W. Harvey (London: Oxford University Press, 1950).

[14] See Karl Barth, *Church Dogmatics*, trans. G. W. Bromily and T.F Torrance, eds. (Edinburgh: T. & T. Clark, 1956), vol. I, part 2.

and above all a sense of real self, appear. The earliest stage of religion is that of prehistoric hunters, in which there is typically a sense of the animal or its guardians as sacred and needing to be placated; there is also initiation and shamanism. After the discovery of agriculture, new emphasis is placed on mother goddesses, seasonal festivals, and sacrifice, all understandable among sedentary farmers dependent on the fertility of the earth, seasonable weather, and the power of new life unleashed by death.

When societies coalesced into the large units we may call the ancient empires, such as those of Egypt, Mesopotamia, or China, the underlying desire of these agricultural communities was for stability, expressed in sacred kingship, seasonal rites, and a bureaucratic polytheism. Underneath, however, a thirst for new revelation, monotheism or monism, and personal liberation or salvation was on the increase.

That tendency was expressed in the great religions which emerged in the world of the ancient empires. They are characterized by emphasis on sacred scripture, a historical founder who is in some way a unique expression of divine reality, revelation in historical time, a monotheistic or monistic thrust, and means of personal salvation or liberation. (Not all the great religions have all these characteristics to the same degree or at all, but all have most of them.)

The great religions have subsequently gone through several stages of internal development, which may be summarized as apostolic, consolidation, devotional, reform, and modern, the last representing the crisis that all religions have undergone in the last century or two in responding to the modern world.

One feature of modernity has been the academic study of religion from historical, sociological, and philosophical perspectives: positions range from seeing religion as the historical evolution of spirit (Hegel) to cohesion of society (Durkheim) to the existential, which stresses that faith is a matter of free choice (Kierkegaard).

Alan Carey/The Image Works

Female Zen Buddhist monk in evening meditation.

Oases of the Mind: The Psychology of Religion

Chapter Objectives

- Describe the shifts in "state of consciousness" that we go through as we move from one mood or mode of mental and emotional activity to another; and then discuss how religion accepts the reality of these shifting states of consciousness and evaluates some as better, higher, and closer to the real self in relation to ultimate reality than others.

- Show how our human capacity for development and change through life interacts with religion and religious experience.

- Discuss some important *religious* states of consciousness, that is, states of consciousness often highly valued by religion or usually interpreted religiously, such as the "peak experience," meditation, guilt, power, and dependency.

- Describe what Maslow means by the "peak experience" and what Turner means by "liminality"; discuss the meaning of both in and for religion.

- Summarize the position of such major psychological interpreters of religion as Freud, Jung, and the humanistic psychology school.

- Construct your own model, based on the section on religious development and your own observation and experience, for the role of religion in the various stages of human growth, from infancy to old age.

- Present your views on why childhood seems to be so important to religion, both as an ideal and as something to be gone beyond.

MENTAL SHIFTS

The discussion of psychology of religion centers on the concept of different **states of consciousness**, that is, different ways in which one is aware of oneself and feels oneself, together with the resultant shifts in the way one perceives the world.

In ordinary life we pass through many transitions of consciousness every day. To pass from sleep to wakefulness, or from sleep without dreams to sleep with dreams, is to go from one state of consciousness to another. So is passing, as one nods over studies, from focused attention to diffuse reverie. The state of consciousness during a game is quite different from that in war, or from the deadly serious hunt of a famished man. Intense emotional states, such as fear or rage, bring about their own state of consciousness. Psychological researcher Stanley Krippner has listed twenty basic states of consciousness that range from dreaming, lethargy, hysteria, and rapture to trance, reverie, and the expanded states of consciousness often (though not necessarily) induced by psychedelic drugs.[1]

Think of spending a summer day at the beach. The day may seem wholly uneventful and pointless except for relaxation and fun. Even on such a day, though, one moves through a number of states of mind, most of which in fact have religious parallels. Strenuous physical activity such as swimming or playing ball makes the mind alert and under a certain tension to perform, and it bathes the mind in a mild joy as performance is achieved. In times of quiet reading, the mind is passively receptive and the body is relaxed. A special concentration and excitement ripples through one's senses when talking animatedly with friends, playing out conversation full of warmth and humor. Parents and children together at the beach feel the special warmth of enjoying one another in a situation of considerable freedom and lack of pressure. Finally, there are those contemplative moods that the beach seems especially able to induce. One looks at the enjoyment of others and the sun sinking over the sparkling water in an almost godlike way, and begins to intuit some sort of unity behind it all.

Our streams of consciousness are comprised of unceasing series of shifts like these. One can think of the mind as a piano or organ and of these transitions as the ongoing music. Musical possibilities are virtually infinite,

[1] Stanley Krippner, "Altered States of Consciousness," in *The Highest State of Consciousness*, ed. John White (Garden City, N.Y.: Doubleday & Company, Inc., 1972), pp. 1–5.

owing to the great number of possible combinations of a much smaller number of notes and tempos. In the same way, the almost infinite shadings of consciousness we experience are the product of combinations of a smaller number of basics, like Stanley Krippner's twenty, with each other and with circumstantial factors.

The idea that different states of consciousness have their own reality and that moving from one to another can both provide valid knowledge of ultimate reality and facilitate self-transformation, becoming a real self, is fundamental to religion. Equally fundamental are religion's assumption that some states of consciousness are better—more valuable to these ends—than others and its provision of extrinsic guidelines for evaluating them. These presuppositions underlie religion's emphasis on such states as meditation, conversion, worship, and philosophic or moral reflection and its characteristic denigration of strongly sensual or negatively emotive states. Each of these is an altered or discrete state of consciousness in the sense of Krippner.

In the first chapter, we took note of Robert Bellah's concept of religion as a transcendent experience, which implies that religion is ultimately a particular kind of consciousness, rather than a particular sort of belief or activity. Religion is not so much affirming specific ideas or behaving in certain ways as it is thinking or doing almost anything when these things are thought or done at a level of consciousness that gives them transcendent reference—in other words, makes them symbols of a meaning-giving pattern and a relation to the ultimate source.

To be sure, religion is associated with some of the most striking human behavior, and some actions may be so uniquely religious it would be hard to think of them as anything else. This is not surprising if religion were partly defined as ideas and acts inexplicable in terms of meeting ordinary practical or biological needs. The unusual, even bizarre, quality of much religion (at least to outsiders to the tradition) is, however, itself a symbol—a symbol that it pertains to a sphere that *is* different and not oriented toward the ordinary, practical means and ends of this world but those of another. Religious acts indicate another kind of consciousness, transcendent in implicit intent at least (suggested by the indifference to this world shown in many religious acts). Indeed, much of religion is like a science for exploring a state of consciousness. The phenomena of religion—liturgies, asceticism, methods of prayer, joyful hymns, or whatever—are ways of exploring and then acting out what various transcendent experiences are like.

Entering into a religious situation always, at least on a symbolic level, implies entering a different state of consciousness with its own way of seeing things. A rock in a temple may be a divinity; a rock outside may be just a rock. Standing or kneeling in church may be praising or praying to God; outside it may be just standing to look out the window or kneeling to work in the garden.

If religion means moving into (and later out of) a different reality, the process of moving in and out is of great interest. We need to reflect on this process and these realities.

SUBUNIVERSES

Any concept of different realities interplaned with different states of consciousness is reminiscent of the great nineteenth-century psychologist William James's concept of **subuniverses**. For James, reality in any sense meaningful to humans is what interacts, with our emotional and active lives. When something stimulates one's interest and so comes into relationship with that person, the combination creates a special reality, a subuniverse of meaning.[2]

James's subuniverses have more recently been explored by Alfred Schutz.[3] He sees our experience as made up of countless "finite provinces of meaning." The paramount one is the world of everyday life, or working world. It is the mode of experiencing oneself and the universe that is the point of reference for all others. (This may be true insofar as it is probably the reality created by the culture whose worldview one accepts, and so is in practice the norm for evaluating other perceptions.) Schutz tells us there are other worlds too—"the world of dreams, of imageries and phantasms, the world of scientific contemplation, the play world of the child, and the world of the insane."[4] These each have a "cognitive style," a way of knowing, unique to that world, and so each creates a realm of experience with inner consistency, even if different from the cognitive style of working, or everyday life.

A particularly important point in Schutz's discussion is transition from working reality to one of the others. The transition, he says, is accompanied by a sort of shock, such as falling asleep to enter the world of dreams or awakening to leave it. The transition may be marked by signs that indicate one is suspending one reality in favor of another while reading or hearing a story, playing a game, or starting a ritual. Anyone who has known the subtle but meaningful inward jolt or transition that marks entry into a meditation state or the outward thrill of response to the drums or organ music or processional panoply opening a splendid religious service knows the meaning of Schutz's words for understanding religious states of consciousness and their entry. More intense examples would be the jerking phenomena often observed as shamans or mediums

[2] William James, *The Principles of Psychology* (New York: H. Holt & Co., 1890), vol. II, ch. 21.

[3] Alfred Schutz, *Collected Papers*, ed. Maurice Natanson (The Hague: Martinus Nijhoff, 1973), vol. I, pp. 207–59.

[4] Ibid., p. 232.

go into trance or the strong psychoemotional effects, sometimes experienced as rhythmic waves of feeling, that can accompany intense spiritual conversion or rapture.

Religion fully and enthusiastically accepts the reality of different states of consciousness. If it did not, it would not be easy for it to postulate, as it must, transcendent patterns and the possibility that the real meaning of things can be better perceived if looked at in other than the ordinary way. Peter Berger has said that religion is man's audacious attempt to see the whole universe as humanly significant.[5] This statement implies that ordinary perception does not render the universe humanly significant but that religion's task requires looking at things in a nonordinary way. Entering the reality of other subuniverses and their corresponding states of consciousness (for it can be postulated that different realities and different states of consciousness come and go together), it sees, for example, the same deity behind sea and stars as behind human love.

What religion does is establish a scale of values among states of consciousness. It says that certain states are highly valuable for perception of transcendent reality and for acting out the dramas in which one is a real self, and others are counterproductive to this end. Therefore, religion provides techniques and situations to induce the desired states and sanctions to discourage the undesirable ones. Religion is a matter of the mind, and with its continuing music of ongoing states of consciousness, the mind is an instrument on which one can learn to play different scores. Thus, states of consciousness are the raw material with which religion works, as an artist works with oils or clay. With states of consciousness, religion makes a picture of a real self in tune with infinite reality.

This artistry can work because the psychology of religion has certain principles. It is extremely important to understand that states of consciousness do not remain the same. Not only do they change, but also we humans appear to have a need for them to change. It seems to be almost a natural law that a particular state of consciousness sooner or later wants to be supplanted by a contrasting state—a calm contemplative state with an active one, a highly emotional state with a clear tranquil one. When these changes do not occur, it is a sign of severe mental illness.

Religion, therefore, can speak of getting to more desirable states of consciousness because all of us have gone through at least a limited range of different states and through the realities that accompany them. Moreover, the principle of alteration in states of consciousness indicates that we have a need for states and realities that contrast with what we take to be ordinary consciousness and reality, since every state wants to be followed by a contrasting state. The more monochromatic a person's life is, doubtless the more intense is that need.

[5] Berger, *The Sacred Canopy*, p. 28.

There are innumerable people around the world who generally live practical, commonsense lives close to the soil and to family and friends. They are concerned mostly with crops and prices, buying homes and planning parties—except in certain religious situations, when events long ago and far away but kept alive in stories and temples arise in vivid color in their minds and conversation. They may perceive miracles or real-life dramas that repeat the power of those times today. This other world is a part, a necessary contrasting part, of the lives of crops, houses, and families. Just as the people need the commonplaces of life, they also need the states of consciousness that open doors to an alternative reality of prophets, gods, and wonders. Tradition, temple, music, rites, preaching, and feeling open invisible doors to that other world, utterly remote though it may be in time and place, can brighten the skies of this world more than a thousand sunrises. Indeed, that other world goes into this one like milk and love, giving point to the institutions that cement families and communities.

DEVELOPMENT AND CHANGE

Another feature of human consciousness that supports religion is our capacity for development and permanent change. Alterations of consciousness do not need to go around and around a limited cycle. People can experience changes in the whole structure of the cycle, and very often religion is the major symbolic factor in this change. Something in nearly everybody wants to find a way of life in which he or she knows a more desirable, perhaps because it is more intense, state of consciousness a larger part of the time. For this some turn to adventure, romance, or drugs. Others, feeling that religion deals in states of consciousness and with the highest and widest ranges of being, turn to it.

Sometimes the permanently changing effect of religion is sudden. Consider a young man following a very ordinary life—getting up, getting dressed, going to work or school, worshipping perfunctorily in the way of his people, eating, sleeping. One fine day he has an experience. A tremendous power enters his life, in a vision or jarring psychological experience along the road or at the back of the barnyard, and he knows that from then on his life will be entirely different. Afterwards, he leaves home, wandering and possessing nothing, yet (in his mind) possessing all things. In ancient times, he might have become a disciple of the Buddha or Jesus, in the Middle Ages a Franciscan friar or itinerant yogi or dervish, nowadays a missionary or Zen monk. The religion-connected change was fast and deep; the new states of consciousness that now ring his mind make him feel more like a real self.

The change may also be gradual and, rather than wholly spontaneous, may well be deliberately sought through religion. Indeed, it is a mistake to think the sudden, unexpected conversion is typical. Without going into the issue of what sort of unconscious psychological preparation there may be even for a change as dramatic as Paul's on the road to Damascus, it is safe to say that most people are first drawn to religion by a hope for change, sudden or gradual, and that many subsequently find it.

On the other hand, personality change is not necessary to the practice of religion as such; there is also the way of those ordinary believers for whom religion is a contrast within normal life rather than a radically new life. Even when extensive change occurs, it may be more a spiritual parallel to the radical enough changes nature itself gives than something of a wholly different order.

Quite apart from any effects of religion, everyone's life is a series of immense changes. We move from infant to child, from child to adult, and from student to sage, from maiden to mother. All these require giving up one pattern of thought and life and taking on another. The reprogramming of mind and feelings is never easy. It requires effort, some tension, and probably some symbolic reinforcement through such means as graduation and wedding ceremonies. New titles and status may go with the new role to uphold the individual's sense of identity and meaning during a difficult adjustment.

Everyone who survives infancy goes through changes like these. In the course of these transitions almost everyone experiences significant problems, moments of poignant regret for what he or she is leaving behind, and the excitement of attaining the new. The adult may wish to be a secure and happy child once more, the harried mother a glamorous maiden again.

Here, in conjunction with the ordinary transitions of life, religion provides assistance. It does so in three ways that may appear contradictory but that nevertheless seem to work well enough together.

One way is to offer times and places for symbolic returns to earlier stages, such as childhood, under controlled conditions. It can hardly be denied that much of religion does suggest, in contrast to the ambiguous adult world, a return to the subuniverse of the child's perception of things. Morality may be delineated by simple rules, like those of the nursery. Practices such as kneeling, chanting, and singing simple songs symbolically hint at returning to the child's height and modes of expression. Pentecostalists often talk of their tongues as "babbling like babes," which shows the speakers are reborn "babes in Christ." For many people, temporary returns to the world of childlike values, actions, and perceptions is doubtless of great benefit in maintaining psychological equilibrium.

Yet religion also works to support adult life and to reinforce the idea

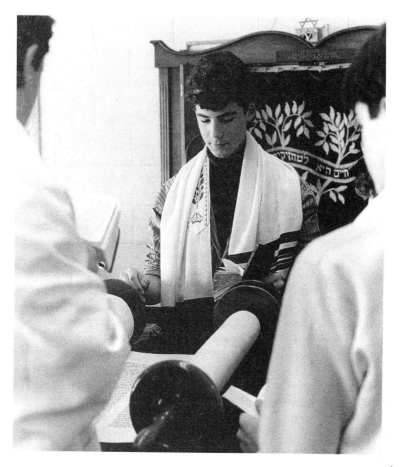

Shirley Zeiberg

The Jewish bar-mitzvah ceremony, when a young man first reads publicly from the scriptures and undertakes the spiritual responsibilities of adulthood, is typical of religious rites of transition from one state of life to another.

that one can and must transit from earlier to later stages. It marks these transitions with rites like confirmation and marriage. It gives prestige to heads of families and the elderly, and it supports their authority. It portrays adult vocations as divine callings that must be exercised morally and cannot rightly be refused; they are parts of the pattern that makes each person within society a real self. These two sides of religion—the return to childhood and the sanctification of adult life—are ideally kept in equilibrium.

Finally, religion contends that there can be religious parallels to the transitions of life. If one has found life after physical birth to be empty and off-center, one can be reborn spiritually, start again, and make right what went wrong the first time out. If one has inadequately moved from childhood to adulthood, one can become an adult spiritually, doing right through a new process of spiritual growth what was done wrong when the process was only physical and social. Mystics talk of spiritual marriage to Christ or deities. Just as one can grow, learn, and marry in secular life, so one can in spiritual life.

The greatest natural and spiritual transition of all is birth itself, apart from the equally great transition of death. Birth is the transition from nonexistence, at least in terms of this world, to existence. Beside the momentousness of this event, other transitions, such as those of maturation or marriage, pale.

It is no wonder, then, that religion has seized on birth and often made it the most important symbol of all of its dynamic side. The idea of **rebirth** is a concept around which the most powerful forces of religious psychology revolve. In this idea everything potent is pulled together. Through rebirth one is able to negate his or her previous life and to start again, doing right what then went wrong. This experience immediately suggests the reality of two contrasting modes of being and so of ordinary versus transcendent planes of reference. Rebirth suggests the return to childhood, indeed to the womb and the very roots of childhood, yet it also indicates sanctifying a new life here and now as an adult. It also infers a passing through a mysterious alternative reality, thereby indicating that one who is truly reborn has knowledge, if not mastery, of other realities. He or she is one who has spiritually passed through death and come back and has dealt with all significant corners of the sacred, has met the numinous and taken it into himself or herself, and has built the symbolic bridge from here to there. Above all, by being reborn he or she has been reborn as a real self.

Not all religion, of course, puts equal emphasis on the symbols and language of rebirth. But if it is interpreted broadly to include any extensive change in one's state of consciousness, whether sudden or gradual, rebirth seems an apt symbol for the dynamics of religion within personality. Rebirth can also be called initiation, and the rites of initiation are often full of rebirth symbolism. We do not speak of just those traditions in which spiritual rebirth is expected to be sudden and dramatic. In an arduous but gradual process like yoga, undertaken as serious spiritual training, much in the traditional literature suggests a psychic return to the womb, gestation, and reemergence as a new person with a new and powerful mode of being in the world. In all sorts of religion and amid all kinds of technique, however, the prevalence of initiatory and rebirth motifs reminds us that at heart religion is, in Frederick Streng's term, "means toward ultimate transformation."[6]

---

[6] Frederick J. Streng. *Understanding Religious Life*, 2nd ed. (Encino, Calif.: Dickenson Publishing Co., Inc., 1976), pp. 7–9.

Indeed, virtually every religious tradition has some process of initiation, for all members, for religious specialists, or for both. These are commonly rife with symbolism of dying and then coming to life again, or returning to the womb and being reborn.[7] One good example is Christian baptism. Going into the waters or into a grave and then emerging clearly represents, as the apostle Paul stated, dying with Christ and rising again with him. It also suggests returning to the watery depths of the womb and being reborn as a new person with new values and a new life.

Among Native American tribes, such as the Algonquin of the Northeast, a young man undergoing initiation spends several days in a round sweat lodge. In its center is a fire, representing the center of the world, surrounded by rocks on which water is thrown to produce steam. While in this hut full of fire and steam, the initiate neither eats nor drinks nor sleeps. He does, however, occasionally smoke the sacred pipe and endeavor to travel to the realm of the gods, see a vision of his guardian spirit, and perhaps receive from him a new name. After this experience in the warm, dark, and mystical world of the lodge, he emerges, clad only in a blanket like a baby, and ritually receives his first food and drink.[8]

Yoga in India and elsewhere is a comparable process but enacted more within the self—although sacred environments and regimens reminiscent of the Algonquin are not unknown to yoga. Indeed, yoga as we know it has partial roots in ancient sacrificial rites centering on fire. Its main emphasis is on inward control of the mind and senses, and inwardly the yogi strives to pass through a mystical death and rebirth. After mastering techniques of posture and breathing that give yogis tranquility together with mastery over their moods and desires, they are able to withdraw their senses from the outer world and become unaware of external events. They then find developing within themselves a whole new equivalent of the nervous system and the mind, as though a new person were forming. The power of the new yogic men and women compared to that of the old is as a superman to a baby; they have access to marvelous psychic senses (the tradition tells us) that enable them to know and control things near and far, and their consciousness is bathed with a calm light beyond the keenest joy of ordinary folk.[9]

These examples suggest deliberate techniques for inducing subjective rebirth, or moving from one state of consciousness to another, more desirable one. It is important to realize that much of religion consists of just such techniques and the concepts that go with them.

It is equally important to balance that realization with the understanding that although experiences of transformation can be prepared for

---

[7] Mircea Eliade, *Rites and Symbols of Initiation* (New York: Harper Torchbooks, 1965).

[8] Evelyn Eaton, "Towards Initiation," *Parabola*, 1, 3 (Spring 1976), 42–46.

[9] Eliade, *Rites and Symbols of Initiation*, pp. 106–8.

by prayer, study, meditation, psychosomatic procedures, and association with spiritually significant people, when religious experiences occur they feel unexpected and spontaneous. They are a breakthrough that liberates something previously dammed up within the self. Far from feeling induced, they may feel like the most free and genuine being the self ever had. One thinks of the great **conversion** accounts, from those of Paul and Augustine in the West and Chaitanya or Shinran in the East to modern converts like Charles Finney and John Newman. The experience may have been sudden or gradual; in many cases it can be convincingly argued there was unconscious preparation; it may also have been strongly suggested by factors in the cultural environment or by specific events in the individual's prior life. The fact remains, however, that conversion differs from something planned. It feels like a new and unexpected gift, a grace. Instead of merely employing a technique based on an already accepted worldview (though this may come later, as the convert endeavors to hold or recapitulate his or her experience), it moves the recipient into an altered worldview and behavior pattern along with the new state of consciousness.

The following account is that of the American evangelist Charles Finney:[10]

> I went to my dinner, and found I had no appetite to eat. I then went to the office, and found that Squire W— had gone to dinner. I took down my bass-viol, and, as I was accustomed to do, began to play and sing some pieces of sacred music.
>
> But as soon as I began to sing those sacred words, I began to weep. It seemed as if my heart was all liquid; and my feelings were in such a state that I could not hear my own voice in singing without causing my sensibility to overflow. I wondered at this, and tried to suppress my tears, but could not. After trying in vain to suppress my tears, I put up my instrument and stopped singing.
>
> After dinner we were engaged in removing our books and furniture to another office. We were very busy in this, and had but little conversation all the afternoon. My mind, however, remained in that profoundly tranquil state. There was a great sweetness and tenderness in my thoughts and feelings. Everything appeared to be going right, and nothing seemed to ruffle or disturb me in the least.
>
> Just before evening the thought took possession of my mind, that as soon as I was left alone in the new office, I would try to pray again—that I was not going to abandon the subject of religion and give it up, at any rate; and therefore, although I no longer had any concern about my soul, still I would continue to pray.
>
> By evening we got the books and furniture adjusted; and I made up, in an open fire-place, a good fire, hoping to spend the evening alone. Just at dark Squire W—, seeing that everything was adjusted, bade me good-night

and went to his home. I had accompanied him to the door; and as I closed the door and turned around, my heart seemed to be liquid within me. All my feelings seemed to rise and flow out: and the utterance of my heart was, "I want to pour my whole soul out to God." The rising of my soul was so great that I rushed into the room back of the front office, to pray.

There was no fire, and no light, in the room; nevertheless it appeared to me as if it were perfectly light. As I went in and shut the door after me, it seemed as if I met the Lord Jesus Christ face to face. It did not occur to me then, nor did it for some time afterward, that it was wholly a mental state. On the contrary it seemed to me that I saw him as I would see any other man. He said nothing, but looked at me in such a manner as to break me right down at his feet. I have always since regarded this as a most remarkable state of mind; for it seemed to me a reality, that he stood before me, and I fell down at his feet and poured out my soul to him. I wept aloud like a child, and made such confessions as I could with my choked utterance. It seemed to me that I bathed his feet with my tears; and yet I had no distinct impression that I touched him, that I recollect.

I must have continued in this state for a good while; but my mind was too much absorbed with the interview to recollect anything that I said. But I know, as soon as my mind became calm enough to break off from the interview, I returned to the front office, and found that the fire that I had made of large wood was nearly burned out. But as I turned and was about to take a seat by the fire, I received a mighty baptism of the Holy Ghost. Without any expectation of it, without ever having the thought in my mind that there was any such thing for me, without any recollection that I had ever heard the thing mentioned by any person in the world, the Holy Spirit descended upon me in a manner that seemed to go through me, body and soul. I could feel the impression, like a wave of electricity, going through and through me. Indeed it seemed to come in waves and waves of liquid love; for I could not express it in any other way. It seemed like the very breath of God. I can recollect distinctly that it seemed to fan me, like immense wings.

No words can express the wonderful love that was shed abroad in my heart. I wept aloud with joy and love; and I do not know but I should say, I literally bellowed out the unutterable gushings of my heart. These waves came over me, and over me, and over me, one after the other, until I recollect I cried out, "I shall die if these waves continue to pass over me." I said, "Lord, I cannot bear any more"; yet I had no fear of death.

How long I continued in this state, with this baptism continuing to roll over me and go through me, I do not know. But I know it was late in the evening when a member of my choir—for I was the leader of the choir—came into the office to see me. He was a member of the church. He found me in this state of loud weeping, and said to me, "Mr. Finney, what ails you?" I could make him no answer for some time. He then said, "Are you in pain?" I gathered myself up as best I could, and replied, "No, but so happy that I cannot live."

Many conversions, particularly those as apparently sudden as Finney's, have involved significant symbols that seemed to trigger the transformation. St. Augustine heard a child chanting in a singsong voice from some neighboring garden, "Take and read, take and read," and opened a New Testament to a passage that deeply changed his life. Hui-neng, a Ch'an, or Zen, patriarch of the seventh century C.E. in China, sold firewood to support his mother after his father's death. One day he carried wood to a customer's shop. As he left he saw a man reciting a sutra. It was the Diamond Sutra, with such lines as the following: "As the raft is of no further use after the river is crossed, it should be discarded. So these arbitrary conceptions of things and about things should be wholly given up as one attains enlightenment. So much more should one give up conceptions of non-existent things, and everything is non-existent."

Hui-neng was immediately awakened. He talked with the man and found he was a monk from a certain monastery. After provision was made for his mother, the young Hui-neng left to join the monastery and eventually became one of the most influential figures in the history of Chinese Buddhism and Zen.[11]

A modern spiritual figure of India, Meher Baba, first awakened to his spiritual vocation from a rather ordinary student life when, at the age of nineteen, he passed a famous and very aged Muslim female saint called Hazrat Babajan. She was sitting under a tree but silently arose and embraced the young man unexpectedly. Not a word was spoken, but from then on the youth's life was deeply changed. He visited her every day for a time thereafter and soon was spending many hours in deep meditation.[12]

AWARENESS OF SELF

So far our reflections on the psychology of religion have led to the following observations: (1) human beings are capable of different states of consciousness; (2) religion accepts this fact enthusiastically and is concerned with distinguishing the states and giving them differing values; (3) religion offers techniques and symbols for inducing or giving meaning to changes in consciousness of religious significance. These operations of religion work against the background of the changes of consciousness that inevitably occur with human growth and alterations in life. Life is a series of initiations—of developmental changes, natural or induced, that produce lasting changes in one's *patterns* of states of consciousness, or at least in the meaning and symbolization one gives them—from birth through education, marriage, and parenthood. Religion relates itself to this process of initiation both by providing occasions of release from its inevitable tensions and by providing parallel ritual or psychologically transformative initia-

[11] Charles Luk, *Ch'an and Zen Teaching* (London: Rider & Co., 1962), vol. 3, pp. 19–20.
[12] C. B. Purdom, *The God-Man* (London: George Allen & Unwin, 1964), pp. 18–19.

tions with religious symbolic completion—rites for transition in life, re-birth, and conversion. We next look at some important states of consciousness to see what meaning religion gives to them.

RELIGIOUS STATES OF CONSCIOUSNESS

Psychologist Abraham Maslow has called one state of consciousness that favorably contrasts with self-awareness the **peak experience**.[13] Although Maslow's peak experience is not explicitly or necessarily a religious state, he has taken pains to show its general similarity to the experiences reported by religious mystics in the past. It is primarily the feeling of joy and creativity that comes to anyone at high moments, whether in something done well, in love, or in spiritual ecstasy. It is a state suffused with absolute being, sufficiency, wholeness, and effortlessness. In a peak experience, Maslow says, a person feels integrated, able to fuse with the world, at the height of his or her powers, spontaneous, natural. Creativity flows out of the person, and he or she needs nothing outside of himself or herself. Because the person has no sense of dependence or goal-orientation toward anything outside, he or she is complete within and so has little sense of time or space. It is akin to joyfully playing a piece of music one has mastered, so that the performance seems effortless. The person in a peak experience often has a sense of luck, fortune, or grace.

The ways in which this state can offer a contrast to ordinary self-cognition should be obvious. Here is a condition in which, for the moment, meaningful awareness of bounding by birth and death, and the stress engendered by unfulfilled needs, falls away. When you are swimming, skiing, loving, writing, painting, reading, or just contemplating and there wells up a sense of deep fullness in the here and now so great it needs no outside justification, that is the peak experience. Give it a religious content, call it an experience of God, and it is explicitly a religious experience. Intense conversion and mystical experiences have qualities of peak experience (although they may include others too, such as intense awareness of guilt, especially related to the religious content). Both involve a melting down, so to speak, of the ordinary structures of thought shaped by self-cognition or self-awareness, thus enabling these structures to be re-formed. One emerges from the experience with new systems or states of consciousness and new symbols interiorized to stimulate them.

This is what really happens psychologically during an initiation, rebirth, or conversion such as those previously described. The anthropologist Victor Turner, following the classic work of Arnold van Gennep, has

---

[13] See Abraham Maslow, *Toward the Psychology of Being* (New York: Van Nostrand Reinhold Company, 1968); and *Religion, Values, and Peak Experiences* (Columbus: Ohio State University Press, 1964).

distinguished three stages of initiation: separation, **liminality**, and reag-gregation.[14] The Algonquin Indian initiate, for example, first passes through a process of separation from ordinary life—he undergoes a prelim-inary fast and purification, then enters the hut. Next follows the most interesting state, the liminal, or marginal, state of the novice during the heart of the transition, when he is in neither his former nor his new status, but is cut off from both as well as from the mode of existence on which ordinary self-awareness or self-cognition is based. He is in a place with virtually no contact with the structural world but open to the depths of his consciousness and to the gods. The liminal state is tomorrow's knight during his nocturnal vigil, a future king during his coronation, the novice in the initiatory lodge.

In a broader sense, Turner points out, certain categories of people are in a permanent state of liminality against the structures of society: outcasts, monks, hoboes, unassimilated minorities, alienated youth, or whoever finds his or her role to be on the borders or margins of structure. Often this role, as in the case of the monk or holy man, may be a symbolic gesture toward antistructure accepted and semiritualized by society, and so (like initiation) a part of its structure in a larger sense. Nonetheless the liminal person is in principle not bound by all of society's rules or a participant in all its privileges and thinks thoughts of a different sort since he or she is oriented toward different values. The liminal person serves as a standard symbol of the possibility of alternative ways of life and climates of con-sciousness, as do all sorts of people in American life, from Trappist monks to black jazz musicians. Also, at certain times or occasions, groups of people, or society as a whole, enter a state of liminality in comparison with ordinary life—in festival or carnival, in pilgrimage, in revolution.

The ordinary initiate, however, only briefly passes out of structure into antistructure, with the aim of returning to the same structural world as a person changed within. The initiate is, as we have seen, spiritually reborn; he or she has returned to the forge of his or her making and has built new structures out of the breaking-down of previous ones. The new structures include the purport of the divine vision and the new name. The initiatory experience, in other words, functions to induce a transition state comparable to that of a peak experience. Both provide an alternative to ordinary self-cognition.

The conversion experiences already discussed, which could be called spontaneous initiations, are an important subcategory of transformative peak experience. Regardless of their cause, they also break down previous self-cognition, as do peak experiences, and facilitate new identity construc-tions. What seems to happen *psychologically* in conversion and related

---

[14] Victor Turner, *The Ritual Process* (Chicago: Aldine Publishing Co., 1969), chaps. 3–5. See also Arnold van Gennep, *Rites of Passage* (Chicago, Ill.: University of Chicago Press, 1960).

experiences (much more can be happening on other levels, of course) is that a buildup of emotional stimulation caused by conflict, anxiety, depression, or simply the excitement of something new causes an overload that blurs the ordinary self-cognition, with all its sense of limits and qualifications. Issues are reduced to very simple, strong, primordial choices; symbols emerge with decisive power. In this fluid situation, the personality can be turned around to focus on a new symbol as representative of the new self; choices that before seemed too complex can now be made because they are simplified into polarities. For the mind, then, conversion is a kind of rebirth; it goes some distance back toward the unshaped plastic of the newborn's mind and is remolded.

At the same time, it should be observed that the conversion process can be more apparent than real. Important subsystems of consciousness can remain in place, with only their direction and conscious symbolization changed. A drive for success in business, for example, may be changed to a drive for evangelistic success.

Another state of consciousness related to the peak experience is that of **meditation**. Meditation is basically a pleasant and restful quietness or stillness of mind. It may involve imagery (of a religious nature, if the meditation is religious), or it may be focused on a chant, a point of visual concentration, or a formless mental quietude. Claudio Naranjo and Robert Ornstein have defined meditation still more broadly. It is, they say, a quality that infuses whatever is done, be it worship, sitting, dance, or play, through a *dwelling upon*, that is, a stopping of the mind on a single thing.[15] This singleness makes one feel he or she is living close to the ground of consciousness and so is a real self. Meditation, whether in prayer or dance, is a common religious way of perpetuating or recovering or, one could say, enjoying the effects of a transformative experience.

Still another religious state of consciousness, related to the foregoing in a negative way, is **guilt**. A sense of guilt—that is, of severe dislocation between what one feels oneself to be and one's ideal self-image—is a state of consciousness markedly different from both ordinary self-cognition and the peak experience. It implies an intense feeling-laden state of introspection. In it, as in conversion, values are polarized into broad-gauged blocs of feeling, essentially good versus bad, with the present self identified with bad. One can continue in a state of moderate guilt for some time and be motivated by it to a high level of religious activity that simultaneously activates and alleviates it. The guilt state can also lead to conversion, especially as it becomes intense. It is perhaps less likely, psychologically, that a person with a strong sense of guilt would be successful in meditation or other peak experience, since they fundamentally require a positive

---

[15] Claudio Naranjo and Robert Ornstein, *On the Psychology of Meditation* (New York: The Viking Press, Inc., 1971), pp. 8–12.

valuation of the accessible self. It can be observed that religious traditions in which the guilt state is prominent tend to stress active or emotionally intense forms of religious expression more than meditation.

Often, religion is also connected with a state of consciousness centered on a sense of immense power. One may emerge from initiation or conversion feeling that one has transcended all ordinary limits and is full of great power, immune to what can hurt and able to do almost anything. The power state of consciousness may result from the very close identification of self with the paramount symbol that the rebirth experience can afford, so that symbolically one *is* Christ or Buddha and is as immune and transcendentally powerful as he; or it may simply be that because one has enjoyed the sort of peak experience that alternates with ordinary self-cognition, one is infused with the alternative consciousness's indifference to the normal awareness of bounding and finitude.

Another characteristic religious state that can be psychologically defined is attachment or dependency. The religious personality frequently attaches itself in an emotionally powerful way as a disciple to a particular person, a savior, teacher, or guru. The attachment can also be to a particular symbol, idea, or slogan that is emotively powerful, perhaps one that emerges in a transformative process. One can see religious dependency psychologically (again, much else may be operative on levels beyond the psychological) as a process interiorizing something initially outside the self as a pivot around which the consciousness revolves. Because the symbol is still outside as well, continual contact with it is needed to maintain the pivot in a central place, at least until it is well fixed. Thus, disciples may spend several years in almost continual attendance upon their master, then leave and not see him again physically for many years. Yet they continue to keep him in mind and heart, worship him from far off, and perhaps believe he is still teaching and guiding them in their thoughts.

Two very common religious beliefs are clearly affirmations of the peak experience. A nearly universal belief is that in some way or another, one's existence is not exhausted of meaning with physical death but that one has psychological relationships with those higher states of consciousness that negate the ordinary sense of bounding by birth and death. In nearly all religious tradition there is a concept of continuing personal existence, in heaven or hell, in a reincarnate state, or in a realm of continuing spiritual growth. (This is true even in Hinduism and Buddhism; most people have many more lives to lead before attaining the ultimate transpersonal Nirvana state.) It is a way of affirming the awareness, especially strong in peak experience or even in guilt and dependency, that there is more to life than the ordinary, that one's real self is unbounded. The internal awareness is perhaps deeper and stronger than the formal doctrine or belief, but however the latter is put, it is a way of affirming the primal and normative value of certain states of consciousness.

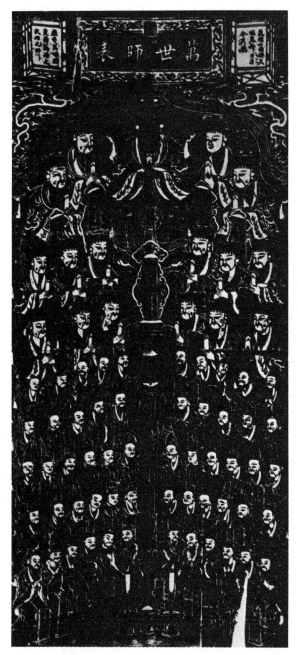

The Granger Collection

The dependency relationship between master and disciple is suggested by this modern Chinese print of the sage Confucius and seventy-two scholars of his school.

The same can be said, psychologically, about another very basic religious affirmation, that of the existence of a God or gods. If one looks at God or gods from the perspective of the psychological meaning of belief in divine beings, one can see that they can represent models of the unbounded or peak state of consciousness, since that is the consciousness that deities themselves are generally said to have—unbounded by birth or death and without human limits on knowledge or power. It is as though a deity, or a figure like a Buddha, lives in the peak experience state all the time and wholly fulfills the promise of one's moments of sensing power and immortality. Insofar as one identifies with the deity, the object of much traditional religious devotion, one shares in his or her fullness of consciousness. Even if one is simply attached to the divine figure, the latter becomes a symbol around which one's own high experiences can form.

PSYCHOLOGICAL INTERPRETATIONS
OF RELIGION

We shall now look at some important psychological interpretations of religion past and present.

For the father of psychoanalysis, Sigmund Freud (1856–1939), religion was a symptom of an incomplete or pathological development within a personality. Religion is individual in its roots, although it took social form, since civilization itself is an expression of neuroses (that is, the channeling of drives within the self in ways that may be socially necessary but that create frustration, tension, and anxiety). Religion comes from a lack of a full, well-resolved relation of self and environment. It perpetuates childish or repressive attitudes toward the world in place of the "reality principle," that is, the way things really are. Religious notions are retentions of childhood concepts of father, magical omnipotence, and so forth, as a means of rationalizing to oneself adult behavior that has neurotic rather than reality motivation.

For example, a person facing a difficult problem in adult life might turn to a divine father figure, recalling the time in childhood when the father seemed able to solve all problems, or he or she might turn to a magical rite or **mystical** state of consciousness, harking back to the infancy in which cause and effect or the limits of the self were not well understood. It is an assumption of the Freudian tradition, so basic as to be almost unspoken, that what we have called the ordinary self-awareness or self-cognition view of the self is the most accurate one, that is, the one that best corresponds to the reality principle. An equally basic Freudian assumption is that the sane adult is wiser in assessing reality than the child, and indeed the mature personality as a psychoanalytic ideal and goal seems to take the mentally healthy adult male as a model.

Freudians would suggest that most religion endeavors to go in other directions; it denies one's best perceptions of reality to return to the comfortable misperceptions of childhood. Although these misperceptions may be of limited benefit to some people, they cannot ultimately solve one's problems of adjustment to life because they are based on false premises. Since they conflict with other aspects of oneself that have to be perceived as reality, religion may well induce those deep-seated tensions and anxieties known as neuroses even as one tries through religion to alleviate them.[16]

A more positive assessment of religion was made by a student of Freud who later broke with him, Carl G. Jung (1875–1961). Jung taught that life is a quest for *individuation*, that is, for unifying the various constituents of one's mind into a harmonious pattern. These constituents are basically aspects of masculinity and femininity, together with the dark negative principle, called the Shadow, and the emerging ideal self. Each of these parts has a root image called an archetype. Traditional religious myth and ritual, together with dreams and fantasies, are seen by Jungians as treasure troves of images that represent these archetypes. The feminine side, for example, presents itself to us as the elderly and wise Great Mother (goddesses like Cybele or Isis) or as the eternally young anima (youthful maidens such as Persephone or the Virgin Mary). The masculine may be the Wise Old Man, like Merlin, or the Hero. The emerging individuated self may be represented by the archetype of the Marvelous Child or by a Hero triumphant through a struggle, such as Christ.

The archetypes and the psychic force behind them are normal constituents of the mind. Everyone has something of all of them, and if any are repressed it may cause trouble. Equally unhealthy is inflation by an archetype, so that one acts *only* as the Great Mother or the Hero. They must instead be arranged into a pattern, a Mandala, so that they balance each other off and the ideal self emerges in the center. Religious rites, myths, and art (as well as those of traditions such as alchemy) are seen by Jungians as able to help one greatly in the process of rightly placing the archetypes and attaining the individuation process. They give one symbols for understanding aspects of himself or herself that correspond to the dynamics of the Great Mother or the Hero. Traditional rites can help insofar as they are basically aimed at aligning the archetypes and enabling a true self to emerge out of them.[17]

We have alluded to the approach to the psychology of religion of

---

[16] See Sigmund Freud, *Totem and Taboo*, trans. James Strachey (London: Routledge and Kegan Paul, 1950); and *The Future of an Illusion*, trans. W. D. Robson-Scott (Garden City, N.Y.: Doubleday & Company, Inc., 1957).

[17] For summaries of the position see Carl G. Jung et al., *Man and His Symbols* (Garden City, N.Y.: Doubleday & Company, Inc., 1969); and Frieda Fordham, *An Introduction to Jung's Psychology* (Harmondsworth, England: Penguin Books, 1956).

Abraham Maslow (1905–1970), Claudio Naranjo, and others. This approach is grounded in the movement known as humanistic psychology, though a significant wing of it has come to be known as transpersonal psychology.[18] Maslow's fundamental premise is implicit in his exposition of the peak experience; one is most fully *actualized* (that is, what a human being should be and potentially can be) in peak moments, when one is most full of a sense of sufficiency and creativity and least aware of needs outside the self. To know the truth about human beings, then, we should proceed from these states and what they tell us, not from pathological states as Freud was accused of doing. Maslow's approach has obvious philosophical and religious ramifications. Many have used the work of humanistic psychology to present a view that religion is grounded in the peak experience and is a resource of methods for inducing it.

RELIGIOUS DEVELOPMENT

We have observed that life is a series of initiations that religion can help to correlate. We have also noted—and this could be very richly substantiated—that religious traditions tend to idealize various stages of religious development in a person. The following is a brief discussion of the major stages of development and of what, at least in modern American culture, tends to be characteristic of religion in each of them.[19]

Stages of Development

Infancy. In infancy and early childhood there is, of course, little if any separation of religion from the rest of life. Yet in the eyes of many psychological theorists, this is the age that is really all-important for religion. According to Freudians, it is the locus of the oceanic, infantile omnipotence and the parent-dependency stages one later endeavors to recover through mysticism, magic, or personal gods. Motor activity at this age is also one of the main ways of knowing, which could be the basis of religious ritual, dance, and ecstatic release. On the other hand, if religion really is a matter of knowledge acquired through philosophy, scripture, and tradition—media of the distance senses, a matter of words and

---

[18] There are several anthologies that provide an introductory sampling of the literature of these movements and particularly stress their interaction with traditional mysticism and religion. These include John White, ed., *The Highest State of Consciousness* (Garden City, N.Y.: Doubleday Anchor Books, 1972); John White, ed., *Frontiers of Consciousness* (New York: Julian Press, Inc., 1974); Robert Ornstein, ed., *The Nature of Human Consciousness* (San Francisco: W. H. Freeman and Co. Publishers, 1973); and Charles T. Tart, ed., *Transpersonal Psychologies* (New York: Harper & Row, Publishers, Inc., 1975).

[19] An older but classic book on the psychology of religion, which provides a useful discussion of stages of typical development, is Gordon W. Allport, *The Individual and His Religion* (New York: The Macmillan Company, 1950).

cognition—then infancy would have very little relevance for it. Perhaps we can at least say that the quest for a real self begins in infancy and is continued through every stage by whatever means are accessible.

Childhood.   Many stages are really contained within childhood, but we must here collapse them all into one. The basic operation is reality construction, pursued in many ways, such as stories, fantasies, games, learning, and relating to parents and peers. Religion may be learned and practiced but is not likely to be a genuinely distinct area of life so much as a matter of acquiring the ways of parents and friends. At the same time, however, the child through stories and imaginary games (though he or she does not distinguish clearly between imagination and reality) is also acquiring an interest in alternative realities and moving in and out of them. With sensorimotor knowing still very important, even though the child also is coming to know through words and concepts (the adult way), he or she has a strong capacity for ritual and dramatic experience. If these capabilities become attached to religion, as is often the case, religion becomes very much a live and precious thing, and this attachment can easily continue into adulthood. Religion acted out in play goes deep.

Adolescence.   For many people, though certainly not all, adolescence is the golden age of religion. It is first of all a time of intense feeling that indicates a lively capacity for religious experience. It is also a time when one is striving desperately to find one's place in life, to sort out difficult relations with parents and the opposite sex. The adolescent has strong sexual drives, sometimes so disturbingly strong he or she would like to transmute them into something else or to have other drives just as strong to counterbalance them. He or she also has a new capacity for logical, abstract thinking and wants a logical, coherent picture of the world and his or her place in it. He or she wants something highly persuasive to which an intense emotional commitment can be made. All of these drives together make the religious commitments and intense personal experiences characteristic of adolescence very understandable. For many, of course, these drives find other outlets and adolescence is not especially religious. Indeed, the strong drive for self-identity that underlies all other drives may well take the form of deeply felt rebellion against one's past; and if religion is included in that past, it may be one object of rebellion.

Adulthood.   Early adulthood is often marked by a greater flexibility of thought than in adolescence. If one explores the nature of religion more deeply, he or she may be led to a fuller religious commitment or to a greater inclination to see the relativity and symbolic nature of religious language. The emotional commitment side of religion may diminish as he or she moves further into adulthood, but the importance of religion as a social construction of reality (that is, its rich meaning in family and community) and its ability to help one manage the tragedies, frustrations, and emptiness of adult life become more important. Religion becomes a vehicle for the interpersonal expression that undergirds adult society; it is like a vocabulary, to religious persons, for expressing the meaning of family and community and for finding meaning in the absurdities of a good deal of adult life.

Old Age. Finally, in old age, religion can sometimes grow in importance. Not because it is easier to believe then or because one is closer to death (which is, perhaps surprisingly, often less of a problem to old people than to children or adolescents), but just because one finally becomes more emotionally contained and better able to live in the present. One can enjoy more calmly the beauty, sociality, and wisdom of religion. A rigorously logical interpretation tends to matter less, with emphasis shifting to a symbolic environment that links one to one's own past and present.

Religion and Childhood

This scheme of the religious significance of life's stages is, of course, very general. Undoubtedly the reader can think of numerous exceptions. Moreover, one final problem that should be discussed is the relation of religion and childhood. Much of what we have said could create an impression that religion is little more than a perpetuation of childish things. The matter is not that simple. Although the importance of childhood experiences for religion is immense, this may not be the same thing as saying religion is childish.

The affinity between religion and childhood is, in fact, generally accepted. Great religious personalities, such as Jesus when he admonished his disciples to become like little children, acknowledged it from one point of view, even as those who discredit religion as immature do from another. Although some may say that one should leave behind all childish or immature areas of life, it can be argued with equal force that it is crucially important to accept and unify within one's total personality all of one's past as well as one's present. The person who does not wisely and knowingly give place to the child within may find that child expressing itself in highly undesirable ways.

Even more important, the assumption that what is earlier in development is necessarily less adequate than what is later is only an assumption. Religion around the world, through innumerable myths, symbols, and ties, has commonly made an opposite assumption, that however valuable adulthood may be, there are ways and occasions in which children have a far keener perception of right values and truths than do adults. (Thus, the savior is a babe, the youngest son is a hero, or a boy or girl opens a religious rite or divines in a sacred oracle.)

It needs to be understood that when we talk about mysticism and the infantile oceanic consciousness, or childhood fantasies and religious myth or alternative realities, these words should be taken only metaphorically.

Steve and Mary Skjold/The Image Works

Religious life in a modern family.

The child within may open for an adult the capacity for mysticism or understanding myth, but he or she is still an *adult* mystic or myth-maker, not literally a child again. The adult brings to the experience everything that has happened since he or she was a child, including perhaps considerable education, and this makes the experience quite different from what it would be if he or she were still a child.

SUMMARY

Psychologically, religion is based on the self-evident fact that we experience varying, shifting states of consciousness. Religion accepts the reality of these states and evaluates some of them as better and truer—more expressive of the real self in the right relationship with ultimate reality—than others. States such as the "peak experience," meditation, sense of guilt for one's sins, sense of infusion with divine power, and sense of dependency upon God and spiritual teachers are usually highly valued by religion.

The psychology of religion also focuses attention on how religion interacts with changes in life. First, there can be experiences that definitely point one in a particular direction spiritually: conversion and mystical experiences. These may apparently come spontaneously and may profoundly affect one's religion for life. Conversion may be either intellectual or emotional or a combination of both. Second, there are structured rites of initiation or transition which are designed to induce religious experiences that also have a lifelong effect. Third, the ordinary stages of life—maturation, marriage, children, sickness, death—are marked in most religions with rites and teachings that bring out their spiritual implications. Finally, there can be devised a model for understanding how religion is experienced and what it is likely to mean to people in different ages of life, from early childhood to old age.

Understanding religion psychologically is inseparable from the problem of understanding the self psychologically, especially when our basic concept of religion is that it expresses scenarios for the real self. Seeing oneself as a self if both biologically and socially conditioned; establishing selfhood is an ongoing process with which religion often interacts by providing symbols and ideals for the true self as well as vehicles for expressing it.

Religion has been understood differently by various important psychological thinkers. For Freud it meant basically an unrealistic desire to return to childish attitudes; for Jung, archetypal symbols for aspects of personality; for humanistic psychologists, names and techniques for the "peak experience" which is the highest state of consciousness. Childhood itself has a continual fascination for religion, both as symbol of the primal innocence and nearness to the divine it idealizes and as something to be transcended.

United Nations

The doorways of this restored twelfth-century Buddhist temple at Angkor, Cambodia, suggest the role of religious symbols, including symbols in architecture, as portals to mysterious other worlds.

Magic Doorways: Symbol, Rite, and Religion

Chapter Objectives

- Understand the difference between sign and symbol and present a good definition of the religious meaning of symbol.

- Discuss how religious symbols help the mind relate particular issues to general religious patterns of meanings, like those of Christianity or Buddhism, and thereby make decisions. Think of some concrete examples of how this relationship might work.

- List and define the categories of symbols presented in this book: focal symbols, general symbols, and secondary specific symbols.

- Discuss how sounds and words, including stories and doctrines, can also serve as symbols, that is, audio symbols. Define the main categories of audio symbols in religion: nonverbal, nonconceptual verbal, and conceptual verbal.

- Interpret the meaning of myth in religion, as the term is understood in religious studies (as a story which expresses in narrative form important aspects of the religion or culture's worldview). Explain two main types of religious myth, the cosmogonic and the hero/savior.

- Explain how doctrine, as a statement of a religion's beliefs in abstract, propositional form, differs from its narrative expression. Explain the nature and use of "religious rhetoric" in preaching and inspirational writing.

- Distinguish between public and private symbols and give religious examples of both.

- Tell how religious symbols, especially in rite, perpetuate the sacred past and help us to simplify and clarify feelings.

- Discuss rite as "orchestration of symbols," by which a special time and place are set apart wherein the religion's world comes alive and its reality is enacted. Summarize the stages a worship rite typically goes through.

As you read the chapter, also look for important words. The key words defined in the glossary at the end of the book are in boldface type at their first use in the text.

SIGNS AND SYMBOLS

Perhaps you have read a story in which a very ordinary entryway, a closet door, or a garden gate, turns out to lead into a fabulous other world. Sometimes even the flick of a television dial, when it moves to a drama like *Star Trek*, can reveal another world. This chapter is about symbols in religion, and symbols for religious believers are like such doors, gates, and television controls. Even the plainest symbols can open up a virtual universe of transcendent feeling and meaning for those who understand. They are magic portals into the other world where the truth of one's religion is visible, felt, and far overshadows the inconsistent ordinary. A symbol may be a work of art, the architecture of a temple, a church service, or a sacred book. The Ise shrine and the figure of Jesus, as described in the first chapter, are good examples of religious symbols that have this kind of magic power.

To comprehend how all this symbolism works, several distinctions have to be made. There is a distinction between a **sign** and a **symbol**, and there is a distinction between the *religious* and *nonreligious* use of both terms. All sorts of indicators bombard us from all sides, and the structures of our thought processes continually construe them to tell us things not literally contained in the words as noises or the objects as things. We constantly make out certain squiggles of ink, like those before you now, to be more than just black-on-white patterns, just as we read significance into colors, gestures, and even the arrangement of the stars. We understand significance through associations we have been taught or that the mind makes on its own from past experience and its own intrinsic structures. Language itself is sign and symbol; the noise of most words has no relation to the meaning, yet words immediately call to mind, to one who knows the language, what is being communicated. *Cat* does not sound or look like the animal, yet when we hear or see the word we call up a visual and even audio idea of the furry creature that meows.

Many such verbal units as well as countless nonverbal indicators, from traffic lights to the dial tone on the telephone, come to us as little more than signs. They are just indicators that have no essential relation, except convention, to the thing signified. Susanne Langer speaks of them as *references*. They may be, she suggests, a very truncated form of the original, such as the code word or gesture in some game. Unlike a true *symbol*, however, they are not necessary to the *completion* of some experience, much less a miniature of life itself, as would be the "miniature" eating or washing of a sacrament such as holy communion or baptism.[1]

The sign can be thought of as the traffic light, and the symbol as the cross or holy communion (though, as we shall see, matters may not in the end be quite this simple). Signs are generally taught, or based on language that is taught, since they have little intrinsic relation to the thing signified. Signs saying stop, exit, keep right, no parking, this side up, hotel, cafe; gestures of pointing, guiding, or even hostility; and footprints one is following are all examples of signs.

Some indicators, however, are more involved. If you come to a restaurant featuring the cuisine of a particular nationality, and you are familiar with that culture, the sign might do more for you than just reveal the existence of the restaurant. It would probably evoke in your mind the whole world of the culture—memories of travel, of the smell of the kitchens of relatives who came from that country, of a few bars of ethnic music heard with the inward ear, maybe even a few scenes from a childhood long past.

Recall from Chapter One Alfred North Whitehead's statement that the mind is functioning symbolically when some components of its experience elicit consciousness, beliefs, emotions, and usages respecting other components of its experience. The former set are symbols; the latter, the meaning of the symbols. If the restaurant sign evokes the sort of emotions and nostalgia suggested, the sign would clearly be a symbol, and the culture of the evoked nationality, as you had interiorized it, would be the meaning of the symbol for you.

The theologian Paul Tillich has also discussed the distinction between sign and symbol, defining the latter as that which participates in what it symbolizes.[2] One could argue that the restaurant sign is still not quite a symbol in this sense. However positive the feelings it elicits, it is not really

---

[1] Susanne K. Langer, *Philosophy in a New Key* (Cambridge, Mass.: Harvard Press, 1957), pp. 153–59.

[2] Paul Tillich, *Systematic Theology* (Chicago, Ill.: University of Chicago Press, 1951), vol. I, p. 239.

a participant in the culture it evokes, any more than would be the colored blotch representing the country on a map.

If you were to enter the restaurant (just as you might enter a religious building or service, attracted by the sign or token outside), any doubt about the extent of real participation in the culture would probably disappear. You would see decor representative of the homeland, hear its music, smell the spices used in its cooking,and perhaps notice a patron or two in the corner reading a foreign language newspaper. The restaurant would become for you a symbol, indeed an experience, of the culture in the fullest sense.

The distinction between sign and symbol is intricate but important. What is a symbol to one person may be only a sign to someone else. If you are Hungarian, a Hungarian restaurant may function as a major symbol for you, evoking memory and meaning. For another person, who never eats there and has no particular interest in Hungary, it may be only another routine building along the street. Meaning is not a quality inherent in events or objects themselves but a product of what is brought to the objects by the associations, memories, and psychological makeup of the observer, especially if he or she is also a participant.

Thus there are situations in which even the traffic light becomes a symbol that participates in what it symbolizes. It is a part of modern technological society and representative of how the authority of the state must operate in such a society. To this extent it is a *bona fide* symbol of authority in a society that depends on immensely powerful vehicles and must regulate their movements, even when they are under individual control, with a precision unknown in the streets of ancient Athens or medieval London. Fortunately, the same society that produces powerful private automobiles can also mass-produce traffic lights. The latter can evoke responses that are really responses to the whole meaning of modern technological society and the sort of state authority that goes with it.

Every part of a culture is a symbol of the whole of the culture.[3] Advertisers constantly tell us that how one brushes one's teeth or what kind of soft drink one imbibes can identify the person's whole lifestyle and generation. The principle behind such claims, however excessive they may be, contains some truth. For a cultural style, like a personality, is made up of a thousand details that are interrelated, reveal something of the totality, and are capable of serving as a symbol of the whole that participates in it. Toothpaste tubes and carbonated soft drinks, like stop signs, are significant symbols of modern American civilization. They participate in it not only metaphorically but also as million-dollar industries with high advertising visibility. They reveal important attitudes in the culture toward

[3] For example, see Claude Lévi-Strauss, *The Raw and the Cooked* (New York: Harper and Row, Publishers, Inc., 1969).

John Coletti/Stock, Boston

A modern American highway scene with its multitude of signs and symbols—advertising traffic instructions, license plates, endless words.

health and happiness. They could not have existed in the same way, as mass-produced, mass-marketed products, in any previous culture. Trivial as they may seem, without them modern American civilization would be something different.

If the part serves as symbol of the whole in ordinary society, it does so to the highest degree in religion. (It is, however, sometimes misleading to regard the religion of a society as a part that symbolically reveals the values of the whole. That relationship is often complex, with the religion being more dialectical—challenging as well as interpreting—than continuous with the cultural values.) Religion is the greatest of all redoubts of symbolism, especially if the vast realms of art and music associated with religion are included. Everything in religion is a symbol, since the object of religion is the transcendent and the real self, and these are beyond immediate representation.

All the forms of religious expression, the theoretical, practical, and sociological, are symbols of the total message and experience of the religious system in which they coexist. Each participates in that total experience, but each is only a part of it. For example, the doctrinal statement of a religion tells us something about its vision, but the message for the actual participant is modified by what is told him or her through the kind of worship and the kind of group experienced.

Religious symbols, however, are not merely passive clues to identity or meaning. They are also aids to thought, and so to decision, just as are language symbols. Thus, in the example of the girl converted to Christ presented in the first chapter, accepting Jesus really meant accepting the whole of Christian life, doctrine, worship, and fellowship as she understood it along with transforming grace through Christ; but focusing just on the figure of Jesus clearly facilitated her decision. Encapsulating a total word or experience in a single symbol or a discrete symbol system can sometimes be misleading, but it also helps one to clarify distinctions, make choices, and so find or create one's own identity. In any case, for better or worse, that is the pattern of human thought.

We want maps to chart the separate choices we encounter into a simple, comprehensive pattern, as scrambled iron filings leap into line when a magnet is brought near. We want a *pattern* that fits over them and lines them all up—right versus wrong, good versus bad. We want this pattern to have ultimate meaning, to be actually the sacred network versus the profane discussed in Chapter One. Then, as we pick the right side, we feel part of the pattern too—a somebody, a real self, who also fits in. The pattern is really a way of *seeing*; whatever the outer reality, the important thing is that it has an inner reality for the one who sees, which empowers one to make the right choices.

We want usually to choose what is right and good when it involves a deliberate choice and not just an emotional reaction. Religion helps us focus on choice and subordinate emotion to the right and good by making personal issues and feelings fit into a universal pattern of sacred meaning. Religion's symbols are the tools by which it performs this action.

CATEGORIES OF RELIGIOUS SYMBOLS

Let us now look at some of the major types of religious symbols, which are major tools in religious thinking, used for making the kinds of pairings and distinctions—between right and wrong, the sacred and the outer realms, and between one religion and another—that the religious mentality wants to make. What we deal with are symbols in the most exacting sense of the word; each is a specific, discrete object that is seen, like an image or diagram, or heard, like a story or a piece of music, and is distinguishable from other objects. The sociological structure of a religious group can also be highly symbolic, but this is a symbolic statement of a somewhat different type from that communicated by discrete visual and audio objects and is considered in Chapter 6. Later in this chapter religious rites as orchestrations of symbols are discussed. First, it is useful to examine some categories of religious symbols.

Focal Symbols

To start with, there are **focal symbols** in religion. Some of these are the cross in Christianity, the image of the Buddha in Buddhism, or Mecca for Muslims. Although the details of their function and meaning may be different, they have qualities in common: each is specific to the religion, is obvious in its role as a symbol, and serves as a standard focus for worship and identity within the religious community. Focal symbols convey a central and generally recognized message about the religion—the importance of Christ's death on the cross, the importance of the Buddha's enlightenment—so that even outsiders can identify with the religion if they know anything at all about it.

Focal symbols, however, should not be reduced to the bare signs by which places of worship are marked. A religion may well have several objects that serve obviously as focal symbols. In Judaism there is not only the star of David and the menorah but also the Torah and the ark within

John Pitkin

This eight-branch *menorah* or candlestick (with an additional socket for the lighter) and wine-cup used in the celebration of the eight-day Jewish festival of Hanukkah recall the symbols of religion.

the synagogue; in Hinduism, all the principal deities are focal symbols, as is the sacred Ganges River.

Focal symbols generally have some specific visual form by which they are remembered and recognized, but there is more to them than a visible shape. When we say the Torah is a focal symbol in Judaism, do we mean the elaborate scroll on which the first five books of the scripture, containing the law, are written, and which will probably spring to the minds of those accustomed to synagogue or temple worship when the word is pronounced, or do we mean the actual words these five books of the Bible and the commandments therein? When we say a Hindu deity like Krishna is a focal symbol, do we mean the image of Krishna in a Hindu temple, myths and teaching related to Krishna, the concept (or reality) of Krishna as a transcendent deity, or the name Krishna chanted in a formula mantra like the "Hare Krishna"? Obviously, we have to mean all these together because in practice they go together. A characteristic, in fact, of major symbols is ability to work on several levels at once, so the composite experience says in a moment what it would take many pages to express in writing. Each level of meaning supports the others and adds to the others' symbolic power.

Focal symbols are not necessarily visual. The cry to prayer five times a day by the muezzin from the minaret of a Muslim mosque is as powerful a focal symbol as any. So are the organ music and church bells of Christendom.

Focal symbols contain suggestions of other parts of the religion's full symbolic constellation; they are undoubtedly related to its most important myths or narratives and to its central doctrines and have an important role in its major acts of worship and in legitimation of its principal sociological structures. The image of the Buddha is not enthroned passively on the altars of Buddhist temples but receives flowers and incense in private and public worship. Seated in meditation, it suggests the major act by which spiritual realization arrives. Standing to teach, the form of the Blessed One recalls the sutras that contain the basic doctrines of Buddhism and are attributed to his lips. Finally, the image of Buddha serves as the model and spiritual master of the monastic brotherhood that is Buddhism's fundamental sociological expression.

General Symbols

Another category of religious symbols could be called *general symbols*. These are constructed forms, like the cross and circle, or natural objects, like the tree and moon, that recur over and over in the religious world as components of symbolic constellations. These symbols move from one culture to another or appear independently in many cultures. The meaning may be somewhat altered in each use, yet the general symbol also retains something of what might be called the core meaning of the symbol. To

Although the cross, as on this church, is a symbol in Christianity, it is also a general symbol found in other religions as well.

Peter Simon/Stock, Boston

what extent symbols are universal, and to what extent their recurrence is independent and accidental, is a debated issue.

Also subject to much debate is the related issue of the precision with which the universal meaning of general symbols can be specified. Some, perhaps following a Freudian or Jungian school of psychological interpretation of religious motifs, would say, for example, that a symbolic circle is bound to represent female sexuality and the womb—even if only unconsciously—and that on a more abstract level it represents wholeness and eternity. Others would say that the meaning of each symbol can only be determined in the context of its own culture.

As in most arguments over such abstract matters as these, some truth can be rightly claimed by both sides. The cross in Christianity is a symbol of Jesus Christ and of redemptive suffering. Both of these meanings, one historical and one conceptual, are highly specific to Christianity and are by far the most important meanings of the cross in that faith. Cross symbols, however, appear widely outside of Christianity, from the sand paintings of

Navaho Indians to the mandala diagrams of esoteric Buddhism. Outside of Christianity, the cross characteristically suggests the earth with its four directions and access to a mystic center integrating the four corners of the earth and of one's psyche. This meaning is not stressed in Christian discussion of the cross but is consistent with the central Christian meaning. It has appeared in the past as a minor theme, related to the lordship of Christ over the earth and his place at the spiritual center of the world providing the way of access to heaven.

The tree is a widespread symbol suggesting life and access to transcendence. Compare the tree under which the Buddha sat at his enlightenment and the old tradition of referring to the cross of Christ as the "tree."

The moon as a symbol has a highly specific meaning in Islam: it suggests the flight of Muhammad from Mecca to Medina, which marked the turning point in his career and is the beginning date of the Muslim calendar. In Christianity it is associated with the Blessed Virgin Mary and particularly with the annunciation. In Chinese and Japanese popular religion it is a heavenly abode of immortals. In all its uses as a religious symbol, the moon seems to suggest or mark renewal, the triumph of life over death, and supernatural aid—no doubt suggested by the phases through which the moon goes as it seems to die and then to return to life, by its relation to the female cycle, and by widespread belief that the moon gives rain and fertility. This combination of near universality, versatility, and broad but deep underlying themes illustrates the nature of general symbols. They often provide elements, or even the basic theme of particular focal symbols.

Secondary Specific Symbols

Still another class could be called *secondary specific symbols*. These are symbols specific to a particular religion but not as important for identification with the religion as the focal. Examples are the triangle or three interlocking circles that symbolize the Trinity in Christianity, the many arms of the bodhisattva Kannon in Japanese Buddhism, and the mace and discus of Vishnu in Hinduism. Secondary specific symbols are typically those of particular doctrines or religious figures such as saints, gods, and bodhisattvas, but they may well incorporate simpler general symbols as do focal symbols—the circle representing eternity (or the womb) multiplied *three* times to express the trinitarian Christian God.

AUDIO SYMBOLS

Focal, general, and secondary specific symbols may be either visual or *audio*. Most people think of symbols as something seen, but it is important to realize that sounds, not to mention stories and ideas, can function just as powerfully as visual symbols. When a worshipper enters a church, he or she is lifted into the religious world just as much by the organ music, the choir, the words of prayer, or the sermon as by what is seen. Now we turn our attention to the religious symbolic role of what is heard. The symbolic role of the written word is included in this discussion because in religion it is never wholly detached from its parentage in the spoken word and shares its meaning.

It should not be thought that visual and audio symbols work together in religion in mutual reinforcement and grand harmony. In fact, an underlying dynamic aspect of the history of religion that might seem very puzzling to the proverbial man from Mars has been a seesaw war between the respective symbolisms of the two distance senses—a war sometimes only latent but sometimes rising to furious battle in which men have killed and died for the sake of the word against the picture or vice versa. Sometimes religion has been most conspicuous as the patron of sacred painting and sculpture, has made the fruits of this patronage the foci of worship, and has communicated to most people a preeminently visual suggestion of the sacred. Medieval Catholicism and Mahayana Buddhism veered in this direction. At other times religion has generated iconoclasm (the destruction of images) in favor of upholding the spoken and written word as the most reliable conveyor of truth. Protestantism and Islam are examples.

The written word in religion is an extension of the spoken word and shares its psychological attributes. Reading may be visual but is not usually mistrusted by those who suspect visual symbols of a nonverbal nature. The origin of writing in the spoken word is more decisively recognized in religion than anywhere else; reading is rarely allowed to stand alone as the formal expression of one's relation to the verbal symbols of faith. In Protestantism one is certainly encouraged to read the Bible and religious books, but doing so does not take the place of formally hearing the Bible read in church and a sermon preached.

Audio symbols fall into three categories: nonverbal—music and sound; nonconceptual verbal—words such as chants and spells used chiefly for effectiveness in the word itself rather than the concept is conveys as verbal communication; and conceptual verbal—story, myth, rhetoric, and doctrine.

Nonverbal

Music is virtually universal as an important accompaniment of religion, except in Islam in which chanting and rhythmic recitation take its place. Music's importance in facilitating the basic task of religious symbolism, helping the participant to make the transition from ordinary to sacred reality, is unsurpassed. Whether the solemn and mystical Gregorian chant, the fast-paced hums of Buddhist sutra reading, or the gladsome notes of gospel singing, music in religious worship sets the altered emotional tone and universe of meaning of the rite and does much to bring the participant into it. Religious music is mostly a secondary specific symbol. Despite its immense and pervasive importance, there are few instances of single discrete pieces of music having quite the status of the focal symbol, and there are surprisingly few musical motifs that, like general symbols, find their way into the worship of a diversity of religions with a core meaning intact. Rather, the music of a religion is mostly specific to its cultural context and drawn from it, although a great religion may spread across many cultures and carry musical traditions with it, along with other cultural baggage. We will look more at religious music in the next chapter.

Nonconceptual Verbal

Although it may be less familiar to some Westerners, sacred words as **nonconceptual verbal expression** are extremely important in the history of religion. In some cases, such as the distinctive chants of Japanese Pure Land and Nichiren Buddhism, they rise to the role of focal symbol.

Very often the nonconceptual feature is not absolute. Religious scholars within the tradition may appreciate the meaning, and it may in fact be known to ordinary practitioners. Nevertheless, as in the case of the Nichiren chant *Namu Myoho Renge Kyo* ("Hail the Marvelous Truth of the Lotus Sutra"), the literal meaning is not as important to ordinary devotion as the mantic or evocative power of the formula, which just through the vibrations of the sounds themselves is believed to align one with rich spiritual forces.[4] Examples are the mantra of Hinduism and Buddhism, recited in formal prayer and private meditation to create an atmosphere of the presence of divinity and peace; the *dhikr* or chanted ascriptions of praise to Allah in Islam; and such comparable Christian devotions as the Jesus prayer in Eastern Orthodoxy, the rosary in Roman Catholicism, and the repeated utterance of familiar prayer phrases and hymns in Protestantism.

The use of special or sacred language, from Latin and Sanskrit to the archaic English of the King James Bible, is a closely related matter. Most nonconceptual verbal expression is predominantly secondary specific symbolism, although the *idea* of some of its modalities, such as the use of sacred language, rosary, or mantra, has spread through several religions.

Conceptual Verbal

Conceptual verbal expression in religion takes several different forms. As one grows older, the words about religion that one hears

[4] See, for example, the description of Nichiren chanting in Robert Ellwood, *The Eagle and the Rising Sun: Americans and the New Religions of Japan* (Philadelphia, Pa.: The Westminster Press, 1974).

change. One may at first be told stories about religious heroes, later may learn the faith's creeds and catechisms and be taught something about the abstract meaning of the doctrine, and finally may have it expounded in mature philosophical form. Without implying that one or the other forms is better, most religions have words that fit all these categories.

MYTH AND DOCTRINE AS SYMBOL

Myth is one example of conceptual verbal expression. Myth in religious studies means a story that expresses in narrative form the basic world view of the culture. Myths are of two basic types, the **cosmogonic** and the **hero/savior**. The first tells how the cosmos came into being, and the second tells how a way has been found back to the primordial unity of humankind with the transcendent.

How one says that the world came into being tells a great deal about how one thinks of the world, and one's place in it, today. In India one of many accounts of the beginning of this world tells of a primal man who is also God dividing himself up in a sacrifice to make the many things. The Judaeo-Christian account in the Book of Genesis relates that God literally created the universe as something outside of himself and subject to him. These two narratives suggest two views of the total meaning of the world in relation to God. In the first, God is hidden in the world. All parts of the cosmos, stars, mountains, trees, and people, are really God in veiled form, self-sacrificed so their multiplicity can flourish. In the second, God is not the same as the world but views it as a craftsperson views the exquisite work of his or her hands and as a sovereign views his or her subjects, expecting love and obedience from them. In both cases, the myth implies that if we know the real origin of something, we can understand it now. In this light, the myth is indeed a symbol, because it both participates in what it symbolizes and is part of the conceptual reality that interprets the meaning of the whole.

The hero/savior narrative recounts the way back to this beginning. It presents a model of the accomplisher of the way who is a pioneer of salvation, opening and demonstrating the path for others. Examples are warrior-heroes such as Rama in India or more peaceful figures such as the Buddha and Jesus. Religions may advance both classic examples that are part of its memory from the past and recent saints and heroes who exemplify its way of life in the present. People such as Albert Schweitzer, Mohandas Gandhi, Martin Luther King, and Mother Teresa of Calcutta have been widely regarded as religious heroes of the twentieth century.

Regardless of whether it is classic or modern, the hero/savior story comes to be told according to a fairly predictable structure (which makes the hero/savior myth per se a general symbol, even though of course the specific contents vary widely). The mythologist Joseph Campbell, for example, describes the pattern of what he calls the *monomyth*—the basic structure of the myth of the hero that is repeated over and over behind a thousand names and settings.[5] Simplified, his scenario can be compared with the three initiatory stages of van Gennep and Turner, previously discussed, of separation, liminality, and reincorporation.

There is first the *departure* of the hero—his or her call, crossing the first threshold of trial and temptation, and entry into what Campbell calls the "deep sea journey" or (from the example in the Book of Jonah) the "belly of the whale," a long and arduous passage out of ordinary reality to the place of true transformation. The second part, the time of real *initiation* through struggle and triumph, involves experiences such as those called the "road of trials," the "meeting with the goddess," the "atonement with the father," "apotheosis," and the "ultimate boon." It would be the Buddha's enlightenment, the passion and resurrection of Jesus, or in J. R. R. Tolkien's *The Lord of the Rings*, the struggles of Frodo from the last meeting with Galadriel to the destruction of the Ring and the coronation of Aragorn. Finally, there is the stage of *return*, when the hero is reincorporated into society as a changed person and one able to change others to enable them to go more easily through what he or she has experienced.

There are other kinds of structural patterns that can also be seen; Claude Lévi-Strauss made three basic points about myth in his essay "The Structural Study of Myth."[6]

1. Myth is a kind of language—that is, it has a message and is trying to make a statement.

2. A myth is composed of all its variants—to know what the message is, one looks not only, as a historical scholar might, for the earliest form but also at every way the myth is expressed. To know the full message of the Buddha in human experience, for example, one would not only look at the life of the historical Buddha but also at all the ways he has been represented and talked about down through two and a half millennia of Buddhist history.

3. The movement of myth is from awareness of opposites to mediation. Polarities like male and female, man and nature, youth and age, or locality and world are reconciled. Lévi-Strauss shows how this is done in a way by the "trickster" figure, like Coyote in North American Indian mythology, who manages by his wits to make his way

---

[5] Joseph Campbell, *The Hero with a Thousand Faces* (New York: Bollengen Foundation, 1949).

[6] Claude Lévi-Strauss, "The Structural Study of Myth," *Journal of American Folklore*, LXXXVIII, 270 (October–December 1955), 428–44. Reprinted in Richard and Fernande De-George, eds., *The Structuralists: From Marx to Lévi-Strauss* (Garden City, N.Y.: Doubleday Anchor Books, 1972), pp. 169–94.

among gods and men, alternately bamboozling and befriending them. The same task of mediation is done more formally by the hero in his or her initiatory adventure.

Doctrine is also a symbol of the religious world one is in. It differs from myth and narrative in that it usually comes later and sums up in more abstract language what they said in story format. Doctrine asks and answers the question, "If such and such is what the divine did on this and that occasion, what can we say about it that is true all the time?" Responses are such general statements as that God, or the sacred reality, is always near at hand, knows all things, can transform people, and so forth. Specific religious doctrines are discussed in a later chapter.

Religious rhetoric, language that is conceptual but intended to persuade or to construct religious reality through its interweaving of concepts, is found in preaching and inspirational writing. It blends the second and third forms of audio symbolism, verbal nonconceptual and verbal conceptual, and perhaps even has a hint of the first, music, when the rhythm and intonation of a voice are used to create a special state of consciousness. Chiefly, though, preaching and other rhetoric is the use of words and concepts not so much as doctrinal statement or sustained logical argument but as triggers to enable the hearers (and perhaps the speaker) to make the leap of transition into the religion's alternative worlds where its values are plain and true. Key words, phrases, and ideas potently recall the root images and metaphors and experiences of the faith, bringing them back if one has known them before, suggesting their transformative power if one has not. Religious rhetoric constructs religious reality rather than describing it and enables experiences of it rather than mere knowledge about it.

PUBLIC AND PRIVATE SYMBOLS

One last categorization of symbols that ought to be made is between *public* and *private*.[7] Symbols pervade both outside social landscapes and the private landscapes within each person's head. They affect both the way one relates to the community and the way one lines up ideas in one's own mind.

Symbols that relate people chiefly to larger social units and are widely known and understood, at least in terms of their social role, are public symbols. Examples are the flag or the cross. They are accepted in the society as symbols of its identity. They can also, of course, dwell within one's mind as an interiorized public symbol—a soldier may die with an image of

---

[7] Kenneth Boulding, *The Image* (Ann Arbor: University of Michigan Press, 1956).

the flag in his mind; a devout Christian may bear the cross in his or her heart and mind even when not seeing it visibly on steeple or altar.

Between public and private symbols is a realm of what may be called conventional symbols. Such symbols are widely understood and almost a kind of language but have no official status in any community as does flag or cross. Functionally they are often little more than signs. Examples are such favorites of editorial cartoonists as the dove of peace and the sword of war.

Private symbols in the strict sense are most meaningful just to one individual because they have come out of one's personal experience and imagination. Every person, however plain and unpoetic, must have some mental image—a special place, a scene from some significant dream or fantasy, a favorite picture or memory—that has importance as a symbol for that person but no one else. For that person, the image participates in an important greater reality, and he or she may look at it, go to it, or recall it from time to time.

Symbols in the original creative work of artists and poets are basically in the private category and may derive from each artist's personal roots. They have a fuller destiny as they become known and bring others into the poet's or artist's private world. They do not, however, become official in the public symbol sense, though a few may become conventional.

Of course, it is a relative matter; to be a symbol in a religious or poetic sense the entity must have a communicable meaning. It cannot be purely and flatly personal. It must call up some kind of response in the minds of percipients. Many of the most effective symbols in religious art and poetry are based on general symbols (tree, moon, circle, and so forth) but are used in such a fresh way as to seem novel and evocative.

SYMBOLS AND MEANING

Let us look again at what religious symbols are. They are discrete visual or audio objects or sets that offer a paradigmatic concept of the real self and the way to it. Ultimately, stories and pictures of gods, religious heroes, or other religious topics are powerful because they suggest oneself at one's highest, the real self. They are like seeing or hearing outside of oneself, or perhaps recognizing outside of oneself, what one would most like to be, in rapport with ultimate reality. Alternatively, symbols can be said to become most powerful when one is already in touch with the real self—they are like doors to the infinite divine reality accessible only to the real self.

Moreover, symbols are triggers facilitating transition to an alternative reality in which the real self, or infinity, is actualized. Visual symbols, words, or music may express tremendous reality to some people and be just a passing entertainment to others, but for those to whom the other

George Holton/Photo Researchers

Shinto *torii* or shrine gate

world behind them is part of life, the symbol is enough. Seeing or hearing the symbol can work almost like a posthypnotic suggestion, calling up emotional and conceptual responses of immense power. At the least, these images or tones make entry into the other world seem inviting and serve to make the person open to it. That achievement depends on the evocative ability of symbols to reconstruct times past, to simplify emotional attitudes, to provide the sort of mental rearrangement around a new center that makes this world look different. Symbols energize such shifts by jolting one with a transitional shock.

Let us now look at some symbolic functions. Symbols recall the past as public or private memory jogs. S. G. F. Brandon has spoken of religion as "ritual perpetuation of the past."[8] To a great extent this is an accurate characterization. Religion's services and festivals, like the secular rites of societies, are based on events that happened, or are believed to have hap-

[8] S. G. F. Brandon, *Time and Mankind* (London: Hutchinson, 1951), p. 19.

pened, at some point in the past and are of vital importance to the present. They are moreover events that go a great way toward giving the people of the present their identity. Rites are a kind of collective memory, and memory and the story it tells are important to identity.

Because the past cannot be re-created completely, it must be done symbolically, even as the individual consciously recalls only a few representative moments from the distant past. Just as one does not remember everything one did in one's ninth summer, recalling just one trip to the beach or one baseball game that encapsulates and represents the whole, so the founder of a religion or a nation may be represented by just celebrating his birth and death or by just one characteristic gesture, such as Jesus at his Last Supper or Muhammad returning to Mecca for his final visit. Through such joggings of the collective memory, Christianity and Islam perpetuate their pasts with symbols to recall to the minds of their present followers who they are. Through rites like the holy communion or the pilgrimage to Mecca, they make the entire past live symbolically in the present.

It could be argued, of course, that the ritual reenactment of single events in the lives of men as spontaneous and original as Jesus or Muhammad grossly distorts their lives. That may be, although perhaps no more so than our own memories distort our past lives, but it must also be acknowledged that to a religion the meaning of its own past is more than simply historical. The ritual repetition of keys to the religion's spiritual meaning is essential to unveiling the larger meaning of the past. The further meaning is that the past evoked is a sacred time, when a special divine power and wisdom were available. The symbol, music or rite or image, becomes a way of getting into that past time. The very fact that it is familiar and perhaps repeated makes it most effective for this purpose: time travel (even if only subjective and even if only back to a stylized version of the original time) is not an easy gambit and so is best done over familiar roads. One becomes accustomed to responding to familiar clues or concepts.

Religious symbols can also recall one's own past. Some symbols clearly suggest the world of childhood. It is religiously valuable to be taken back into it, since memories of happy childhoods always have a glow about them that reinforces other concepts, whether paradises or divine maternal or paternal figures. Religious symbols may also recall the intense religious experiences of one's past. To hear the music once played at one's most meaningful religious service or to see again the place of one's conversion or warmest devotion can understandably strengthen a desire to remain loyal to those moments.

These reflections evoke another feature of symbols. Symbols have the capacity to simplify feelings and ideas into strong, undifferentiated monoliths that can easily be polarized to their opposites—the sacred and the profane, the good and the bad, our world versus the outside. By simplifying religious decision to acceptance or rejection of the symbol, worship or nonworship, the symbol makes commitment easier. That is particularly the case when the symbol represents a god, Buddha, savior, patron saint, or teacher who personifies an absolute divine claim or is the center of identity for a city or culture.

It is important to remember, though, that even as symbols simplify they are also complex. Every symbol conveys a complex set of messages, because symbols are able to handle several matters at once. The same symbol—say the ancestral tablets of a Chinese family—can suggest at once loyalty and commitment to the family watched over by these ancestors, adherence to the traditional Confucian system of values that so emphasizes ancestral piety, and transcendence over ordinary life indicated by the supernatural aspect of the ancestral spirits. More developed symbols, such as the Buddha who dwells in a family or community temple in Thailand or Japan, might even suggest conflicting values that the individual would have to resolve—for example, between loyalty to the family supporting the temple and to the Buddha's call to his followers to free themselves from all worldly ties. Within Christianity, some have felt the same kind of conflict between the message of Jesus and the church as they know it.

Nonverbal symbols may oversimplify issues, compared to the kinds of nuances and qualifications that can be raised by verbal discussion, although we must remember that language too is symbolic and words as symbols also oversimplify the realities behind them. Symbols, however, bring out certain complexities, either resolving them in the symbol or presenting them to the individual to resolve, by bringing together in one discrete point several otherwise different areas of experience—the self, the family, the community, the past, the numinous, the transcendent.

All these are important aspects of what is contained in most religious symbolism. The symbol's purpose is to put them all together or to lead the individual to do so. Thus loyalty to the past and the family, or leaving the family for a holier life and rejecting the past to build a brighter future, may both be tinged with numinous, transcendent value.

THE ORCHESTRATION OF SYMBOLS IN RITE

It remains to say a few words about symbols in relation to the practical form of religious expression, that is, expression in acts such as worship, pilgrimage, art, architecture, or private prayer and meditation. *Rite* or public worship, the fullest of all these practical forms, is an orchestration of symbols to evoke the religious alternative world through several media simultaneously—vision, hearing, perhaps also smell, touch, and taste. The most effective worship is a network of many small things, all of which converge to bring the participant into the alternative reality of the religion. It becomes a total perception. When such a total environment is constructed, there is no objective reference point from which to judge it, and even one's inner thoughts are brought into alignment with it.

These concepts have been applied to theater by the dramatist and critic Richard Schechner.[9] His approach to theater, centering on the ideas of environment and performance, depends heavily on studies in traditional religion, especially shamanism, and in turn does much to illuminate the meaning of rite as orchestration of symbols. Schechner emphasizes the theatrical experience as a total experience—a "total immersion" in the drama, which therefore becomes transformative for cast and audience alike. For there to be a total environment, of course, the audience cannot be just spectators *outside* the drama but must be participants, a part of the environment that makes the drama. The fact that there are people present is a major factor in what goes on.

In the same way, a religious rite (whether a shaman's trance, a High Mass, or a Protestant service with sermon) may be an effective performance by the religious specialist, but the total experience for those present is affected also by the presence of the whole group of participant-observers. The rite is probably the act of a community of some sort, and its meaning is completed by the fact that there are others besides the performers present and by the transformative impact it has on those others.

Transformation means subjective movement from one world or reality to another in which one becomes a real self. This transformation must finally be brought about by a communication of the reality of the alternative by a person or setting for which it *is* real. The alternative reality cannot be feigned; although human motives and consciousness may always be mixed, if religious specialists or players on the stage are *only* acting and have no involvement in the reality of what they are doing, that strange and indefinable but real sense of entering another world through their operations is likely to be missing. For this reason Schechner speaks of performance, not acting, in the theater.

Notice, though, that the term *performance* does imply actions performed according to definite patterns for which one can prepare and that can indeed be a highly programmed break with the diffuseness and unpredictability of ordinary life. Doing something that seems real and that points toward another level of reality is likely to be *more* controlled and structured—in a word, cultural—than the ordinary. (Even such seemingly spontaneous worship as speaking in tongues and falling to the ground in ecstasy usually occurs within the structured situation of a service in which it is expected.) It is Peter L. Berger's social or cultural construction of a sacred cosmos, discussed in Chapter 1, in which the human capacity to change reality as we perceive it by symbols and management of time and

---

[9] Richard Schechner, *Environmental Theater* (New York: Hawthorn Books, Inc., 1973).

environment is carried to a high degree. This change is often accomplished by gestures whose point, in fact, seems to be reversing the natural to show the power of culture and, thence, of the gods transcendent over it. Claude Lévi-Strauss has set up several transformational pairs of opposites:

continuous	intermittent
spoken	sung/chanted
profane	sacred
everyday	mythic
unadorned	masked
nature	culture[10]

Consider how often the transformative movement of religious rite is from the first column to the second—singing when in ordinary life one would speak, being masked (or otherwise dressed in special garb) when in ordinary life one is not, doing something that happens only occasionally instead of any time or all the time. All this suggests a cultural and sacred reversal of the natural and ordinary. Precisely by performance (doing things in the second column), rite begins the transformative process. When a shaman or priest comes out robed in rich colors to begin a dance or rite, that immediately tells us something different is about to happen and begins the transition to, in Alfred Schutz's term, another province of meaning.

All rite and worship involve a combination of symbols. Even worship as simple as a Quaker meeting speaks through several symbols and senses—silence, the spoken voice and words, austerity of surroundings, the presence of other people. There is a message about any religion in the structure and symbolism of its worship, just as much as in what is outwardly said. In all religion worship is a form of expression. It is simply a matter of ascertaining *what* its message is wordlessly saying about how one best comes into rapport with the transcendent through this form of expression. If it is an elaborate and traditional rite, it says one best transcends finitude through participation in something with strong aesthetic appeal and a sense of getting beyond the present through forms that come out of the past. If it is very plain or free-form, it says one achieves the same end best through a minimization of impediments to knowing the divine inwardly or to expressing oneself freely. The same can be seen in the messages carried in strong centralized leadership versus widespread participation, largely visual versus largely verbal communication, and so forth. The messages about the nature of humanity and God on this level, although surely there, are not often fully articulated and have to be felt or intuited.

---

[10] Cited in Schechner, *Environmental Theater*, p. 171.

We shall now look at some of the stages by which worship as orchestration of symbols typically enables the transformative process. The order of the internal stages may vary.

Opening.   The rite begins with a gesture that marks and enables a transition from the ordinary to religious reality. It may be a rite of purification, such as the Shinto priest waving a wand over the assembly of worshippers. It may be a hymn, a dramatic procession, the beat of drums or the sound of a conch, but it marks a transition and may even induce a sort of shock to assist the subjective shift.

Prayer or establishment of rapport with transcendence.   The next stage is likely to be a verbal process of becoming synchronous with the sacred—chanting, praying, or reading of sacred texts. It is quieter but more prolonged than the opening drama, indicating a more deeply meditative adjustment to the other reality.

Katrina Thomas/Photo Researchers

A religious procession in an Eastern Orthodox church, suggesting the role of traditional ritual in religion.

Presentation of offerings.   This stage is many things, such as placing of food on Shinto or Hindu altars, offering the sacramental bread and wine in Roman Catholic and Eastern Orthodox liturgies, offering money in Protestant churches. Some rather ceremonial collection or presentation relates important material symbols to the divine. This is a somewhat more active and dramatic moment than the preceding.

The message.   In most, but not all, worship there is a sermon or at least the reading of a sacred text by a religious specialist as instruction or inspiration and the use of religious rhetoric in the very supportive setting of temple and rite. This is a reversal of the previous action—the people then communicated to the divine; now the divine communicates to them.

Participation.   In this the culminating stage, the people and the divine come most together and are thoroughly mixed. Divine life comes into the people, perhaps altering behavior, and people feel closest to God. There is likely to be some motor activity and the use of some of the proximity sense. This is the point of holy communion, of pentecostal speaking in tongues, of the Shinto festival climaxing in sacred dance, carnival, and the rapid procession of the deity through the streets.

Closing.   At the end there is another shock of transition in the termination of the sacred experience and return to ordinary life, though it may be eased by blessing, music, final prayers, and socializing among participants.

Practical expression is not limited to settings of worship. It can also be done individually. A person alone can move himself or herself through these stages and enter the alternative world or actualize the real self in prayer and meditation. The process can be achieved with the aid of sound or visual accoutrements, such as a sacred picture or image upon which one concentrates, or it can be accomplished with only the evocation of what is within one's mind.

The process of transformation through orchestration of symbols can be accomplished geographically. Pilgrimage—travel for religious renewal to a special place that is itself a sacred symbol, such as Rome, Jerusalem, or Mecca—is a prolonged and spatially expressed rite. Traditional customs of pilgrimage have the same sense of opening, transition, offering, learning, and participation, but they may go on over days or weeks, and each stage is done at a different place along the route. The entire journey is like a rite and amounts to a temporary movement into the religious alternative world or into liminality, to a place where the map of the alternative world coincides with geography as we know it. The pilgrimage site is a place where one can be a real self.

For example, the well-known Muslim pilgrimage to Mecca begins with separation from ordinary life as the visitor dons simple pilgrim's garb at the port of Jidda several miles from the holy city. From then on he or she will take no life, cut neither hair nor nails, and abstain from sex. At Mecca, he or she will circumambulate the shrine of the Kaaba seven times, stand on the side of Mount Arafat (to hear a sermon) all afternoon, and then, leaving the sacred state, ritually sacrifice a goat or sheep and have a haircut—all over a period of two or three days.

Traditional pilgrimage sites, like Mecca and many others, are themselves complex symbols. Their buildings and temples reproduce the organization of the heavenly realm of their gods or God. In Mecca, for example, the throne of Allah above is said to be directly over the Kaaba, and angels continually circle around it even as do the faithful below. Kyoto, the ancient capital of Japan, is patterned on a mandala or Buddhist sacred diagram of the relationships of cosmic Buddhas and has monasteries or temples guarding its approaches.

Religious symbols, then, are magic doorways into worlds where religious meaning becomes the overt and apparent meaning of things, rather than the hidden meaning as in our ordinary world.

SUMMARY

The fundamental distinction between sign and symbol needs to be understood. A sign, like a road sign, merely points to what it indicates, but a symbol participates deeply in what it symbolizes, being derived from a figure or object close to its heart—the cross in Christianity or the figure of the meditating Buddha in Buddhism. It is not only a signpost but also of itself helps a person enter into the experience of the religion. Further, each symbol is a part of the whole religion and opens into the whole pattern of meaning it sets up. By thinking of what is compatible with the major symbols—the cross or the Buddha—and what is not, we are aided in making choices. That is, by letting the symbol lead us into the religion's "world," with its values and experiences, our eyes are opened to its pattern of meaning and so much further helped in decision making.

Symbols can be usefully divided into several categories, such as focal, general, and secondary specific. There are also several categories of audio or word symbols. These are all defined in the glossary.

A particularly important vehicle of symbol is myth. In religious studies myth means a story which expresses in narrative form important aspects of the religion or culture's view of the world and of being human before God or the gods. Two main types are the cosmogonic myth and the hero/savior myth. Doctrine and religious rhetoric are other important bearers of verbal symbols.

Some symbols are public, in that they are recognized by a community to pertain to community beliefs and institutions and have a generally accepted meaning; others are private symbols, rooted in individual experience, though they may be expressed in art and writing and may be just a fresh interpretation of a traditional public religious symbol.

Religious rite may be spoken of as an "orchestration of symbols." Visual and verbal symbols, perhaps also symbols reaching the senses of smell, taste, and touch, are brought together. Religious rites perpetuate the sacred times and persons of the past, help to simplify and clarify feelings, and above all create through the impact of many symbols at once a special time and place in which the religion's view of reality is enacted, making it, for those able to respond fully to the symbols, entirely real.

New York Public Library, Spencer Collection

The prophet Muhammad, Abu Bakr, and Ali on the Way to Mecca, painting from a copy of the life of the Prophet, Ottoman court style, 1594.

Chapter
5

Faith Through Form: Religion and Art

Chapter Objectives

- Give reasons why art is important to religion.

- Trace the story of painting from the earliest examples in cave art on, noting the role of animals, nature, and the human form in religious art.

- Tell how sculpture can differ from painting in its treatment of religious subjects.

- Speculate about how and why religious images became more anthropomorphic, especially at the time of the rise of the great religions.

- Summarize the role of music in religion, mentioning why it has sometimes been seen as dangerous, but more often as helpful in the creation of religious sentiments.

- Discuss poetry as expressive of feelings and responses to religion, sometimes in a complex way. Select a favorite religious poem and analyze it in terms of its combination of words, pictures, and feelings.

- Describe how drama can create archetypal divine or human images, and also present human beings with all of their flaws.

• Summarize the role of religion in literature and tell how novels and stories can present profound images of human nature with which religion can work, and how they can also chronicle human experience in all its fullness. Give examples from stories you have read.

As you read the chapter, also look for important words. The key words defined in the glossary at the end of the book are in boldface type at their first use in the text.

STAINED-GLASS WINDOWS

Many older churches have windows of stained glass in which the white light of the sun is colored and shaped to take on the form of haloed saints and conventional symbols of faith. In a real sense that is what all of religion does. We noted in Chapter One the difference religions make between sacred and profane realities. Now let us go a step farther back and see what lies behind this distinction by using a set of relatively neutral terms from the Buddhist tradition: *unconditioned* and *conditioned reality.*

Conditioned reality is what most of us know most of the time. Conditions mean limitations. We are, first of all, conditioned or limited in space and time. If we are, say, in a city in the U.S., we are not also situated in Hong Kong or on the planet Neptune. If we are living in the late twentieth century, we are not also in the ninth century with Charlemagne or in the twenty-fifth century with Buck Rogers. Our minds are also of limited capacity. Most of us cannot think of more than one thing at a time or multiply more than two two-digit numbers in our heads, and we forget far more than we remember. Further, we notice that this conditioning is the state of all ordinary reality around us.

But what if another reality existed which was the opposite of all this; which was equally present in all times and places, unlimited in mind, all-seeing and all-knowing, as unconditioned as we are conditioned? This reality would, in a word, be what religions ordinarily postulate God, Brahman, or **Nirvana**—however ultimate reality is named—to be.[1]

All religions, one way or another, think that there is a different kind of reality, made up of gods and spirits, transcendent over the ordinary conditioned reality plane. The great religions generally go on to think of a "split-level" universe, made up of unconditioned and conditioned reality, of God or the Absolute on the one side, and the human realm on the other.

One could, of course, deny that there is any such thing as unconditioned reality, or say that if there is it could not be known by conditioned

[1] Note, however, that philosophical Hindus and Buddhists do not conceive of Brahman or Nirvana as having personal consciousness in the way that Jewish, Christian, or Muslim monotheists think of God as possessing.

beings like ourselves, so we might as well just live in the world we know. Religions, however, believe that both sides can be known and that the borderline between the two is, so to speak, filled with doors and windows. Indeed, this porous boundary is the realm in which religion works.

In the eyes of traditional religion, visitors from the other side—gods, saviours, saints, angels, spirits—have entered and may continually enter our conditioned homeland. Messages in the form of revelations and spiritual gifts are regularly sent. The symbols and worship forms of religion say significant things about the nature of unconditioned reality, as do its doctrines. Conversely, persons from the conditioned level like ourselves can inwardly enter, or taste something of, unconditioned reality through rite, prayer, and mystical experience.

This borderland is also the territory of religious art. The term *art* is used here in the broad sense, to include painting, sculpture, architecture, music, poetry, drama, and fiction—and even such "minor" arts as garden landscaping and jewelry making. Art therefore is obviously congruent with symbolism as presented in the preceding chapter, though our emphasis here will not be on core religious expression such as official scriptures and the media of major forms of worship. We shall look rather at how great artists in all these visual, audio, and literary forms have dealt with themes drawn from religion.

Sometimes they have portrayed the splendor of unconditioned reality as transmitted through the window of a particular faith, sometimes they have voiced the anguish of guilt or doubt through which a religious quest can lead. But in any case, the virtue of great art is that it expresses feelings or visions that many have had, but have not been able to put into form or word; in its presence we may find ourselves saying, "This experience of seeing, hearing, or reading has clarified something important for me; now I understand both myself and reality better."

The poet Shelley wrote that "Life, like a dome of many-colored glass/ Stains the white radiance of eternity"; so great art, reflecting life, should refract the light of unconditioned reality into hues and forms that bring it closer to home yet still make it seem like something from another world. Like a stained-glass window, it should be an inviting portal between two worlds.

Art also connects parts of our own human selves. The one thing that unites all the art media, whether painting, sculpture, architecture, music, poetry, or prose, is that they are things made by humans and not solely to meet practical needs. Rather, like religion, they also meet a different kind of need, in this case to express something specifically human, indeed specific to the artist however well the artwork also expresses what others feel. Art says in ways *humans* can understand things seen, heard, and felt; it helps us know feelings of beauty, awe, or dread enhanced through the power of art to the point where they are strong and clear.

Art may draw themes from nature, or from human society, but it does not leave them just as they are, pure and simple. Rather, it filters them through the artist's own human nature, to come out in ways that show us how *humans* see, hear, and emotionally respond to what is around them. Or, art may draw from themes that seem more inward, from the realm of dreams, or of symbols (as discussed in the last chapter), or of moods and feelings and mental images; these too it gives forms that show what they are and how we can see them and respond to them. Art, in other words, is a mysterious process that links three vitally important human arenas: nature, the subjectivity of the artist, and the audience of the art in human society.

When an artist works with religion, she or he is not just presenting the images and symbols of the religion in some untouched form. To be sure, religious art has a very important role in preserving the myths, history, and symbols of the faith, generation after generation. When closely associated with worship, it also has the role of helping create the *expected* feelings and reactions to them, that is, of facilitating faith by taking part in worship's *orchestration of symbols*.

Yet if it is great art it will also have something of the artist in it, and that artist will in some sense be a great person, full of texture and complexity. Religious art will say things superbly about the objects of faith and the varied human ways of responding to them. We know that being a human is not easy. Great religious art can lead us into hours of tremendous spiritual exaltation, and also into times of despair; of faith lost and faith found, of shallow faith and deep faith.

PAINTING

One of the earliest forms of art must be the painting of pictures, for if one excludes the quasi-artistic aspects of intentional burial, little that can be called human art antedates the famous cave paintings of the Old Stone Age Cro-Magnons who lived in the Europe of 25,000 to 35,000 years B.C.E. As is well-known, these pictures are largely accurate and remarkably dynamic studies of bison, horses,and other large game animals that were probably important to the economic life, and certainly to the spiritual life, of the people who drew them.

The caves containing these works of art were not mere picture galleries, nor were the paintings only the ornaments of homes where people dwelt. The illustrations are located very deep in the caverns, where then as now they could be reached only after an arduous and dangerous quest. It is difficult to envision these places as other than religious sanctuaries, where

Peter Buckley

Cave painting, Lascaux, France.

sacred rites believed to be crucially important for the life of the tribe were carried out.

If so, it is not surprising that the representations were mostly of animals, for to these hunting and gathering peoples, the animal was the source of life. In early nature-oriented religion the main source of food, and so of life, was inevitably also a central religious symbol—the animal for hunters, the plant represented by a dying and rising vegetation god for archaic agriculturists. Of course for Cro-Magnons, as for most hunters and gatherers, no doubt wild-plant foodstuffs and smaller creatures like fish and rodents constituted a large part of the diet, but it is big game—bison, horse, deer, bear—that are on the cave walls. These mighty beasts were the hunters' greatest physical challenge, and so also the greatest spiritual challenge to their skill, stamina, and inner rapport with the animal spirits.

These deep cave sanctuaries were probably the site of hunting magic designed to bring success in the field. But they may well have been more than that. There is reason to think they were places of initiation for tribal youth, and that the positioning of the animal pictures, often superimposed

Alinari/Art Resource

Painting of the Blessed Virgin

one on another, encoded some kind of story or record. The depths of these caverns may well have been not only the temples, but also the schools and libraries, of the people. Whatever the full meaning, their religious life must have centered around an idea that the animal, and so a painted representation of it, was a portal to a sacred world.[2]

Comparable ideas can be found in the long history of religious painting. The **icons** used in Eastern Orthodox churches are particularly clear examples of paintings that are windows to the transcendent world. These paintings of saints, the Blessed Virgin, Christ, and even the Trinity are done in a highly stylized, traditional way that emphasizes the spiritual nature of the subject: large soulful eyes, conventional gestures, haloes to show the inner radiance of a holy person, a golden or starry background indicating eternity. To believers, the icon shows the subject as he or she is

[2] See John E. Pfeiffer, *The Creative Explosion: An Inquiry into the Origins of Art and Religion.* New York: Harper & Row, 1982, pp. 210–25.

Allnari/Art Resource

The Baptism of Christ by Giotto described in the text.

now in heaven, and these pictures are treated with the profoundest reverence whether in churches or a prayer corner in the home.

The traditional Christian religious painting of Western Europe is somewhat more flexible in subject matter and style, often developing themes from biblical stories or the legends of saints. Yet, at least in medieval or early modern examples, the picture is certainly also intended to be an entry into another world of wonder, miracle, and supernatural reality.

For example, the treatment of the baptism of Christ by the Florentine master Giotto (1266?–1337) makes Jesus, standing nearly naked in the water of the Jordan river, a quite human young man of about thirty. No less manly is John the Baptist, in his camel's hair tunic and rose-colored cape, reaching out to his messiah in a natural way from the shore. Yet both have a nimbus or halo, and above the two, reaching down from heaven, his finger pointing at Christ, is God the Father. On the two banks of the river are saints and winged angels watching the scene intently. The typically Western European attention to physical detail, especially of the human form, and to the drama of events, is thus combined with features making it clear that in these bodies and this happening nature and supernature are united.[3]

[3] This painting is presented and discussed in Beverly Moon, ed., *An Encyclopedia of Archetypal Symbolism.* Boston: Shambhala, 1991, pp. 454–57.

Sometimes it is nature itself that conveys that which is behind or within ordinary nature. This is especially true of Chinese and Japanese landscape paintings in the **Zen** Buddhist tradition, such as those of Sesshu (1420–1506), widely regarded as the greatest of all Japanese artists. In Zen, everything, even the humblest bird or leaf, seen just as it is, reveals the Buddha nature, the essence of the universe as perceived by a Buddha in his enlightenment.

The point of all the famous Zen arts, whether rock gardens or flower arrangement or **chanoyu** (the "tea ceremony"), is to bring out that hidden nature by letting things reveal the whole universe down to its innermost heart through being just what they are. A rock in a rock garden is not just a rock, but also a rock that is an outcropping of the universe as a whole in one particular time and space, a rock in Nirvana as well as in conditioned reality. A tea-ceremony cup of tea is a cup of tea enjoyed as nothing but a cup of tea. All the attention of an adept of this rite is to be on nothing but its aroma and flavor, just as a saint's might be on nothing but God. But because the tea is simply **Nirvana** in disguise, the tea adept is no less liberated than any other devotee who is in harmony with unconditioned reality.

This is why much of the great Zen *suiboku*, or ink-wash painting, is of the ordinary but grand things of nature: mountains, trees, water. Yet they reveal something else as well, something even older and deeper, from the Buddhist point of view. For these landscape paintings can be seen as divided into three layers from bottom to top, each corresponding to one of the three great bodies, or forms of manifestation of the Buddha nature according to **Mahayana** Buddhism: in the plain outer world of physical manifestation and conditioned reality where we usually dwell; in the heavenly worlds, no different from the intrapsychic realms where dreams and visions come from; and in the *dharmakaya*, or essence of the universe itself, where the whole is seen as the Void, and the dance of molecules and galaxies takes place.

Thus at the bottom of a Sesshu painting will be something like a lake and a beached boat, and perhaps a humble figure in straw raincoat, at the foot of a mighty cliff and mountain. Halfway up the mountain will be a jewel-like, or dreamlike, temple, and perchance the dwelling of a wizardly hermit-sage. Still higher up, the peaks will disappear into mists and empty skies, washing into the formlessness of timeless eternity.

Yet another perspective is given by those painters who represent religious subjects or moods in abstract or symbolist forms. For meditation purposes, Hindu deities can be presented as **yantras**, abstract diagrams. For example, Shiva as universal essence and his Shakti, or consort—earth and manifested reality—can become a series of interlocking triangles, those pointing upward representing Shakti, those pointing downward, Shiva. In certain Tibetan meditation paintings, the tokens and body parts of a powerful Buddha or bodhisattva or consort-goddess are scattered randomly; it is the exercise of the meditator to bring them together by the force of his concentration.

Marc Chagall (1887–1985), artistic chronicler of Jewish life in the villages of old Russia, in his unforgettable "Fiddler on the Roof" studies, presents what seems at first to be the rather bizarre image of a musician playing on, indeed almost floating above, the ridgepole of a peasant cabin. Yet after a few moments of letting our conscious and subconscious minds absorb the spirit of the painting, we understand how the player's music, and sheer joy of life, soars above the squalor of his earth-plane existence.

Many other modern artists, adherents of such schools as impressionism, surrealism, or cubism, have also clearly been on a spiritual quest through the medium of paint. Their rejection of ordinary realism, in fact, arises from a passionate desire to see and reveal realities beneath the surface that often converge with spiritual lines of perception. Van Gogh's superluminous starry night shows the heavens with a splendor perceived by no ordinary eyes, but true to the divine glory behind them—behind both the eye and the star. Piet Mondrian's straight lines and blocks in his cubist period hint at the saying attributed to Plato, "God geometrizes." Many if not most of such artists have not been believers in any conventionally orthodox sense, but they have shown anew how art can be a reflection of nature, the artist's own subjectivity and that of a human audience—and Ultimate Reality or windows and doors thereto.[4]

SCULPTURE

Alongside of paintings and other two-dimensional (or bas-relief) representations of religious subjects, one sees the full-figure forms of wood, metal, or stone known as statues or sculpture. Indeed, when a physical object of human construction is a visible focus of religious worship, whether the image of a god or Buddha, or the cross or crucifix of a Christian altar, it is—with the notable exception of the Eastern Orthodox icons already mentioned—most likely to be a three-dimensional sculpture of some kind. Paintings of religious figures or stories are commonly found on the walls of churches, temples, abbeys, or pious private homes, but statues may be the focal point of worship on the altars and in the shrines themselves.

For this reason, human-form statues are suspect in some great religious traditions. They are not found in Eastern Orthodox or Protestant Christianity, Judaism, Islam, Shinto, or Confucianism, unless in a very secondary ornamental capacity. For these religionists, devotion directed

---

[4] A useful introduction to this topic is Kathleen J. Regier, compiler, *The Spiritual Images in Modern Art*. Wheaton, IL: Theosophical Publishing House, 1987.

toward such a physical form comes too close to idolatry, or the worship of something other than the true God. (Three-dimensional symbols, though, like the Protestant cross or the Confucian tablet bearing the name and title of the Great Sage, may be acceptable.)

For other faiths, however, the artistry of statues can interact with worship. The carved form, though strictly speaking not worshipped for its own sake, serves to align the worshipper's thoughts and feelings. It becomes a focus of prayer, an aid to devout visualization, and sometimes is seen as an outward repository of divine energies.

Our concern now, however, is not with the religious use of sculpture but simply with it as a form of religious art. Here we may first of all observe that statues are particularly good at capturing the archetypal meaning of a religious figure or symbol. A statue usually tells less of a story than many paintings, but may do even more to freeze its subject in a single timeless gesture that sums up its meaning as a window to unconditioned reality. The subject, in other words, becomes an **archetype**, the embodiment of a great universal theme, like those of which Carl Jung wrote. She or he is just the Great Mother, the Hero, the Sage, the King, captured in a single gesture of compassion or fortitude. While paintings, of course, can do this also, statues do it especially well, facilitating concentration without distraction on just that one aspect of the sacred in rounded form. Great religious sculpture, as it combines a single significant gesture by an eternal being with the solid durability of a medium like marble or metal, powerfully bespeaks the transcendence of religious reality over ordinary time, and of divinity over corruptible human flesh.

In much religious sculpture, the archetypal significance swallows up any serious realism. The figure may display only fertility, as does the "Venus of Willendorf" and many similar round, faceless, sometimes multiple-breasted female forms from early Europe. Or they may be only stern guardians, like the famous, giant stone Easter Island heads, or ancestral eyes quick to anger, or the sly trickster (crafty mythological god sometimes helpful but unpredictable) with his crooked smile. Whatever it is, these images show no human complexity of personality, but are limited to a single function.

The archetypal function undoubtedly controls another great wing of religious sculpture, the **theriomorphic** (animal-shaped) form. Divine animals, or animals with a divine mission, are exceedingly plentiful in religious myth and folklore, and there are examples in religious sculpture: Hanuman the Hindu monkey-god, Bast the sacred Egyptian cat, Quetzalcoatl the feathered serpent of Mayan lore. An animal can clearly present an archetype very well.

But animal-god statues are somewhat less common than those of deities with animal heads and human bodies. In them, the archetypal and the human are significantly joined. Examples include many of the ancient Egyptian gods: the jackel-headed Anubis, the mortuary god; ibis-headed Thoth, god of wisdom; the lion-headed goddess Sekhmet. There is also the Hindu Ganesha, the elephant-headed remover of obstacles. Still another variation is the animal companion of an anthropomorphic (human-shaped) or abstract deity. Many of the Hindu deities have such a follower: Nandi the bull with Shiva, the owl with the wisdom-bearing goddess Saraswati.

Then there are **anthropomorphic** deities as such. Many of them also possess "unnatural" features suggesting archetypal functions, such as those Hindu gods and Buddhist bodhisattvas with multiple arms and faces. These indicate supernatural capacity to do many works of mercy in many worlds simultaneously, or to see in all directions—that is, with infinite omniscience—at once.

Other sculpted gods simply possess artful human form. The ancient Greeks developed this type of expression to its greatest glory. To them, it was the natural but ideally beautiful human form that best mediated divinity. Their Aphrodite, Ares, Athena, Poseidon, and Zeus were women and men of normal attributes, perfectly proportioned for their age and gender.

The Greek ideal has had a wide influence, particularly in the sculptured art of the great religions that arose in the wake of the axial age. The influence of Greek models on indigenous trends cannot always be measured exactly. But it is of interest that Greek influence at its most far-reaching coincided, broadly speaking, with the rise of new, artistically and devotionally more human-centered religions, especially Buddhism, Christianity, and emergent forms of Hinduism.

In the East, the Greek ideal of human-form gods spread through the conquests of Alexander the Great, culminating about 326 B.C.E., in the West, through Greek cultural influence on Rome and its empire. These new religions gave fresh and central roles to the sanctified human, the saint, Buddha, bodhisattva, saviour, and avatar (Hindu god who has come into the world in human form), as well as to anthropomorphic gods and angels. For them, the Greek ideal was well suited, and, though with considerable adaptation, its reflection can be seen from the Buddhas of Kyoto's famous temples to the saints in medieval European cathedrals.

ARCHITECTURE

Those temples and cathedrals call to mind the next important religious art form, architecture, the construction of great buildings in the name of faith. Religion's buildings, its temples, shrines, churches, and mosques, can be edifices of great beauty in themselves, by virtue of their materials and proportions, and so reflect the beauty most believe to be latent in unconditioned reality. Their arrangements also make important statements about the nature of the religion.

Religious buildings have two possible roles in relation to their religious purpose. They can serve, either symbolically or concretely, as the home of the deity, the *House of God*. They also can serve as a place of worship, an assembly place for the *People of God* when they gather for worship and visibly become a religious community. And, of course, religious buildings can be both simultaneously.

Shinto shrines, Hindu temples, and many others are primarily houses of the deity. They are built as one would, in that culture, build the home of a great person, even a king, who is venerated and honored. They boast courts where visitors may come to pay respects, offer gifts, and submit petitions, as if in audience before such a kingly personage. Food and other services may be offered regularly with all the ceremony of a royal repast. But there is no room for an entire congregation or community to be inside at once. That is not the purpose of what is essentially the private house of a deity. At major festivals, when the assembly is large, people may pass before the honored deity in a steady stream or gather in a courtyard or foreground.

Muslim mosques, Protestant churches, Jewish synagogues, and some other religious buildings are today primarily places of congregational worship. They may also be politely called the House of God, and treated with due respect, but that epithet is not taken as literally as in the courtly sort of temple. The architectural emphasis is instead on providing an adequate facility for large gatherings, with good acoustics for music and sermons, and an inspirational atmosphere for the corporate worship experience.

Roman Catholic churches, some Buddhist temples, and a few others are really both. Their altars are sanctified by the presence of the Blessed Sacrament incarnating divine presence, or by venerated Buddhist images, yet they are also places for both services and individual prayers.

Thus religious buildings may, first of all, be divided into those that are divine houses or palaces, those that are essentially auditoria, and those that are both. The first may be divided into many rooms and courtyards, and so cover a large area, but particular chambers may be relatively small. The auditorium-type structures, conversely, are likely to be quite large. Indeed, the interior open spaces and vistas they require pose difficult architectural problems. These were met in some places by the development of the dome and the vaulted roofs of Gothic cathedrals.

Then there are various architectural styles of sacred buildings, each bearing its own message through the layout of the structure as well as through the religion it serves. It would not be possible here to present all the religious architectural styles in the world, but an example, the traditional Western Christian church, may be of help. They have passed through several stages of dominant styles.

The first large-scale church, appearing with the fourth-century liberation of Christianity, was the basilica, an oblong building with a central nave or passageway, based on the Roman court of law. It suggested the church as a place of important meetings and proclamations, where a community could be gathered, and the gathering presided over by duly authorized officials at the front.

The next development was the Romanesque church, a squarish domed building, often with high narrow windows, which appeared in the early Middle Ages. In those troubled times, it strongly suggested the church as a fortress, a place of refuge and security. One variation often found in England and the U.S. is the square-towered Norman church. But as the medieval period advanced, the Romanesque bastion of faith was succeeded by Gothic churches and cathedrals, with their high-pitched ceilings, soaring steeples, and larger stained-glass windows, frequently including round *rose windows*. These edifices seemed to speak not only of security but also of human aspiration toward the heights and the heavens.

The Baroque church of about 1600 to 1750 is represented in the U.S. by Spanish missions and other buildings in that style, as well as by churches of different Baroque schools. The Baroque style is characterized by graceful curving lines, a sense of proportion and perspective, and above all by elaborate ornamentation. Nothing could be left plain; Baroque columns were twisted and creased, altars gilded, and the walls behind them featured cascades of carved foliage, scallops, and polychrome saints. This fashion obviously reflects the new wealth, artistic creativity, technical advances, and exuberant self-confidence of Europe in the Renaissance and subsequent Baroque eras. While often criticized by later generations as pretentious and overdone, Baroque at its best communicates a sense of the overflowing richness and color of sacred reality, and the divinely playful joy of artistic creativity.

At around the same time, the simpler Georgian or Palladian style, represented in many Colonial American churches, took hold in England. It is characterized by proportioned steeples, arched clear windows, simple but elegant lines, and much use of plain white woodwork in both the interior and the exterior. These churches seem somehow to reflect both Protestant restraint and the clarity of thought that was the ideal of the Age of Reason in which they flourished.

The nineteenth century, though a great age of church building, brought Romanesque, Gothic, and other revivals, but little that was truly innovative. In the twentieth century, in contrast, a new age of religious-building art commenced. On the one hand, economic changes effectively sealed off the past. Costs, plus a dearth of traditionally trained craftsmen, made it now nearly impossible to build new medieval-type Gothic cathedrals, although the National Cathedral in Washington, D.C., and St. John the Divine in New York were ambitious and attractive, though controversial, attempts.

On the other hand, new techniques in glass, poured cement, and construction, combined with new inspiration from various schools of streamlined modern architecture, made a fresh plasticity available to churches. They were now shaped like ships, tents, or skyscrapers, were elevated or half-sunken, were built in the round with the altar or pulpit at the center, and sent out numerous novel messages about churches to the world around them. We cannot decode all these communiqués here; perhaps you could study one or more of the contemporary church, temple, or synagogue buildings in your area, and decide what they are saying through the architecture of the edifices themselves.

MUSIC

Churches, temples, synagogues—all evoke not only sights but also sounds, above all perhaps the sound of music. From the stomps and drums of tribal dances to the strains of a mighty pipe organ, from the haunting sound of the shofar, or ram's horn, at the Jewish high holy days to the gravelly chants of Tibetan Buddhist monks, music has been religion's companion. It has elevated the spirit, made sacred words memorable, galvanized individuals toward conversion and assemblies toward action.

To be sure, the very power of music has caused some to suspect it, at least in public religion. They have feared with Plato its appeal to feeling rather than to reason or to the still, small inward voice, and have viewed with apprehension the way the hypnotic rhythm of drums, say, can reportedly counterfeit true mystical states. Many Quakers, unlike most other Christians, have given music only a minor religious role. Unless one counts the rhythmic recitation of the Koran or the muezzin's call from the minaret, melody is not heard in Muslim mosques, though many **Sufi** or Islamic mystical orders employ hymns, chants, and dances in their fervent devotionalism.

For most of the rest, though, music is inseparably part of religion. In the Confucianism of traditional China, music was seen as an important indicator of the spiritual constitution of a society. A militaristic state would have martial music, and a peaceful one idyllic music. Music was also important as an instrument of education and social control. Good music promoted virtue, and as Arthur Waley commented in his translation of *The Analects of Confucius*, music "is an intrinsic part of the Way that causes gentlemen to love other gentlemen and makes small men easy to rule."[5]

[5] Arthur Waley, trans., *The Analects of Confucius*. London: George Allen & Unwin, 1938. Vintage book ed., p. 69.

We have spoken in the last chapter about the role of religious music as audio symbol. Now it remains to distinguish different kinds of religious music.

In many tribal societies, music is closely connected to the dance. These are both communal, community-creating dances and performances of specialist shamans. Both entail heavy rhythm and percussion, and may also include shaman songs, chants or melodies uttered by shamans and shamanesses when in a trance or when calling spirits. This music survives not only in remaining tribal societies, but also in such forms as the music of **kagura** Shinto sacred dance.

Chants, or the rhythmic, repetitious, monotone or quasi-monotone singing of religious words or texts, undoubtedly had their origin in the recitation of tribal myths and lore before the invention of writing. In those days, as in many folk cultures to this day, remarkably long pieces of song and story were committed to memory by the wise and presented on solemn occasions. Rhythm and a clear chanting tone of voice were aids to memorization, hearing, and creating the special atmosphere called for by the reverent recounting of the past. Chanting of magical formulae was also done, as in those Vedic chants called **mantras**, and their peculiar tone added to the sense of a different use of language than the ordinary; in these cases the very sound—vibrations—of the words themselves was part of the power.

In later religions, chanting of both mantras and longer texts became the particular province of such specialists as Brahmin priests, nuns, and monks. Sometimes the words and their meanings became obscure to all but scholars, because they were often in a nonvernacular language, Sanskrit in the East or Latin in much of the Christian West. But literal meanings are superseded by other religious meanings of chants, the symbolic creation of a monastic community singing in common, the creation of a religious aura, and the channeling of prayerful feeling by the haunting sacred melodies.

In this connection, it is interesting to contrast the sounds of chants in different traditions. The chant of Zen monks in Japan, for example, is a deep monotone that has been compared to the drone of a pond full of frogs; it may even be reminiscent of a Japanese tradition that compares the Buddha seated in meditation to an old bullfrog. In any case, the Zen sense of spiritual closeness to nature is evoked. Much Roman Catholic monastic recitation, on the other hand, is in what is called Gregorian chant, or plainsong. Its elegant but simple and repetitious melodies are somewhat farther from nature than those of Zen, somewhat closer to a purely human concept of sweetness and beauty.

That brings us to another form of religious music, what may be called **liturgical** because it is intended for use in the services of faiths with a formal **liturgy**, such as the Roman Catholic, Anglican, Lutheran, or Eastern Orthodox. Jewish service music led by a cantor has a comparable role.

This music is just a setting for regular parts of the service, though often sung by choirs and musically much more elaborate than chants.

Hymns are also sung in services—though of course they may be at other times as well—but are more variable and occasional than liturgical music. Hymns are often devotional in intent, and so express tender feelings in their words and melodies (for example, "Jesus, The Very Thought of Thee, With Sweetness Fills the Breast," and similar Hindu **bhakti**, or devotional hymns to Krishna and other gods), although they may also be martial, like "Onward, Christian Soldiers."

Finally, there is religious performance music: oratorios (for example, Handel's "Messiah"), spiritual songs, organ voluntaries, and the like. They are based on religious themes and create a religious mood, though they may not be strictly parts of worship and its orchestration of symbols, and may well be performed separately from formal worship, at concerts and festivals.

POETRY

We come now to religious artistry in words. Poetry, of course, is not too far removed from religious music in that the words sung to the latter are generally poetic. But now we shall look at poetry with emphasis on the words. Poetry may have originally been intended to be sung or recited, especially in a religious setting, and one may argue that it is still best appreciated that way. But today, more often than not, it is just read, or spoken silently in the mind from memory.

Poetry is above all an arrangement of words, vocal rhythms, and sometimes rhymes that create powerful, abiding images in the mind to make a picture, a mood, or a story resonate with one's deepest feelings. It is not intended primarily to impart information or argue a case dialectically, though there are poems that do those tasks more effectively than a hundred books by the force of feeling and/or images they associate with the information or argument. But chiefly, poetry ties together pictures and emotions, and in so doing it is ultimately close to religion and its roots in myth and symbol.

Poetry is religious when the pictures and feelings it calls forth move into the areas of the doors and windows between conditioned and unconditioned reality, of what the theologian Paul Tillich called *ultimate concern*, whether or not the theme is explicitly religious. Indeed, there is much bad poetry on religious topics which may not really move us in that way. And some very good poetry that, though free of religious language, does so move us through its ability to stir up deep thoughts and forcefully ask the ultimate questions about the origin, purpose, and end of our lives. (However, we should bear in mind also that, as was the case with religious painting, sculpture, and music, not all sacred poetry has to be truly great; some religious examples that are merely serviceable do have the valuable function of keeping alive traditions with their symbols and stories.)

We have mentioned the Japanese identification of the Buddha with a frog—sitting as though in meditation—on the banks, or atop a lotus, in one of the innumerable temple ponds of the island nation. The *haiku* is a concise seventeen-syllable (in Japanese) poem focusing on a single significant image, though perhaps with a "spring" or change in the middle. This haiku by the great Zen poet Basho (1644–1694) is perhaps the most famous of all, and has been said to sum up the whole of Buddhism in three lines, as it speaks of the Buddha's entry into the world, or into Nirvana from the world, and the spreading out from that entry of the *dharma*, or Buddhist gospel.

> *An old pond—*
> *A frog jumps in—*
> *The sound of water.*

Like a Zen painting or the tea ceremony or a Zen garden, this verse says what has to be said in veiled, simple, concise language.

In a real sense, the English poet William Blake (1757–1827) attained the same end in poems like "The Tiger." Without directly mentioning God, he raises the problem of evil—why is there evil in the world, why are there tigers that eat lambs?—as boldly as it has ever been presented in literature, as he asks whether the same hand that made the lamb also made the tiger. And if not, whence came the tiger?

The Tiger

> TIGER! Tiger! burning bright
> In the forests of the night,
> What immortal hand or eye
> Could frame thy fearful symmetry?
>
> In what distant deeps or skies
> Burned the fire of thine eyes?
> On what wings dare he aspire?
> What the hand dare seize the fire?
>
> And what shoulder, and what art,
> Could twist the sinews of thy heart?
> And when thy heart began to beat,
> What dread hand? And what dread feet?
>
> What the hammer? What the chain?
> In what furnace was thy brain?
> What the anvil? What dread grasp
> Dare its deadly terrors clasp?

> *When the stars threw down their spears,*
> *And watered heaven with their tears,*
> *Did he smile his work to see?*
> *Did he who made the Lamb make thee?*
>
> *Tiger! Tiger! burning bright*
> *In the forests of the night,*
> *What immortal hand or eye*
> *Dare frame thy fearful symmetry?*

Blake was influenced by the ancient Gnostic school of Christianity, which believed the present world was created not by the High God, but by a lower deity who bungled the job. This explains why there is so much evil where, one might think, an omnipotent creator could have done better— why there are carnivorous animals, and humans; why limitation after limitation is built into the realms of conditioned reality.

But Blake's poetry is subtle and not dogmatic. He does not sermonize, but points to evils from the victimized lamb to victimized human children like the chimney sweeps and prostitutes of his day—and no less the abused or abandoned children of our own—and simply asks, straightforwardly and unavoidably, what hand framed all this?

And moreover, claiming the usual religious separation of soul and body to be an idea from the devil, Blake affirmed, "Energy is the only life, and is from the Body; and . . . Energy is Eternal Delight."[6] It is the "mind-forged manacles" ("London"), not the flesh and its innocent desires, that truly bring us under the hammer and chain of whoever could frame this world of tigers and weeping children.

Gerard Manley Hopkins (1844–1889), a celebrated religious poet of the Victorian era (like Blake more appreciated in the twentieth century than in his own time), presents here, in "God's Grandeur," a more affirmative view of God's subtle presence in the world.

God's Grandeur

> *The world is charged with the grandeur of God.*
> *It will flame out, like shining from shook foil;*
> *It gathers to a greatness, like the ooze of oil*
> *Crushed. Why do men then now not reck his rod?*
> *Generations have trod, have trod, have trod;*
> *And all is seared with trade; bleared, smeared with toil*
> *And wears man's smudge and shares man's smell: the soil*
> *Is bare now, nor can foot feel, being shod.*
>
> *And for all this, nature is never spent;*
> *There lives the dearest freshness deep down things;*

---

[6] "The Voice of the Devil." Alfred Kazin, ed., *The Portable Blake.* New York: Viking, 1953, pp. 250–251.

And though the last lights off the black West went
Oh, morning, at the brown brink eastward, springs—
Because the Holy Ghost over the bent
World broods with warm breast and with ah! bright wings.

Perhaps this divine vision benefits Hopkin's vocation as a Jesuit priest, though despite this calling, his spiritual path was often difficult, and the ecstatic consciousness of God's omnipresence such as poems like this reveal was not easily won. We, however, can appreciate how he is saying what Blake in his own way also tried to say: that despite all that the humans who infest this world have done to obscure it, there is nonetheless a deep splendor beneath the surface, or in the flash of a bright wing, that connects to unconditioned reality. Hopkins could see that smudged radiance as none other than the hidden God of orthodox Catholic Christianity. For Blake, the glory was the fleshly "Eternal Delight" represented by the energies of Jesus and the human world in which Christ was embodied, and was not at all from tyrannical old Nobodaddy, the bungling "spiritual" Father-God of this suffering planet.

But in both cases, the visionary religious poet sees with distaste a smeared and smudged outer world, stained by tears and greed, and peeking out from behind it almost invisible realms of glory. Blake also wrote:

Eternity

He who bends to himself a joy
Does the winged life destroy;
But he who kisses the joy as it flies
Lives in eternity's sunrise.

And in "Jerusalem" he sang:

I will not cease from Mental Fight,
Nor shall my Sword sleep in my hand,
Till we have built Jerusalem
In England's green and pleasant land.

DRAMA

Like many other art forms, drama has its ultimate roots in religion. The first plays were probably little different from rituals, the acted-out or danced-out myths and services of a people, connected with times of festival. Remnants of this background remain in some places. In the No drama of Japan, among the most sophisticated of all dramatic performances in the world, the backdrop inevitably features a pine tree, sacred in Shinto. The oldest and still most commonly performed of all No dramas is *Okina*, "The Old Man," said to derive from an occasion when an old man was observed dancing under a spreading evergreen at the Kasuga Shrine in Nara; the ancient one turned out to be the god of that shrine.

Traditional drama, like that of No, or the classical Greek theater and Shakespeare in the West, commonly employs verse in its lines and so has an important connection with poetry. On the other hand, the plot has features to be considered in a moment in connection with stories and novels. What is distinctive about drama is that it is to novels as sculpture is to painting. The drama enhances the story in its ability to "freeze-frame" its high, archetypal moments in memory.

At the same time, drama, whether tragedy or comedy, is also particularly good at bringing out the flaws in characters. Greek and Shakespearean tragedy depend on the tragic flaw, the fatal weakness in even the most heroic-seeming personalities that brings them down in the end. And the very essence of comedy is the laughable contrast between human pretension and reality, suggested in the pompous personage who slips on a banana peel, or the public figure trying to explain his private life. In this respect, drama may be more like an opposite than a parallel to sculpture, insofar as statues present only the archetype and leave the flaws and contradictions out.

A No play like Zeami's *Tsunemasa* and English dramas like Shakespeare's *Hamlet* or Shaw's *Saint Joan* contain spiritual questions and religious drama that are made all the more provocative and powerful by the slow dramatic movement and vivid confrontations on stage.

Tsunemasa gets underway as a ghostly voice from offstage begins to chant over the shrill tones of flutes, the complex rhythms of hand drums, and the eerie atonal chants of a chorus,

> . . . but I, because I could not lie at rest,
> Am come back to the World for a while,
> Like a shadow that steals over the grass.
> I am like dews that in the morning
> Still cling to the grasses. Oh pitiful the longing
> That has beset me![7]

The singer now progresses down the runway toward the stage. We see him in the brilliant court dress of a samurai, his face frozen by a small white mask bearing a subtle smile. As the play advances, we learn that this is the spirit of Tsunemasa, a warrior who also had a great love of music and the lute. Because he died in battle, he is condemned to the purgatory of continually battling titans or demons; but now, having heard a lute struck at a service in his memory, he is able to return for a few moments to his

---

[7] From Arthur Waley, trans., *The No Plays of Japan*. New York: Grove Press, 1957, p. 82.

first love, before having to return, wailing, to his torments in the other world. The staged drama of his slow, precise steps, his music, and his hauntingly sad song uttered in low, slow syllables is a triumph of the actor's art. No mere reading of the story could have quite the same effect.

So it is with Hamlet, after having seen his father's ghost, when he utters his famous "To be or not to be" soliloquy; and later, as he confronts his mother in her supposed sins. The look in the eyes, the actor's gestures, the cutting turn of the head—how can these be the same on the printed page, however well-crafted the words? Or Saint Joan, facing in tears her tormentors and even her supposed friends at her trial—and the unforgettable religious questions, the *what ifs?*—all these spectacular plays ask.

What if something one especially loved can call one back for a few moments even from the dead? Would this be a boon, or only a curse if it made leaving, and the rest of one's sentence, all the worse? How much should a son, like Hamlet, heed the ghost of his tormented father and judge the sins of his mother? What if, like Joan, one hears voices supposedly from God? Should one follow them unreservedly, bloodying one's own sword and in the end perhaps tasting blood, or the flames, oneself? Does that do one and the world more good than ill, or not?

If drama raises religious questions, so do cinema and television stories. These newest and liveliest arts, probably those most familiar to many of you, claim many of the characteristics of stage drama, and even more in the way of both close-up intimacy and special effects. Some, in the adventure mode, are like hero-myth stories, to be mentioned in a moment. Others are more subtly psychological, in the mode of plays like those just cited, and raise religious queries as profound. Perhaps you can take one of your own favorite movies, think it over in your mind, and decide what religious *what if* it is really asking, and how it answers it—not only in terms of a final verbal answer, but in terms of how the drama and the characters develop. Is it convincing, or not?

NOVELS AND STORIES

Fiction, the telling of stories, no doubt has its ultimate origin in myth and so in religion. The first stories, in other words, may have been tales having to do with themes covered by religion: the origin and destiny of the world, the meaning and purpose of human life, even the significance of those humorous, anomalous, trivial pains and pleasures that beset human life but make good anecdotes.

All significant stories also have in common with religion the use of symbols. The theologian Paul Tillich once said, "Faith has no other language than symbols," and the same could be said of literature, for in the end, all the characters and incidents of memorable writing are such because they stand not only as themselves but also as symbols of something greater that remains unspoken. Thus they resonate with that which is otherwise unspoken within ourselves as they present human moods, aspirations, and desperations we know are there, but can scarcely name until the story or novel identifies them for us and helps us to say, "I have felt that way too, but hardly realized it until I read such-and-such a story."

Religiously oriented literature may present explicitly religious symbols. A character may be a Christ figure, embodying redemptive suffering as in Morris West's *The Devil's Advocate*, or a Buddha, as in Hermann Hesse's *Siddhartha*. Or the theme may be presented only obliquely, and it is up to the reader to make what connections he or she finds meaningful.

Some religious literature, then, continues in the vein of traditional mythology, particularly the myth of the hero, one who embarks on a great quest, overcomes obstacles, endures suffering, and finally triumphs. The major heroes of religion past, such as Rama, the Buddha, or Jesus, are essentially in that pattern. They have set out, have been tempted and suffered like Jesus on the cross, and prevailed not only for their own benefit but that of all humankind.

As we saw in the last chapter, in *The Hero with a Thousand Faces*, the noted mythologist Joseph Campbell outlined fundamental features of this mythic paradigm. These may again be summarized by saying that the hero undertakes an important quest, undergoes important suffering, receives important help, and finally, in attaining victory, experiences important transformation. The hero paradigm is particularly significant in many modern adventure, science-fiction, and fantasy works. One thinks of J.R.R. Tolkien's *The Lord of the Rings*, Ursula LeGuin's *The Wizard of Earthsea*, or Westerns like Zane Gray's *Riders of the Purple Sage*. Though sometimes dismissed by literati, such novels should not be discounted by those attuned to the religious dimension in literature. They represent modern perpetuations of the hero myth, a very important component of religion. Many would say that moderns neglect it, and many other traditional aspects of spirituality, at their own peril. If the hero and the spiritual quest are not acknowledged freely and appropriately—let in through the door— he and it may come back in through the windows in far less desirable guises. One recalls the well-known cults of heroism and pseudo-spirituality in fascist and other totalitarian regimes such as Nazi Germany.

Yet religious sensibility in literature does not stop here either. It can also be indirect. Some works regarded as the most monumental parables of the spirit, heroism, spirituality, and archetypalism are made indirect so the characters have room to be fully human, not merely ciphers for religious values.

In serious literature, the fundamental point is to create and embody a human image, a picture of what a human being is in all the species' diversity. The image may be crafted in the form of a character's experience. But great works of literature will turn the camera on inner experience just as much as outer, and flash the lights into the sub-basements as well as the attics of its protagonists' minds. The wildest science fiction or fantasy stories that humans can imagine are as significant a part of this literary documentation as the most down-to-earth realism. For whether or not those Martian or elfland scenes exist objectively, they have all been *thought* by *homo sapiens*, so presumably say something about those puzzling primates, and go into their bulging literary file.

This documentation of the widest possible human experience, in the depths, in the heights, and in the outward world of action and relationships, is important for religion because it shows what religion has to work with. If religion is to work, it needs to know real humans, real human life, and the innermost thoughts of real humans. In the end, it cannot operate out of just a "theologically correct" view of humankind, but needs a real, authentic human image based on everything. Constructing such images is what great novelists are about.

But though they need each other, as Lynn Ross-Bryant has pointed out in *Imagination and the Life of the Spirit*, religion and literature may interact, but are two different things, and cannot just be equalled.[8]

A fundamental reason is that while religion, in a way like logic or science, deals with what is presumed, at least, to be definitely true, literature can deal with possibilities. Literature, says Ross-Bryant, following Giles Gunn, can present a hypothetical creation. It can ask us "to suspend our ordinary categories of judgment," and say, in the words of Giles Gunn, "If you will grant me my initial premise, or set of conditions, then such and such would, or at least could, follow from them."[9]

This kind of freedom clearly can go much beyond the framework of a collective, or "official," myth, even if like some great works of classical or modern literature it follows mythical models or structures closely. Yet literature can also say, of myth or of any other hypothetical religious reality, "What is this postulated reality, and how does it—or might it—work itself out in the lives of different kinds of people? We might consider those who believe in it easily, those who believe only with difficulty, those who are unbelievers, those for whom it smooths the path of life, and those for whom it presents very hard choices?"

In looking at a religiously significant story or novel, we should ask what the religious and/or character possibility the writer is asking us to accept for the purposes of the story. These two, religion and character possibilities, finally reduce to one, since for any good novelist religion is not just an abstract truth or hypothesis. It is presented in a way that is inseparable from its impact on the lives of convincing characters, just as in

[8] Lynn Ross-Bryant, *Imagination and the Life of the Spirit: An Introduction to the Study of Religion and Literature*. Chico, CA: Scholars Press, 1981, p. 85.

[9] Ross-Bryant, *Imagination and the Life of the Spirit*, p. 87; citing Giles B. Gunn, "Introduction: Literature and its Relation to Religion," in Giles B. Gunn, ed., *Literature and Religion*. New York: Harper & Row, 1971, p. 23. A later version of this essay appears as Chapter 2 of Giles Gunn, *The Interpretation of Otherness: Literature, Religion and the American Imagination*. New York: Oxford University Press, 1979.

real life. Our religion cannot be divorced from who we are and what our life stories have been. This is the same for great fiction writers and the religion in the lives of their characters. It is here that innumerable second-rate religious novelists have failed, making us say, "It sounds nice but I just can't connect with the religion presented in that story, because I can't believe the characters who espouse it are real."

Let us take a few examples of excellent religious literature. Here are some novels whose principal characters are, on the face of it, unedifying figures though in religious roles. But in spite of that—or because of it, since their very imperfection helps us to identify with them—their narratives raise important religious issues. Graham Greene's *The Power and the Glory* is set in Mexico at the time of the fervently anti-clerical revolution of the 1920s, when the Roman Catholic church was harshly persecuted. In this novel we meet a bungling, alcoholic priest who despite being, as he well knows, a poor exemplar of his calling, nonetheless takes serious risks and remains somehow true to God or to something in himself by continuing to say Mass in a string of isolated rural churches. The question asked is, suppose you had a priest like this in a situation of great pressure. Maybe he was being harried unjustly on a personal level, though maybe the revolution also had some valid criticisms to make of the role of the church in that society. How would he respond? What would he want to salvage? And what would that say about the positives and negatives of religion?

In *Kinkakuji*, or *The Temple of the Golden Pavilion*, by the Japanese novelist Yukio Mishima (pseudonym for Hiraoka Mikitake, 1925–1970), we have the story of a disturbed, stuttering novice at a famous Zen temple in Kyoto who finally attains a strange kind of release from his inner torment by setting fire to the supremely beautiful edifice. The story is based on actual fact. In 1950, an unbalanced young monk actually torched this fabled golden dream of a temple out of jealous anger at its uncompromising perfection. (It has since been rebuilt.) Mishima's fictional re-creation of the character and the event is a profound study of abnormal religious psychology.

The young monk-arsonist, Mizoguchi, goes to the temple upon the death of his uncomprehending, well-meaning father, a country priest. The younger man is there under the rule of the abbot, a plump, worldly cleric. But Mizoguchi is far more at the mercy of dark forces within himself that he only dimly understands, and can only express through violent rage, locked as he is in a festering inner world by his ugliness, his stammering, and his limited intellect. The temple itself finally becomes the victim, though its only sin is that of being sublimely beautiful and so the opposite of all that Mizoguchi feels himself to be.[10]

There are superficial similarities between *The Temple of the Golden*

[10] Mishima, Yukio, *The Temple of the Golden Pavilion*. Translation by Ivan Morris. New York: A.A. Knopf, 1958. Introduction by Nancy Wilson Ross.

Pavilion and the novel often considered to be the greatest of all religious novels, *The Brothers Karamazov* by Fyodor Dostoyevsky. The story, set in a small town in nineteenth-century Russia, goes like this. Fyodor Karamazov, a well-to-do but drunken and dissipated old man, has three legitimate sons, Dmitri, Ivan, and Alyosha. The three represent three distinct psychological and spiritual types.

Dmitri, a vital, immoderate, hard-living (and perennially in debt) army officer, full of romantic passion and few principles, represents an essentially physical/emotional life, but one lived to the hilt.

Ivan is an intellectual, a religious sceptic full of the "advanced" Western European scientific and philosophical ideas that Dostoyevsky, like many Russians of his day, found fascinating but also profoundly ominous. Ivan represents an essentially mental life, a person who often seems to have his head in the clouds, but who shows that even seemingly quite abstract ideas—"mere theories"—can have very sharp consequences indeed.

Alyosha, the real heart of the novel, is very spiritual, a mystic when it comes to nature and love. He is a novice in a monastery and a disciple of Father Zossima, a Russian holy man of the old school. Alyosha is no plaster saint, however, for he is sometimes given to doubts and temptations, and is deeply involved in the complex and sordid affairs of his family—but by his temperament and approach, he represents in this context an essentially spiritual life.

Then there is the fourth, Smerdyakov. He is the keen-eyed but unschooled illegitimate son of the old man, and lives in the house as an ill-treated servant; he sees no need for moral scruples in a world that has shown him little pity or concern.

The Brothers Karamazov is a most intricate story, and we cannot trace all of its characters and subplots here. Of most interest are some of the religious discussions in this novel of ideas. Ivan argues to Alyosha that he does not reject God but, on the other hand, cannot put trust in God because he cannot accept the world God has made—and gives horrifying examples of the abuse of innocent children in this world, cruelty which can in no way be reconciled with divine justice. Ivan tells his brother, "It's not that I don't accept God, Alyosha, only I most respectfully return Him the ticket."

Ivan recites to Alyosha a prose-poem he says he wrote several years before, the story of the Grand Inquisitor, the most famous passage in this novel. This narrative tells us that during the sixteenth-century Inquisition in Spain, when numerous people were being arrested and terribly tortured for alleged heresy, Christ or someone resembling him appeared in the streets. He took up again his work of healing the sick and lame, and crowds began to flock around him as of old. But just as in the first century, the Grand Inquisitor recognized him and had him arrested and brought to a cell in the Inquisition dungeons.

That night, the Inquisitor himself came to the cell to visit the unexpected captive. Knowing full well to whom he was speaking, the Grand Inquisitor told Christ that because the Saviour had rejected Satan's three temptations (to turn stones into bread, to cast himself down unharmed from the pinnacle of the temple, to accept rule over all the kingdoms of the earth), Jesus had thereby rejected miracle, mystery, and worldly power. In so doing, he who was the supposed Redeemer of humankind had placed a burden of freedom on humanity too great for most men and women to bear.

It was necessary for the Church to correct those errors—to give people the security of bread, to offer them something miraculous to worship, and to take worldly power unabashedly and use it for human benefit. For these boons most people willingly gave up spiritual freedom, and the Church should help them do so. In following this course, the Grand Inquisitor acknowledged, he was rejecting the purity of Christ and following something of Satan instead, but he was doing so for the good of the great mass of ordinary people whom Christ in that purity could never save.

During all this discourse, Christ remained silent. Then, still silent, he approached the dry-lipped churchman and kissed him. The Grand Inquisitor suddenly freed Christ and told him never to come that way again.

Then the novel climaxes. Smerdyakov heard and grasped just enough of Ivan's talk to take to heart the idea that now all is permitted, and one may, like the Grand Inquisitor, deny God to do good. He therefore murdered the old Karamazov, whom he, like many others, hated. He covered himself well, however, and Dmitri was instead arrested, tried in pages packed with colorful courtroom drama, and to everyone's surprise was convicted by his jury of townsmen and peasants.

But then Dmitri, with his animal passions, and his well-known differences with his father over women and money, should have been the murderer. In fact he was not; the homicide was, Dostoyevsky seems to tell us, instead committed by a combination of too-lofty rational ideas and the dark, abusive, and cruel side of human life. Yet, on another level, all four brothers were guilty, for three of them had in their own way killed their unworthy father in their hearts; and even Alyosha, by omission, had prepared a path for Smerdyakov's crime.

Neither God nor reason come off very well, only faith and love, or rather faith in love, for sinners, for animals, for the earth itself. This was the gospel of Father Zossima, and of Alyosha when he, for all his purity, connives and bribes officials to allow Dmitri to escape the country rather than serve an unjust sentence for a murder he did not, legally, commit.[11]

As we read the end of The Brothers Karamazov, as when we finished The Temple of the Golden Pavilion, we probably feel, as the author intended, a

[11] Fyodor Dostoyevsky, The Brothers Karamazov. Translated with an Introduction by David Magarshack. London: Penguin Books, 1958, 1982.

disturbing awareness of inchoate depths in men and women out of which wrath beyond reason—in a word, sheer evil—can flow. Yet because these characters are drawn nonetheless as fellow humans, they also evoke in us deep, poignant understanding and perhaps even compassion. "I too," we say with a smile and a shudder, "in that time and place, and that body, could have been Mizoguchi, or Ivan, or even Smerdyakov." In that light we can assess their religious significance. This is what religious art can do: make us aware both of human life and of spiritual traditions, and so press us to put the two together.

SUMMARY

We may begin an understanding of religious art by thinking of a distinction between unconditioned and conditioned reality. Conditioned reality is the realm of time and space and limits in which we live; unconditioned reality is the opposite of this, and is what religions call by such names as God, Brahman, or Nirvana. Religious art can be thought of as doors and windows between the two, enabling us to see, hear, or think about something of the other side and its interaction with human life.

Religious painting can take as its subject either nature, showing it as a manifestation or creation of God or Ultimate Reality, or the human form, revealing that reality in the form of gods, Buddhas, saviours, saints, or spiritual scenes. Abstract or surrealistic religious art can reveal religious symbols and forms on subconscious levels. Sculpture, often employed in making figures that are the focus of worship, is particularly good at depicting religious archetypal meaning. Around the time of the origin of the great religions, religious figures often became less theriomorphic and more anthropomorphic in conception, in part under Greek influence, in part because new religions arose with human founders and central figures.

Religious architecture has also gone through many stages. It basically has two roles, either being a House of God or a place of the assembly for worship of a People of God; some buildings, of course, may be both. Religious music, though sometimes regarded with suspicion, generally helps to evoke and channel religious feelings, and has an important place in worship. Its forms vary greatly from chants to devotional hymns.

Religious poetry can convey religious ideas and express feelings and responses to them through combinations of words, pictures in the mind, and emotion; often the feelings are challenging and complex. Drama and fiction, both stories and novels, may be read religiously, particularly in terms of how they create an image of human nature in all its complexity, its nobility and flaws alike, since it is this that religion has to work with. Stories with a religious theme, like Dostoyevsky's *The Brothers Karamazov*, can also ask very important questions about religious meaning, about good and evil in the world, and about the reality of God.

United Nations

A muezzin calling Muslims to prayer.

Traveling Together: The Sociology of Religion

Chapter Objectives

- Discuss whether it is true to say that all religion is social.

- Tell how the nature and structure of a religious group itself gives messages about the meaning and experience of the group, by whether it is close-knit or loose, has authoritarian or democratic leadership, and so forth.

- Present the various ways in which a religious group can relate to the surrounding society.

- Explain Redfield's conception of great and little traditions, emphasizing their meaning for religion.

- Distinguish between established and emergent religion. Describe major forms of each: international, national, and denominational for established; intensive and expansive for emergent.

- Describe the circumstances out of which emergent religion typically derives and some of its fundamental characteristics, such as selection of one central symbol and practice, future orientation, and central, charismatic prophet.

- Briefly describe major types of religious personality.

- Define some leading ways in which religion transforms the society around it.

- Tell how religion interprets history.

As you read the chapter, also look for important words. The key words defined in the glossary at the end of the book are in boldface type at their first use in the text, unless the term serves as a section heading.

ALL RELIGION IS SOCIAL

Religion as we know it is always social, inseparable from the fact that we humans live in societies and in a network of interpersonal relationships. Therefore, for every religious concept, experience, or practice there is a social form of expression—a group formed, or at least a modification of certain relations between certain people. True, people may have subjective yearnings and intuitions and even ecstasies like those of religion independent of any dealings with other people. If our understanding of religion is valid, however, these remain only subjective feelings or musings or even ritualized gestures, unless they are given symbolic completion through words and the experience is related to the social environment.

In this environment we humans inevitably find ourselves, and we cannot ignore it in the completion of any intuition or drive. Even the way we explain the meaning or nature of an inner experience to ourselves is an expression of interpersonal being: postinfantile human mentation without words and concepts could scarcely get beyond feeling. We use words and ideas to understand things about ourselves in our own minds as well as to explain them to others. Conceptualization and reasoning are products of society, since they are products of language. Thought and consciousness themselves, of any sort of which we can possibly conceive, are results of our living in societies, though the separate individual has an innate biological potential for them.

RELIGIOUS GROUPS

Religion then is bound up with the way we live, talk, and learn in groups. A *religious group* is a set of people whose interpersonal relations complete for one another the symbolic expression of religious experience. Since the group itself is a religious symbol, it also stimulates further experience. For one who has been converted to a particular religion, a prayer group made up of like-minded people is a congenial fellowship that both completes the initial experience by supporting it, and by showing that it is, after all, a shared experience, and stimulates more experiences along the same line as the initial one.

The group legitimates the religious experiences of individuals in it by incorporating them into a *social* perception of reality and ultimately into *the* social construction of reality of the culture in which they live, whether as mainstays or dissidents. As a group it has some kind of participation (even if only through withdrawal) in that culture. So any religious group through its very structure and relation to the cultural environment communicates significant messages about self and reality.

The group also establishes a sense of religious power in the individuals within it. When functioning well, religious institutions and groups of all sorts bring together not only heaven and earth but also the individual and effective power. Religious institutions and groups are like miniaturizations of a hard world and an inconceivably vast cosmos in which the hardness and the vastness are replaced with human warmth and manageability, as well as transcendent wonder. Through religion the average person can feel effective and important, close to power and ways of changing things the nonreligious world does not know.

The Chinese peasant prayed in temples to gods who were deified high Mandarin officials. In the flesh he or she would hardly have approached these personages with humble requests, but now that they are elevated to temple gods they are, paradoxically, more accessible to the common person who, though he or she may not be heard by earthly officials, could be heard in heaven.

Ordinary American churchgoers, troubled by news of hunger and revolution in less fortunate areas of the world, mention these places in prayer groups and contribute to missionaries overseas. They believe these gestures help. Religion creates a human-sized, individual-sized world and universe in which, through the religious group, individuals not only can find meaning for themselves but also may be effective in the larger world and universe.

Let us now examine some styles of religious sociological activity. These range from vast international religions numbering hundreds of millions to private visions shared with one or two others. We can mention only a few representative categories—notice that they actually overlap.

GREAT AND LITTLE TRADITIONS

The anthropologist Robert Redfield distinguished between *great traditions* and *little traditions* within a culture and religion, using these terms to point to the fact that within every culture, there are two ways of expressing its motifs.[1] One, the great tradition, has been the way of books and scholars

---

[1] Robert Redfield, *The Little Community and Peasant Society and Culture* (Chicago, Ill.: University of Chicago Press, 1960).

and intellectuals; the other, the little tradition, has been the way of the common people. In older societies, the latter is called folk religion; in modern societies like the American, it is called popular culture.

To comprehend the great tradition, think of scholars at universities and chaplains at the courts of great kings, or in many cases, all those who can read and write and who actually read the major books of the cultural heritage. The great tradition is that of the literate elite. It takes a long perspective; it is oriented toward history and the past out of which the present comes. Intellectual and emotionally cool, it is likely to be the way the religious tradition is presented in the centers of learning, the major cathedrals or temples, and the palaces or centers of power. The great traditions of the world's religions are immensely important. It is to them that we owe the preservation of most of the world's heritage of religious literature—the scriptures, the great commentaries like the Talmud and the Laws of Manu, and the rigorous philosophical defenses of faith such as those of Thomas Aquinas, al-Ghazzali, and Shankara that have made religion able to compete with other kinds of thought. It is also to them that we owe the continuing perception that a religion has historical conditioning. It appeared at a particular point in history, which orthodoxy regards as the pivot of historical time—the place where "the hopes and fears of all the years are met"—and has undergone certain stages of change and development. This is knowledge both hopeful and dangerous but in any case not widely known (or if known, understood) by the masses, who for all practical purposes know things only as they are in the present.

That statement gives an insight into the nature of the little tradition. It is essentially nonliterary, is oriented to the present and to cosmic time rather than to history, concentrates on worship and experience more than theory, and is basically transmitted within family and community rather than through books and academic teachers. For people oriented toward the little tradition, religion centers around the seasonal festivals and the ways things are done in the community, rather than around philosophical teachings in books. Religion is not unemotional; it may become fervent, yet the fervor is associated with pilgrimage, devotion, conversion, or festive joy as venues that have always been there. More often than the great tradition, the little tradition understands that differences in worship and social context make religions different as surely as differences in theory—in fact, it is likely not to understand differences in theory save as they are expressed in differences in worship. All religions are the same on the popular level, except as they *do* different things and attract different people.

I recall that some years ago, in a small town in the Midwest, a woman told me that the Methodist and Presbyterian churches in the same town combined their services during the summer. She added that she did not see any reason why they should not do so all year round, since there was no real difference in their manner of worship. That attitude, centered on

Lawrence Cherney/FPG

The great tradition in religion is brought to mind by England's lovely medieval Salsbury cathedral. This magnificent church was built by cooperative community effort and was the seat of a bishop of the predominant faith.

the experience of worship and the perspective of the local community, was very much from out of the little tradition. Elites of the Methodist and Presbyterian great traditions would immediately have realized that although it is true their forms of worship in America have come to be quite similar, the historical background and theological heritage—the literary and historical dimensions—of the two churches are very different. Among other things, one comes out of the Calvinist tradition with its emphasis on the fallen state of mankind, whereas the other says that after conversion true holiness and Christian perfection are at least lively possibilities. For most people in that small town, those were the issues of long ago and far away, whereas what sort of people attended worship in each church and what they did there were close at hand and well-known. On this score, the Methodists and Presbyterians seemed little different. If the woman to whom I had spoken had visited the local Roman Catholic, Lutheran, or

Episcopal church, whether the doctrine as actually preached and taught was familiar or strange, the differences in worship from Methodism or Presbyterianism—with people standing at altars in colorful vestments and making ritual gestures and so forth—would probably have been enough to convince her that it was a different kind of faith.

In America in general, the distinction between the great tradition and the little tradition follows such lines. To the great tradition, history and ideas are important. To the little, it is the ways of worship and the social rules of religion that count.

Of course, strong links exist between great and little traditions, and the line separating them is often fuzzy. Probably for this reason, some of the most influential religious personalities and movements have been those able to relate convincingly and to borrow freely from both sides. In eighth-century Japan, Buddhism was seriously divided between the learned, wealthy, aristocratic, and officially recognized temples of Nara, the capital, and a popular Buddhistic religion of the countryside that was unorthodox but closely involved in the lives of the peasants and under the leadership of shamanistic, charismatic priests who served as country healers, prophets, wonder workers, mystics, and leaders of such practical enterprises as constructing bridges and irrigation projects. It was a classic case of the split between great and little tradition. The great tradition was scholarly and patronized undying art. Indeed, millions of tourists a year go to Nara to appreciate the glowing cultural legacy of that era. That richness, however, was paid for by the rents and taxes of laboring peasants who themselves had little access to it. The peasants' shamanistic priests sometimes minced few words in decrying the sins of the ruling class and its priests and were in turn sometimes persecuted. Then, in the middle of the century, the Emperor Shomu, aware of the gap and eager to reconcile the countryside so that he could raise money to pay for the Great Buddha he desired as a national shrine, took the step of appointing Gyogi, a leader of the shamanistic Buddhists, chief priest of all Japanese Buddhism. Gyogi was able to bring both groups together through his links with the two sides, and he also helped reconcile Shinto and Buddhism by receiving oracles at the Grand Shrine of Ise favorable to building the Great Buddha. The Great Buddha was erected and is now the noblest of all the cultural attractions of Nara.

Other figures who have linked both traditions could be named, including St. Francis, Gandhi, and many of the great American evangelists. They are people who have some learning representative of the great tradition yet have come out of a popular background or are able to relate deeply to it, so that the ordinary people feel instinctively, "This man is one of us—he thinks and prays like us, yet more effectively. We can understand and trust him." In a word, this person is able to enter the timeless, nonhistorical mood of popular culture by taking the present seriously. He or she can play the role of a folk religion saint or prophet and be appreciated as such, yet also have goals and levels of understanding from the great tradition that motivate his or her actions and may make him or her a motivator of reconciliation and dynamic change.

For obvious reasons, political leaders, such as the Emperor Shomu and many others down to the present, are especially concerned about maintaining links with the little tradition of their country's religion—more so usually than the great tradition's priestly or academic leadership. Rulers may show great favor to such popular religious leaders and linking figures as are deemed politically reliable. This patronage is not necessarily insincere—the leader may be someone who genuinely prefers popular religionists or may earnestly want to reconcile and befriend all segments of the population for the best of motives. Its political value to the leadership, however, is far from negligible. It should be realized that although courts and governments may also patronize the great tradition, its real locus in a religious culture is not so much in its aristocratic and political milieu as in its upper priestly and academic circles. In India, for example, it was not found in the circles of emperors or maharajahs (save for the occasional Ashoka or Akbar) but among learned brahmins or mullahs who might accept the gifts of kings but whose lives were very different from theirs.

Finally, let us consider again the meaning of the little tradition and folk religion. Its usages are called little tradition because, being nonliterary, they seem on the surface limited to small areas and to time as counted in generations. In a deeper sense, however, folk and popular religion is greater than any great tradition; it is a sea out of which great traditions rise and fall. Ultimately, most of the symbols, motifs, and ideas of the great traditions have come out of common little tradition patterns, and even the most appealing aspects of the great traditions—its festivals, rites, social roles—are usually only specific adaptations of common little tradition practices, such as seasonal rites and sacred places. If one can so speak, perhaps 80 percent of all religion is essentially "just religion"—that is, the kind of activity in little tradition or popular religion that does not differ much in role from one culture or faith to another but only in detail, this symbol or this name instead of that. A family gathering with prayers, feasting, and games for the children is not much different whether it is on a Jewish, Christian, Muslim or Hindu joyous holy day. Only the "top 20 percent" represents the specific ideas and doctrines of each faith—over which, because of the particular kinds of identification and experience they may provide, great arguments are sometimes waged.

ESTABLISHED RELIGION

The great and little traditions together represent only one side of religious life. Seen in themselves, they suggest a static sort of spiritual life, tied in with ponderous institutions—whether it is the way of scholars studying the same texts generation after generation or of peasants passing on immemorial folklore for age on age. Although religion is never really changeless, it does have a side that whether scholarly or folkish, likes to think of itself as unchanging and that is closely related to the most deeply rooted structures of the society. This kind of religion can be called **established religion.**

There is, however, another side of religion and another manner of religious social experience. It was hinted at in the discussion of the linking religious figures and movements that often seem to supply the impetus for change. It leads us into the world of new religious movements—movements typically centering around remarkable persons breaking into the placid waters of established religion to denounce many of its beliefs and practices and perhaps especially social structure, to propose radical alternatives, and to make *their* religion a vehicle for protest on many levels. In time, of course, some of these movements may sink back into established religion or become the bases of new established religions. For the time they are at odds with the dominant pattern and show a disjuncture in the spiritual fabric, they are something else—finally a whole different way of being religious. This way may be called **emergent religion.**

Each of these two ways, established and emergent religion, has its own message about the nature of a real self and the way to transcendence. Established religion says that one can find ultimate meaning through living within the religious traditions of one's community. It says that sufficient religious truth can be known by most people, not just an elite. It indicates that even though the great tradition of the religion may be more ample and accurate, the way it is practiced by the little tradition is adequate and perhaps even more devout; although it may seem superficially superstitious, it is informed by what has been called *implicit faith* in the central religious truths. Established religion, then, says it is better to participate in the normative religion with one's relatives, neighbors, and friends than to break with them for the sake of some individual calling.

Established religion comes in many shapes and sizes. We cannot mention every kind of sociological expression it takes, only a few representative categories.[2] First, there are the **international** and intercultural religions. The major faiths that are truly intercultural are Buddhism, Christianity, and Islam; within Christianity the Roman Catholic church stands as a unique example of a very large religious institution that is highly international yet centrally administered. Each of these religions has been a bearer of culture to many lands and so has generated there a particular cultural tone, usually working its way down from the religion's great tradition, which is more international and intercultural than most aspects of the little

---

[2] These categories are based on Ernst Troeltsch, *The Social Teaching of the Christian Churches,* trans. Olive Wyon (New York: The Macmillan Company, 1931), vol. 2; and especially J. Milton Yinger, *Religion, Society, and the Individual* (New York: The Macmillan Company, 1957).

tradition. They have also appeared in each place as something that has come in within historical time, and thus, each exhibits a degree of tension with the indigenous culture.

The message of these religions is that to be a real self and in rapport with infinity, it is better to be aligned with a culturally rich and very numerous movement. Truth is not just for a handful and is not even just the possession of one nation or one culture. One must disdain absolutizing one's own land or way of life for the sake of the higher absolutes of the international religion; one must be detached from any single culture, though far from anticulture.

These faiths are overwhelming majorities in most places where they are found, though minorities in some—as are Christianity in Japan and Buddhism in America. They have the experience of being both broad-based religions and tiny withdrawal groups, depending on circumstances. Where they are greatly preponderant, they are examples of established religion.

Besides such international institutions, established religion can also be manifested as **national religions** shared by the majority of the population, whether predominant churches, such as the Church of England or Lutheran churches in northern Germany and Scandinavia, or one-culture religions, such as Hinduism in India or the traditional religious complexes of China, Japan, and some African states.

Finally, established religion can be expressed through denominationalism. A **denomination** is a particular institutional and sociological organization within a larger religious tradition. In effect it ministers mostly to the spiritual needs of its members, probably a minority of the total society. Collectively in a denominational society, a number of parallel denominations comprise the great majority and represent the society's established religion. America, of course, is a denominational society, as are some British Commonwealth nations and, in many respects, Japanese Buddhism.

Conversely, it is mainly in connection with denominational societies that another manifestation of established religion, called **civil religion,** has been discussed.[3] This name pertains to a belief that society as a whole has a sacred meaning apart from individual religious groups. In America, for example, it is the "religion" (cutting across many denominations of our pluralistic society) of patriotic holidays, such as the Fourth of July and Thanksgiving, and the belief that the nation as a whole has a calling from God and a divine destiny. It has been argued, in fact, that there is a civil religious interpretation of American history that parallels biblical history— the coming of the Pilgrims corresponding to the call of Abraham, the

---

[3] See Russell E. Richey and Donald G. Jones, eds., *American Civil Religion* (New York: Harper & Row, Publishers, Inc., 1974).

Revolutionary War comparable to the Exodus, Washington like Moses, the Civil War the redemptive suffering of this new Israel, and Lincoln like Christ in his wisdom and sorrows. Whether one goes this far or not, there is something spiritually American yet nondenominational that many people feel and that expresses itself in certain attitudes, holy days, and places like the Arlington National Cemetery.

Whether international, national, or denominational, a church connected with established religion tends to have certain characteristics. Because it has a long tradition and an institutionalized structure, in theory it generally has strict, clearly defined doctrinal and moral positions. In practice it has to be fairly tolerant as long as the integrity of the institution is maintained. Since it is the nominal religion of the great majority of the people—of those who have not made a self-conscious, deliberate choice to be something else—it must find ways to accept people in all stages of spirituality. It has ways of incorporating infants of all families into its symbolic network through baptism or comparable **sacraments**; it has a conspicuous role in traditional festivals and community celebrations; its architecture is old and monumental; its leaders are spokespersons for and to the community on moral, and perhaps political, issues of general concern.

The established religion enforces, probably through some pattern of constraint and reward, the normative values of the community. While offering paths to sainthood for those called to follow them, it provides ways for those of more modest ambition to pursue meaningful spiritual lives in some hope of commensurate reward. Thus, in predominantly Buddhist countries, the Buddhist institution offers monks opportunity to make the ultimate meditations that lead to Nirvana and laypeople opportunities to gain merit through good deeds and devotional practices that will result in a desirable reincarnation.

Structures of the established religion tend to parallel those of society as a whole, especially on the national and denominational religious level. Thus in America they have democratic parliamentary forms, in Japan they have hereditary leadership, and in India they center around the charisma of saints.

One could ask whether established religion as a concept still has the meaning today that it did in the past. Modern institutional secularism, loss of belief or interest in religion, and revolutionary changes like those in China have greatly altered the meaning of a notion such as the normative religion of a society. But there is a sense in which religions traditionally considered the national religion have very different roles and meanings in their societies from those long considered non-conformist. One is identified, at least symbolically, with the whole society in national religion, and with a minority segment within it in other groups.

EMERGENT RELIGION

It is this whole pattern of ongoing established religion with which emergent religion contrasts, but in which it has roots. If established religion in a culture is a pervasive sea, emergent religion is a volcanic island breaking through its surface and roiling the waters around it.

The definitions of the word **emergent** suggest several salient characteristics of the sort of religion of which we are now speaking. As an adjective, **emergent** defines something arising out of a fluid which heretofore has covered or concealed it, or something suddenly appearing, or something coming as a natural or logical outcome of a situation (such as a war), or something appearing as novel in a process of evolution. As a noun, the word indicates something that stands out, as a tree above the forest.

These definitions really apply quite well to the counterpart of established religion. New religions emerge out of the fluid sea of popular religion, perhaps suddenly, perhaps in response to situations that impel change such as wars or conquest or new cultural contacts, perhaps as a result, like a mutation, of a process of evolution. They are likely to be recent, for the tendency is for an emergent religion to become a new established religion, or a part of an ongoing complex that makes up established religion, within a few generations. Some emergent religions, like the Amish, remain emergent in the sense of maintaining a distinctive visibility indefinitely; they do not mix and never really become part of the establishment.

An example of emergent religion is Tenrikyo, one of the new religions of Japan, although it is now over a century old. Tenrikyo traces its inception back to 1838, in the last years of old Japan before its phenomenal modernization that began in 1968 under the Emperor Meiji. The final decades before the end of the old regime were times of increasing economic trouble and civil unrest. The traditional popular religion, more than anything else a perpetuation of the shamanistic Buddhism already discussed, persisted, but popular frenzies of dancing and pilgrimage, especially to Ise, swept through from time to time, more and more associated with prophecies of immense change.

In 1838, the son of a prosperous farmer near Nara suffered intense pain in his leg, but a series of shamanistic healing sessions seemed to give him temporary relief. The shaman's female assistant would go into a trance and be possessed by a god, whom the shaman would then worship for healing. On one occasion the shaman's usual assistant was not available, and Miki Nakayama, the farmer's wife, substituted for her. When she went into a trance, however, a very unexpected thing happened: a voice spoke through her lips saying "I am the true and original God" and declared that he would use Miki as his residence in this world.

From then on, according to Tenrikyo belief, Miki Nakayama was the instrument and shrine of God. She lived a busy and holy life; she healed and gave forth words and writings that are believed to be messages of God. Above all, she taught a sacred dance that reenacts the creation of the world by the one God and indicates the sacred spot where the creation of mankind began. A fundamental Tenrikyo belief is that by knowing and dancing out the creation of the world by God the Parent, as the Creator is called, humanity can be brought back into original harmony with God. Now there is, as Miki instructed, a pillar over this spot, and it is the heart of a vast temple, which in turn is the hub of Tenri City, a religious city with administrative headquarters of the faith, pilgrimage hostels, training schools, and a university. Pilgrims come from all over the world to this site, and the sacred dance is performed around the pillar.

Thus, belief in the revelation of God through Miki Nakayama has grown and prospered. It began with a small and often-persecuted band around her. Since her death in 1887, it has become a large and well-organized institution, with an ample structure of classes, churches, and services, as well as missionary zeal.

Other emergent religions could be cited, from the twentieth-century **cargo cults**—typically centering on a prophet who says that if the native people will show enough faith, ships like those of the white men will bring them rich goods—of some colonial areas to a number of well-known religious movements in modern America. Nevertheless, the story of Tenrikyo adequately illustrates several of the most important features of emergent religion.

First, it emerges in a time of change, when many people feel that traditional values are being shaken and the future is uncertain. (This is not too much of a qualification, since most periods appear as times of transition and uncertain future to the people actually living in them, seeming eras of calm and stability only in the retrospective vision of later generations caught up in their own times of change.) In times of change, some classes of society feel left behind or want ways to comprehend and relate to the changes. Emergent religion usually first takes root among groups of people who are relatively powerless within society or not at the center of change—peasants in Japan, colonial peoples, minorities, the young, women. It provides them, as an elect who are in on a divine secret, with a compensatory, even greater power. The emergent religion says that God is doing something in the changes that only they know about, or else that he is doing something even greater than what is happening in the outer world and that this will climax in the near future. This teaching enables the believers to accept change by understanding it in the religious language familiar to them from the older popular and established religion, but with a new twist. As the institution grows, it enables believers to take part in something with a new and modern feel, similar to that of the modern government and business to which they may be outsiders, but *theirs* and for the sake of a faith they can understand.

Second, the emergent religion typically makes the jump from established religion to something new by selecting from out of the amorphous sea of tradition *one* person, place, teaching, practice, and group as its focus, to give it a new, crisp, distinct shape. Established religion tends implicitly toward multiplicity and even polytheism. Whatever the official position, there are likely to be a number of saints and heroes as sacred personalities, of charismatic preachers, of possible institutional affiliations, of sacred churches and places; but when emergent religion breaks through in that scene, it is reversed. As in the case of Miki Nakayama, emergent religion singles out and absolutizes particular examples of these manifold forms. It selects one shaman or spiritual person out of many candidates, one God out of many polytheistic or attributional candidates, one sacred place out of many shrines of established religion, one religious practice or rite out of many possibilities. This selectivity gives it a unique identity within the prevailing religious complex but at the same time sets up the likelihood of conflict. Conflict, however, is the stuff of life for emergent religion, since it enhances the distinctiveness that it craves.

Another characteristic of emergent religion is that it is likely to emphasize a future orientation. It will probably teach that in the near future a utopian kingdom, or a divine judgment that will vindicate its claims, will occur. This sort of prediction can only enhance its appeal to people caught in a time of rapid change when the future is unsure. It is also an expression of the fact that the religion, because it surfaced in a time of rapid change, really represents a discovery, in a new and radical sense, of historical time. Eschatology, or religious teaching about future events, suggests that what the God whom one already understands can do about the future is greater than what any human changes (about which one may in any case feel dubious) can bring about. It says that what you have already seen is nothing compared to what God or the gods will bring to pass.

Emergent religion usually centers around a charismatic personality— an individual who by the radiance of his or her own personality and the appeal of what he or she is, rather than any structural authority, draws people. The centrality of the charismatic person, rather than the institutional appeal of the faith, is very important. Unlike established religion, which can depend on the allegiance of all those not sufficiently moved to protest against it to make a self-conscious adult choice to be something else, emergent religion is mainly made up of converts who *have* made such a choice—which gives it a reservoir of highly committed persons but also means that it must maintain a level of intensity sufficient to counteract the natural pressures of family, community, and inertia that keep people within the established religion of their particular place.

The upshot is, in fact, that after two or three generations most emergent religions become established religions or, at least, a part of whatever established religion is prevalent. This is a result of the process called by the sociologist Max Weber "routinization of charisma"—when the grace and teachings communicated in unexpected ways by the religious founder come to be channeled, or are said to be channeled, through an institution in particular times and places. What he or she did spontaneously now comes through sacraments; what he or she said on odd occasions now comes through preaching at regularly scheduled services.

Two basic kinds of emergent religion should be distinguished, **intensive** and **expansive**. This pair corresponds with what some sociologists of religion have called respectively *sect* and *cult*, but those terms no longer seem to have appropriate connotations.

Intensive emergent religious groups withdraw from ordinary society in favor of a more intense and rigorous commitment to major symbols of the established religion. Within American Christianity, they would be groups such as Seventh-Day Adventists and Jehovah's Witnesses; within Judaism, extreme Hasidic groups. They tend to be legalistic, feeling ordinary followers of the same religion are lukewarm or hypocritical and not really serious about the religion in which, for cultural reasons, they find themselves. Sometimes, as in the case of the Amish or Hutterites, intensive religionists are communal. More often they are not but their members tend to have a high involvement with the group and relatively little relationship, except perhaps for evangelistic purposes, with the society outside of the intensive circle. The intensive religion communicates a message that apart from a very high level of group involvement and intensity of commitment, the full realization of religion's ability to make one feel like a real self and have access to infinite life cannot be realized.

Expansive emergent religion, on the other hand, withdraws from ordinary society in order to found what is, in its adherents' eyes, a more broadly based experience than that of the monochrome religion of the society. It seeks to combine elements of the established religion with new ideas and teachings from science, from far-away places, and from inner vision. In America, examples would be movements such as Spiritualism, Scientology, and various meditation and devotional movements brought in from India or Japan. Expansive religion is generally centered more on mystical experience than on the truth of particular rules or tenets. It is, however, just as likely as intensive emergent religion to be centered around loyalty to a particular charismatic leader and some simple, sure technique for spiritual transformation. It may also be just as much a withdrawal group. Expansive groups, though, are more likely to have outer, diffuse circles of followers of milder fervor, since it is possible to study the teachers and practice the meditation or whatever with a greater or lesser degree of separation from the ordinary world.

It should be emphasized that no specific religion is established or

Ken Kace

Mass wedding in Madison Square Garden, New York, July 1, 1982, performed by the Reverend and Mrs. Sun Myung Moon, leaders of a contemporary "intensive emergent" religion, the Unification Church.

emergent per se; these categories are dependent not on the nature of the religion but on its role. A religion can be emergent in one place and established in another, or it can be one at one point in its history and the other at another. Buddhist faith is established in Thailand and Japan but apt to be emergent in America. Buddhism and Christianity were both emergent at the time of their inception but became established within a few generations. As has been indicated, most religions become established within two or three generations because of routinization of the original charisma and because more and more of their members are born within the faith rather than converted.

The Denomination

The denomination and its founder, who is generally the sort of personality who links great and little traditions (and also links established and emergent religions) are often bridges. The founder—for example, Luther, Wesley, Shinran, and Vivekananda—is typically a reformer within a great, well-established religion who emphasizes a particular aspect of or attitude toward it as a key to the whole. As does emergent religion generally, he or she singles out one simple sure key to the essence of its immense experience and mystery, whether faith scripture, one certain rite, or one doctrine. Shinran, the medieval Japanese founder of Jodo Shinshu, the "True Pure Land" denomination of Buddhism, taught that all of Buddhism can be encompassed in simple faith in the Amita Buddha, who has promised to bring all who call on his name into his paradise, or Pure Land. At the same time, the founder's appeal is usually affected by social factors; it serves as a means of identification for a particular nation, social class, immigrant group, or personality type. Methodism appealed particularly to the working classes in England and to pioneers in America; denominational Lutheranism in America represents the heritage of both state churches and pietistic movements in northern Europe.

Denominationalism says that individuals and movements within the long history of a great religion can provide adequately definitive expressions of the religion's heritage, even though they arrived late in its history and only in particular places. Those individuals and movements can in fact nearly eclipse the rest of the religion. Pure Land Buddhists in Japan, like denominational Protestants in America, know the history, teaching, and ethos of their version of the religion far better than any other. These movements started as emergent religion within an established version of the same faith and have finally become, for all intents and purposes, established themselves. They nevertheless retain a sense of being a sort of spiritual commonwealth, given to activism and belief that activity is good, all the more so because the denomination is not ultimately responsible for the whole faith. In a way, the denomination has the best and worst of both established and emergent religion. It can combine the solid sociological base of established religion with the venturesomeness of emergent religion, being able to take risks it could not if it felt itself responsible as an institution for the whole of the faith to which it is committed. It may, however, also suffer the conservative caution of an established religion, together with the new religion's hypersensitivy to criticism and the precarious sense that it must always justify itself.

Religious Personalities

Intertwined with different kinds of religious groups are different sorts of religious personalities.[4] Each of these, in its own way, communicates a message about what it means to be religious. The number of conceivable types of religious personality is very great; perhaps every religious person is in the last analysis his or her own type. Several that are largely shaped by distinctive and well-known roles within religious history are listed here. These are not so much psychological types as role types that generally

---

[4] These lists are suggested by those in Joachim Wach, *Sociology of Religion* (Chicago, Ill.: University of Chicago Press, 1944), and *The Comparative Study of Religion* (New York: Columbia University Press, 1958); and G. van der Leeuw, *Religion in Essence and Manifestation* (New York: Harper & Row, Publishers, Inc., 1963), 2 vols.

reflect or call forth certain attitudes and styles of behavior toward religion that amount to at least a public personality of a certain sort.

The following are what may be called objective types, types determined by structural role:

The Shaman. The shaman really transcends both objective and subjective categories since, as we have seen, his or her lot is a complex mixture of inner call, spiritistic experience, and socially defined role. Generally, the shaman is an individual in primitive or archaic religion who, having become master of spirits that initially seemed likely to drive him or her mad, now uses them in public and private seances to heal, divine, and perhaps guide him or her to the worlds of the dead and the gods. The shaman's performances, which will follow traditional patterns, are centers of the experience of transcendence for the community and reinforce the sacred view of the universe.

The Priest. This category includes other religious titles, such as bishops, minister, or rabbi. It embraces religious specialists, commonly professional, who hold office through heredity or training and whose primary function is to perform customary religious rites or services in expected ways. While he or she may be personally devout and have had a personal call, it is the priest's position that assures his or her status. The priest mediates the sacred, without necessarily interiorizing it, objectively through rite and word and thus grants the community the necessary ongoing symbol of its presence afforded by institutions and their reliable custodians. Some religious specialists combine attributes of shaman and priest, fervor being a part of their role.

The Monk and Nun. This category includes many sorts of holy people as well, such as the sadhus of India and some Sufi mystics of Islam. Unofficial approximations of its way can be found among the likes of some Protestant missionaries and members of contemporary religious communes. Not all approximations of the monk and nun type are even celibate, but the point of the type is to live a life outside the ordinary structures of society (yet in reality accepted and provided for by the religion) that exemplifies the ideal spiritual life as understood by that tradition. The way of the monk and nun has three goals: to save one's own soul; to exemplify the ideal way of perfection; and to support the tradition through prayer, teaching, and service. It is often (though not always) lived communally for mutual help in this difficult way and to exemplify the ideal social as well as the individual model of perfection. Because its ideal is total dedication, this way may have (when well lived) an aura about it of poverty, abstinence, and inward holiness.

The Layperson. The layperson is one who lives in a community and participates in its religious usages but is in no way a specialist or professional. He or she is the farmer, fisherman, or townsperson who is the ordinary worshipper. His or her place in the religion is not to be defined only negatively, by what he or she is not. Rather, it is a definite and distinctive role, with its own pattern, and is structurally essential to the religion as a whole. His or her religious life has, in practice, different goals and self-interpretation from that of the priest or monk. It is more related to supporting family, community, and ethics and to limited but specific benefits from the deities, as well as ultimate transformation or salvation. In the total life of the religion, the layperson's role is to provide its material support, to make its rites and teachings practically possible by serving as their recipient, and to show the universality of the religion's worldview by manifesting how it structures society and how it can have some kind of effect on the life of everyone.

The Philosopher and Theologian. These are likely to be priests or monks, but some have been laypersons. Their special role is to interpret the religion in terms of the intellectual tradition of their culture. (That tradition may in fact derive from other sources, just as Western intellectual culture derives largely from the Greeks.)

More subjective and spontaneous religious types appear out of a person's inner need rather than out of a wish to fill (even if on the basis of a deeply felt calling) a role or niche already existent in the tradition. The following are some subjective types:

The Founder. The founder of a new religion (the vocation commonly ascribed to persons such as the Buddha, Jesus, Confucius, and Muhammad) is, needless to say, very rare. He or she must have an especially comprehensive religious personality, together with a special charisma and the right historical setting. The founder must become a symbol in his or her personality of both complexity and clarification. The great founders have had a reputation for being able to cover enough of the diverse roles of religion to provide models in themselves for all the strands a great religion needs to have: a spiritual way, an attitude toward society, a common touch, deep wisdom. The founder must also appear at a point of historical transition when religious symbols are still persuasive but new ones or new arrangements of old ones are needed. The founder must be able to facilitate the transition because he or she has links with past, present, and future. People were reassured by Jesus, for example, because he did not reject the tradition, only its abuses; yet he also gave new symbols, himself and his cross, for a new age and suggested meaning for the future as well, in the kingdom of God. An important aspect of the founder is the fact that he or she has a small band of disciples. The disciple is a special type of religious personality in his or her own right and is essential to the founder by providing an intimate audience for the message in a group which will prepare the lasting institutionalization of the newly founded religion.

The Mystic. The mystic is usually within a particular religious tradition, although sometimes, like Kabir in late medieval India, he or she is on the borderline of two and occasionally may seem genuinely independent.

AP/Wide World Photo

Benedictine monks.

The mystic's emphasis is on attaining special states of consciousness considered direct, immediate experience of the religious reality. Understandably, to the mystic these states are more important than religious structures or rites, although their attainment is not necessarily inconsistent with the latter. Within the religion, the mystic has a role as an exemplar of its spiritual reality. He or she may be a teacher and writer, though of course many mystics have not been literary.

The Reformer.   The reformer works within a tradition rather than starting a new one but shares with the founder some sense of a new historical situation that requires a new application of the tradition, particularly in relation to the structures of the social order and the religious institution's own structures. Although the reformer feels these structures ought to be changed, he or she does not believe that the essential doctrines of the faith should be altered. Rather, the reformer has the tradition highly interiorized; he or she does not need to depend on its outward forms and so can urge their extensive modification. In interiorization the reformer may be like the mystic, but unlike the mystic the reformer is critically aware of outward structures and wants to make them conform to the interiorization.

The Popularizer.   This category applies to a wide gamut of effective and charismatic preachers, Sufi saints, Buddhist missionaries, and Christian evangelists. The popularizer is not particularly a reformer or necessarily a mystic (though some have been these, too) but is a dynamic and attractive person able to appeal to the masses as well or even better than the founder. He or she makes no pretense of being original but is a transmitter of faith from out of his or her inner and contagious fervor, chiefly through rhetorical performance. The popularizer may well be an important link between great and little traditions.

Other types of religious personalities could be cited—saint, prophet, seer, convert, penitent, and mystagogue are among those that have been used in lists similar to this. These seem, at least to my mind, either imprecise or too restricted to particular traditions. Close equivalents to the types in the preceding lists can be found in nearly every religion.

On the other hand, it could be argued that the category of founder is not sufficiently distinct from the other three subjective types, especially reformer, since often the figure who becomes—from the perspective of historical hindsight—the founder of a new religion had no intention of being more than a mystic, reformer, or popularizer within the existing religion. From the perspective of his or her own time, the founder may not have played a role much different than that of being a particularly successful exponent of one of those types.

I would contend that historical role as well as the psychology of the figure should be a factor in the typing of religious personalities. The founders did seem to have a psychology and self-understanding somewhat different from mystics, reformers, and popularizers within traditions, even if that difference may have been the product of the distinctive historical circumstances within which they worked and that also enabled their movements to take off as new religions. More than most others, they dealt decisively with issues from all areas of life, interacted with people of all classes of society, were aware of what was going on in history, and sensed that a spiritual new age was starting in them.

All such lists of categories and types as this, in religious studies as in biology, contain elements of historical or evolutionary hindsight. Moreover, they are tentative and useful chiefly for the fact that working with them, rearranging them, and arguing about them can be an excellent aid to study and understanding.

THE TRANSFORMATION OF SOCIETY BY RELIGION

Having considered the effect of historical situations and surrounding society on religion, the reverse, which is equally important, must be noted. That is the transformative impact of religion on society. Religion and other social factors work both together and in reaction against each other to produce spirals of change. Here are some ways religions have effected change in society.

Image of the Normative Nature of Society

All religions contain an image of the normative nature of society. It is not always explicit but is implied in the fundamental myths and symbols of the religion itself, especially in the life of the founder and his or her relations to disciples. For example, Buddhism suggests an aristocratic model of the social order in that the Buddha, however much he embraced ascetic poverty, did so as a prince who deliberately gave up riches. He was, then, always significantly different from a poor man who has never had wealth to sacrifice. In India, and also in China and Japan when it came there, Buddhism appealed most effectively (except in very modified devotional forms) to people of the upper classes, although it marvelously persuaded many of them to endow hospitals, orphanages, and hostels out of Buddhist compassion. Even bodhisattvas (enlightened beings who work out of compassion for the salvation of all) were portrayed as crowned princes. Buddhism has never succeeded on a large scale in relating to a society not basically hierarchical in the traditional aristocratic sense, and it may not as long as its fundamental human metaphor is of the prince who has everything but gives it up for the sake of enlightenment and universal compassion.

The case with Christianity is a little different. A fundamental image in it is *hidden kingship*. Jesus was the *hidden* son of David according to the tradition, and Jesus has often been thought to have known he was the Messiah, or divinely annointed king, who would establish a paradisal rule but to have kept this matter concealed for a time—the "messianic secret." This image suggests the possibility of royal legitimacy, and Christians have often been governed by kings, accepting them as parts of a divinely ordained pattern of society. But the hiddenness of truth, the suffering of Christ at the hands of authority, and the early church's castigation as the "offscouring of the earth," in Paul's term, have all also placed in Christian minds a notion that in society things may not be what they seem. Christianity has thereby been the consolation both of authoritarian traditional regimes, such as those of the Bourbons and Hapsburgs in Europe, and of oppressed people, such as blacks in the New World.

In any case, the implied image or images of society deriving from some of the most basic narratives and doctrines of the religion have profoundly affected societies to which the faith has spread.

Normative Moral Literature

The normative moral literature of a religion—the Ten Commandments, the Confucian classics, and so forth—has an obvious role, but it needs to be understood that the impact of prescriptive ethics of this sort on a society may be less than straightforward. Confucian filial piety (sense of obligation toward parents) shaped the lives of billions in East Asia and probably also led to the explosive rebellion against all that is old and paternalistic in modern China. Upwards of two thousand years of the Ten Commandments in Europe and America have not eliminated adultery, killing, or taking the Lord's name in vain, even among the ostensibly devout or the highly placed; they have instead forced the construction of elaborate explanations of what is and is not justifiable human slaughter and sex. They have produced much wrestling with guilt on these matters and have given sex and violence a double-edged symbolic power—they are both fascinating and forbidden. All this has made societies influenced by Judaism and Christianity genuinely sensitive to moral issues. The sensitivity is reflected in much legislation and in a literature shot through with guilt and justification, but it has not so much eliminated what it regards as sin as set the terms and tone of moral discourse; the same can be said for Confucian, Buddhist, or Muslim societies.

Worship and Sociology of Religion

The worship and sociology of a religion offer models of how it conceptualizes the ideal community, and such models work on deep levels in the minds of people. Whether the worship and the style of leadership imply highly structured forms or mystical freedom, charismatic or routinized leadership, egalitarian or hierarchical patterns; whether worship has mainly verbal or nonverbal symbolism; whether participation is passive or active for most—all these deeply affect the social and political values of the community as well. One can see how Hinduism with its ideal of the holy man prepared India for a leader like Mohandas Gandhi. Denominationalism in America with its models of routinized, egalitarian, and democratic leadership, together with the nonrational charismatic styles of leadership that emerge especially in revivalistic evangelicalism and pentecostalism, help explain American social and political styles.

Historical Impact of Religion

There is also the direct historical impact of religion, especially of the international religions that have conveyed cultures, literary heritages, and political systems across continents. Buddhism, Christianity, Islam, and Confucianism have influenced cultures outside the one in which they began, and not only through formal doctrine. They have come into new lands as models of a different, and often seemingly more advanced style of civilization. Commonly they have either come together with new imperial rule from outside or been catalysts in major political changes internally. At the least, the new religion offers a sense of history, maybe even a discovery of history, that implies the possibility of change in many areas of life by showing that values can be revamped.

Prophetic Teaching and Religious Demands for Justice

Religions have also produced leaders across the centuries who have directly demanded change and justice from those in political and economic power. We have mentioned Gyogi in ancient Japan, and Mohandas Gandhi in the twentieth-century India. In modern America, a good example would be a religious figure like Martin Luther King, with his dream of a land of racial equality, in which his children and everyone's would "one day live in a nation where they will not be judged by the color of their skin, but by the content of their character." Such great persons, speaking boldly out of a moral vision shaped by religious teachings, have had a vast if sometimes indefinable influence on history.

RELIGION AND THE INTERPRETATION OF HISTORY

Finally, religions affect history because they affect the way history is interpreted, understood, and even remembered. Thus they affect the way history is written and the way we come to know it. Confucian historians in China, for example, taught their sense of morality through the medium of history by making good things occur during the reigns of virtuous sovereigns and bad things under evil ones.

The matter can be more complex, however. Donald E. Miller, a sociologist of religion, studied the attitudes of Armenians living in southern California who were survivors of the genocidal massacres of Armenians in the Turkish Empire during World War I.[5] In a two-year period beginning in 1915, some one and one-half million Armenian men, women, and children—over half the Armenian population in Turkey—were slaughtered, often in circumstances of appalling cruelty. Miller found four basic responses among survivors—people now elderly who as children had seen their families killed before their eyes or suffered extremes of hunger and fatigue on forced marches, but who by a seeming miracle managed to escape the fate of most of those around them and to reach a new and happier land.

One response of the survivors was denial. For some, the memory was too painful. They did not want to think about it, and if they did discuss it, they reverted to a childish idiom as though it could only be handled by a subjective reversion to the other time and place.

[5] Donald E. Miller, "Recalling the Past: A Case Study of Survivors of the Armenian Genocide," (unpublished paper presented at the Pacific Regional Meeting, American Academy of Religion, 1976).

Another response was desire for revenge. One way to deal with the trauma of unjust, nonsensical suffering is to seek restitution—that is, to reestablish justice. Some survivors were filled with such thoughts of revenge. (One respondent, a Christian minister, said he was glad he was a Christian because otherwise he would have delighted in killing as many of the other side as possible.)

For others the response was rationalization. They could not accept that their suffering was to no purpose and so tried to find one. Some explained that the Armenians actually provoked the massacre themselves through their insistence on independence. It was better in the eyes of these people to see themselves and their people as guilty than to face a world in which there is suffering for no reason. These people often turned to religion to assist in this line of thought. They said the massacre was a punishment from God for the pride of the slain. They also spoke of its benefits to the survivors—that it led them to turn to God or strengthened their characters.

Finally, there were those whose only response was resignation. They could not deny the massacre, see any satisfaction in revenge, or rationalize it in any way. They could only accept that it happened, but this resignation brought them no peace. Survivors in this category were often melancholic.

The ways in which religious concepts, vocabulary, and symbols are used to enable historical events to be interpreted in situations like these are obvious. Religious symbols, ideas, and practices can deny events by making them seem illusory or by returning the people to childhood in confronting them; they can inspire revenging crusades and a sense of mythic national destiny; they can help explain how a bad event was actually sent from God as punishment or to test and strengthen the people; they can even facilitate a fatalistic resignation. On the other hand, as we have seen in the case of prophets for both ancient and modern justice, from Amos to King, religion can inspire the response of working through righteousness. Religion can accept and sanctify society, but it can also be a force to change it.

SUMMARY

All religion is really social, deriving from the social nature of human beings. Even private religious experiences are conditioned by our social nature through the use of language to interpret the experience to ourselves as religious; without such words and concepts as *God, sacred power,* and so forth, religion as we know it would be unimaginable, and language stems from society.

The great importance of society to religion is also seen in the role of religious groups. Those with religious visions typically try to form groups based on them, for a group gives legitimacy and an accepted role in society. Religious experience becomes more real as it is shared, and the structure of the group itself tells much about its nature and message.

Important messages are also conveyed by the way the group interacts with surrounding society. A large, deeply rooted religion virtually coterminous with the society tells us that truth is broadly based; a small withdrawal group, that it is best found in a small, intense group.

Another way of looking at the social expression of religion is found in the distinction between the great and little tradition. The great tradition of a religion is that which is professed by its elites, who are literate, well aware of history, and usually close to major centers of cultural and political power. The little tradition consists of folk or popular religion, which is nonliterary, historically unaware, and inclined to relate religion to local needs, the seasonal cycle, and the immediate present.

Still another distinction is between established and emergent religion. Established religion embraces both great and little traditions insofar as they together are the stable, dominant religion of society. It may be expressed as a great international religion like Buddhism or Christianity, as a national religion like Hinduism, or as a denomination like Methodism or Baptism.

Emergent religion refers to new religious movements which emerge out of established religion. It may be intensive, striving to practice the dominant religion more strictly and devoutly; or expansive, bringing in new ideas and practices, perhaps combining them with local ones. Emergent religion frequently arises in times of uncertainty and rapid social change. It tends to focus on one central symbol and practice, to be future oriented, and to be built on the authority of a charismatic prophet.

Religion produces distinctive types of personality and personal roles. Those that are basically structural include the shaman, priest, monk or nun, layperson, and philosopher or theologian; those more subjective or spontaneous are the founder, mystic, reformer, and popularizer. They are defined in the word list below.

Religion serves to transform the society around it through the image of the normative or proper nature of society its stories and ideas suggest, through its moral commandments and literature (even though these may not always be followed literally), through the social message embedded in its worship and organization, through prophetic teachers who call for justice, and through the impact it has on the history of society when it arrives, often bearing an outside culture as well as faith.

Religion also affects societies by interpreting their histories, describing historical events as divine judgments, redemptive suffering, calls for crusades, or meaningless illusion. All these ideas affect the behavior of individuals and societies in the present.

New York Public Library Picture Collection

St. Augustine (354–430 C.E.) was one of the most important Christian philosophers and theologians, and well represents the religious thinker.

Truth Messages: The Conceptual Expression of Religion

Chapter Objectives

- Interpret the role of doctrines and concepts in religion.

- Distinguish the content and structural messages of a religious statement: respectively, what is said, and what is said by the *way* it is said.

- Explain what is meant by traditionalist, liberal, and fundamentalist styles of religious belief.

- Explain the general meaning of the word *God* and three basic ways in which God or the deity have been understood: as impersonal absolute, in terms of personal monotheism, and in terms of polytheism.

- Describe the attributes and characteristics traditionally ascribed to the Judaeo-Christian God.

- Tell what some of the main areas usually dealt with by religious doctrine are.

- Discuss and describe different ways of determining truth in religion, such as reason, experience, empiricism, authority, and existential choice.

- Discuss the issue of whether or not religious truth can be convincingly determined.

As you read the chapter, also look for important words. The key words defined in the glossary at the end of the book are in boldface type at their first use in the text.

WHAT IS SAID AND HOW IT IS SAID

Now we come to the part of our study of religion that has to do with what religions "say" and the concepts with which they work: their doctrines about God or gods, the soul, divinely given rewards and punishments in this life and the next, and so forth. It may surprise some readers that it has taken so long to get to these matters, except through various hints and allusions, that to many are virtually the whole point of religion. Religion, they think, is principally a question of beliefs regarding God and life after death and the faith they inspire.

Certainly the verbal and conceptual theoretical expression of religion is extremely important, and the reality construction or universe of meaning that comes out of the interaction of all forms of expression can certainly be called faith. The discussion of religious ideas has been saved until this point to emphasize that they do not comprise the *whole* of human religion but are integral parts of religion as a total experience.

A particular belief may seem to religious participants the main reason for participation in the religion. One is a Christian or Muslim because one believes Christianity or Islam is *true*. But the nature of the total experience one has in religion is deeply colored by the kind of worship that goes with it and the kind of group with which one worships. Immensely different styles of worship and sociology can make the same doctrine seem different, and similar styles of worship can make different doctrines seem compatible, if not almost the same thing in different words.

One could argue, with the philosopher Ludwig Wittgenstein, that religious statements are "language games" with only internal reference within the circle using them. The corollary would be that all religions are equally true and false; you cannot really talk or argue with people outside of your circle but only preach at them—that is, try to bring them through conversion into the circle where that language pattern is meaningful because one has associated it with important experiences.[1]

Moreover, religious myth and doctrine, like other symbols, can be seen as codes; people argue that what they really mean is something other than what they say. To Freudians they encode the worldview of the child

---

[1] See William C. Shepherd, "On the Concept of 'Being Wrong' Religiously," *Journal of the American Academy of Religion*, XLII, 1 (March 1974), 66–81. Shepherd argues that traditional proofs of God really fit the concept of "language game," since they are in the tradition of a particular religious culture and serve to clarify their accepted language—they are "faith speaking to faith." At heart, religious authority does not depend on reason.

within trying to retain the magical universe and omniscient father he or she once knew; to Jungians they express the diverse components of the psyche, such as the Great Mother and the Wise Old Man; to structuralists like Claude Lévi-Strauss they are, so to speak, a code just for the sake of being a code, the patterns of myth and doctrine telling us there are thinking human beings here.

Religious statements can and must also be looked at, and taken seriously, as what they obviously intend to be on the ordinary conscious level, that is, statements of real knowledge and real truth. Whether religious statements should be seen as statements of plain truth or as codes for something else is a decision each person has to make for himself or herself. Nevertheless, one never rightly understands religion and its importance until one has complemented a descriptive approach with endeavors to understand, and wrestle with, the claims of religious statements to be *true*.

Most religious people, then, have perceptions they believe to be true to go with their participation. These are ideas, stories, and mental images about invisible reality and its impingement on the visible. The clarity, logical consistency, and precision of these concepts may vary considerably between the professional elites and the ordinary members of the religion, who may be illiterate or at least religiously illiterate. The religious universe of the latter may be vague and haphazard, albeit deeply felt. However, this only reflects the haphazard way they were acquainted with it—through casual word of mouth, through family and friends, rather than through systematic training. In virtually every religion the professional elite have a different perception, sometimes more liberal and sometimes more rigorous, of its truth statements than the ordinary lay members, though they are often wise enough not to communicate their perception in ways that would unduly unsettle the lay believers.

This does not mean, however, that the elite perception is better or even more accurate in terms of the ultimate meaning of the religion; it is only different. The interpretation of Buddhism by its monks and philosophers, that it shows a path to the cessation of desire and attainment of Nirvana, is immensely important to understanding the role of Buddhism in history and thought—but so also is the more popular role of Buddhism as a bearer of high culture to millions, the sociological meaning of belonging to a temple in Thailand or Japan, and even its role of occasionally providing symbols to revolutionary political movements in China.

It is a matter of messages. In doctrine and myth, as in other areas, there are two messages at once in a religious statement: the **content** and the **structural message**. The content message is what is said; the structural message is what is said by the *way* it is said.

For example, two faiths may postulate the existence of God. One bases its belief in God ostensibly on a tightly reasoned logical argument that there must be a God; the other, on visions or emotional experiences of

God its people have. The content is the same, but the tone, and so the total experience of these two faiths, is quite different.

As another example, imagine a religion in which the elite envision a systematic hierarchy of gods from the supreme ruler of heaven on down. They are arranged in phalanxes, each with its captain and lieutenant, each in charge of a particular area of earthly affairs. The lay people are likely to know of just a few of the gods—the deity of one's village temple or of one's personal occupation or even the god of whom one once had a vision or miracle. Those gods, however, are very deeply embedded in local shrines and festivals, profoundly parts of daily life. Again, the content messages converge, but the structural messages differ. One says the spiritual universe is orderly and reflects the pattern of a well-tempered state or of the reasoning powers of the seasoned philosopher; the other that the universe is as haphazard as the average man's lot is likely to be, but that there is such a thing as community and seasons and that there are points of glory in the cosmos that break through unexpectedly here and there.

The same difference between content message and structural message can be seen in American Christianity. A statement such as "God was in Christ" would be affirmed by all Christians in the same words but would have different meanings because of a different structural context in a traditional church doctrinal statement, in the discourse of a liberal theologian, and in the words of a conservative or fundamentalist theologian.

The adjectives **traditional**, **liberal**, and **fundamentalist** suggest in fact three different structural styles of speaking religious truth messages. Although they are drawn from Christianity, close parallels can be found in Judaism and other major religions. Traditionalist religious statements give a tone to truth indicating that it is interlinked with deep family and ethnic ties, or a desire for the equivalents, and with the oldest and richest art, music, literature, and wisdom of the culture in which the religious tradition is based. Liberal religious statements indicate by their tone and structure that truth must be consistent in all areas of knowledge, including the scientific, and is apprehended through induction and synthesis. Liberals usually see truth as fragmentary and to be held in a way that preserves large areas of inner and outer freedom. Fundamentalist or conservative religious statements are parts of highly consistent systems based on scriptural or ecclesiastical authority. The structural message of the way they are put is that there is absolute truth and absolute authority. The view that human nature has and needs absolute truth and authority may be reflected in family and social values as well.

The structural and content messages are both very important. They may or may not be consistent, but that fact only suggests another message about the ultimate importance of *consistency* in human experience; for there is much to indicate it is important and much to indicate it is not. However, the content message is finally a statement about the human need for

Fosco Marain/Monkmeyer Press Photo Service

The *ka-pa*, or wizard, is an important figure in popular Tibetan religion. He deals with the exorcisms and spells derived from the power of the mighty Buddhas and other beings who animate the Tibetan pantheon. His use of their power is eclectic; he moves with shrewdness among the infinite occult powers by which every Tibetan feels surrounded. Although as a popular religionist he may deal with these deities just one at a time, note that behind him are *tankas*, or meditation paintings, that show the Tibetan pantheon arranged in systematic, hierarchical, and symbolically significant order.

consistency, or unity, from out of diversity. The religious content messages are intended to unify all aspects of religion and life—the group, the worship, the psychological states, the symbols—around a single meaning. It says we have this group, this form of worship, these experiences and symbols, *because* we believe in this kind of God. These religious statements articulate the meaning of it all; they are the points where religion breaks through on the level of the human capacity for reason, mental images, abstractions, and concepts.

These highly verbal articulations are still religion and have all the characteristics of religion. They are the sacred in the mind as surely as the temple is in the city. They are the real self in the realm of ideas as surely as dancing in a sacred place is in the physical realm. These ideas provide a real interpretation of the world different from the ordinary—and although all culture and philosophy does so, religion does it more and relates it to the transcendent, that is, to invisible but more ultimate dimensions.

Religious ideas deal with issues such as suffering, value, and meaning in terms of symbolic forms that focus and concretize them so that the answers can be easily grasped and handled, but the symbols are now ideas and concepts, symbols in the mind. That they are called symbols is not to deny their cognitive value—that is, that they are an actual *knowing of truth* as far as this is humanly possible and as far as it can be known in ways that are transferable through the common coin of human language. Knowing, to oneself as well as in communication to others, requires the invisible symbols of words and ideas, but it may be that some symbols do correspond to absolute reality better than others, and even that some do so as perfectly as possible. Even so, they are also symbols. They are related to our central theme of the real self; as with other kinds of symbols, thinking certain ideas may authenticate one as a real self.

GOD

Virtually all religion affirms the reality of being, knowledge, and joyful power greater than the human; this is the obvious expression of belief in transcendence and of a real self greater than the ordinary. Generally, this belief is concretized in belief in a **God** or gods—self-conscious centers of being, knowledge, and power superior to humanity, upon which ordinary humans must depend and make prayer and offering for their well-being. Even when this ultimate being is not personified, as the Dao, Nirvana, and Brahman of Daoism, Buddhism, and some expressions of Hinduism, respectively, are not personified, there are gods and Buddhas who refract its power and so are symbolic manifestations of it. Significantly, however, in Daoism and Buddhism the superior beings who now personify ultimate being were once human.

Three basic distillations of divinity can, in fact, be isolated. They may be understood in light of H. Richard Niebuhr's understanding of God as *center of value*—that is, as the touchstone of meaning beyond which one cannot go.[2]

First, God can be thought of as an **impersonal absolute**. From this perspective, personality such as you and I have is seen essentially as a limitation. Because we can think about only one thing at a time, there are millions of real things we are not thinking about, and in this way the nature of our consciousness identified with personality makes us terribly limited. Because our personalities are really constructed out of various human desires, anxieties, defenses, and cosmic ignorance, they provide poor models for God. Better, according to impersonalists, to understand God as pure being and consciousness without the hindrance of personality—let the Absolute be like an unstained mirror, out of which all things rise and fall, itself untouched by their vicissitudes. The human correlate is that it is those moments when individual personality is most subdued—in deep meditation, in scientific contemplation—that we best know, or realize, the divine.

Second, God can be thought of in terms of **personal monotheism**. As in the Judaeo-Christian-Islamic tradition, this belief sees the absolute power of the universe as personal, but personality that transcends the human limitations. In its hierarchy of values, personality is at the top. Personal monotheism, therefore, can speak of God as having a sense of purpose, as loving, as being the eternal friend. Its best argument is this: although God may be infinitely greater than personality as we know it, personal existence is the highest form of existence we know, so we can do no better than to start by thinking of God as personal on the model of our own personalities and then try to expand this idea to infinity.

Finally there is **polytheism**, belief in many gods. Polytheism, as Paul Tillich sagely observed, is really a matter of quality rather than quantity— the point is that multiplicity of gods creates a cosmos of very different tone from belief in one center of value. It suggests that every old tree, golden grove, rushing stream, and ponderous mountain may have its gods of independent mood, as does every fertile field and city, and every changing human occasion, from love to war or business to contemplation. At best they may belong to some hierarchy; otherwise they may seem, as often

[2] H. Richard Niebuhr, *Radical Monotheism and Western Culture* (New York: Harper & Row, Publishers, Inc., 1970). Compare it with the following words of C. G. Jung: "The idea of God is an absolutely necessary psychological function of an irrational nature. . . . There is in a psyche some superior power, and if it is not consciously a god, it is the 'belly,' at least, in St. Paul's words. I therefore consider it wiser to acknowledge the idea of God consciously; for, if we do not, something else is made God, usually something quite inappropriate and stupid such as only an 'enlightened' intellect could hatch forth." (In *Two Essays in Analytic Psychology*, Bollengen Series, *Collected Works of C. G. Jung* [Princeton N.J.: Princeton University Press, 1973], vol. VII, p. 71.)

does human life itself, to be running off in several directions at once. In any case, polytheism presents religion not as forcing all of life around a single center of value (something we may often desire if not deserve) but as reflecting our usual experience of it in fragments, with all its many fragments shot through with various inconsistent apertures toward transcendence. The apparent polytheism of Hinduism, Buddhism, and Daoism, as we have seen often goes together with belief in an impersonal absolute.

CREATION

The next step in a formal statement of content is to get from God or the gods to the existing world. In any religious system, the way this step is accounted for, the description of the creation of the world, is extremely revealing of the worldview. The following are some examples.

Some religious traditions, such as the Hindu and Buddhist, see the universe as essentially eternal, without beginning or ending in the stream of time as we know it. Although the universe always stands against timeless reality, from within the stream of time we do not perceive a moment of absolute starting or stopping but only endless cause and effect. The cosmos, however, does undergo immense cycles of creation and destruction, each cycle leading to the next. This view carries with it the implication that conscious existence within this unending chain of worlds would finally become wearisome and sad, leading one to quest for the way to jump off the wheel altogether into unconditioned reality, to find life in God or Nirvana instead.

The way to God, although it may be difficult, would not involve going far; the same traditions show us that God or the Absolute is within all things, their true nature an essence to which only our ignorance blinds us. Another account from India tells us the world as we know it was made when Prajapati, a primal god, offered himself as a sacrifice and divided up his body into many things that make up our world. This myth indicates, as we have seen, that the multitudinous world is God hiding himself behind countless forms.

Still another account of creation is that of the Egyptian and Babylonian myths, among others. This might be called a genetic creation and tells us that the world and its inhabitants are the result of a process of generation analogous to the human but between primal gods. Frequently there is a union of a god and a goddess representing heaven and earth, although in one Egyptian account a solitary deity generates the creation out of himself. In Japan, the primal parents both come down from heaven, and among the Hopi, both come out of the earth. These narratives emphasize above all the continuity of spiritual life with the biological processes and so integrate cosmos with the agriculture and biology of human society.

Finally, there is creation *ex nihilo*, "from nothing," the picture favored by Judaism, Christianity, and Islam. It says that God by an absolute decree called the universe into being, without having to use any preexistent material or any parallel to genetic process. The resultant picture is of God as different in an unqualified way from his creation—the difference between a craftsman and the work of his hands. It establishes that God is sovereign though loving ruler of all he has made and that while his people, who are as grasshoppers in his eyes, have no natural claim to kinship with him, they owe him obedience and can respond to him with love.

The account of creation must explain the existence of that most unusual entity within it, humankind—beings who sense that they are part of creation, yet different from the rest of it, and in some ways close to God, but in others farther from him than the nature that remains as it came from his hand. A major tool of religious thought for dealing with these ambiguities is the concept of the **soul** or its equivalents, such as the Buddhist idea of an ongoing bundle of karmic forces. The soul is an immaterial substance within the individual that provides his or her ultimate identity and is in rapport with deity or infinite reality—a function that includes the capacity to receive the supernatural judgment or punishment and reward incurred by the individual's needs.

Beliefs about the soul have varied. Some cultures have conceived of multiple souls having different destinies after death—some going to paradise, some lingering around the grave or the household shrines. Some very important cultures have thought that according to its deeds, the soul reincarnates in human or animal or even ghostly or divine forms. Others have held that it goes directly to a post-mortem reward or punishment in heaven or hell or perhaps to an intermediate state, a purgatory, where the demerit of sins less than fatal can be worn away. Others emphasize the association of the spiritual principle in man with the physical body and do not expect the soul to live a meaningful life apart from it; they wait for God to raise the body and the spirit to newness of life on the Last Day. Still others stress the closeness of ancestral spirits to the living of their family; the departed remain near them in tomb and altar to bless and watch.

In all these beliefs, the soul or something comparable to it is like a reflection of God in a small mirror; it shares the nature of God or the gods in that it is immaterial and deathless, yet it shares the nature of human clay in that it can receive the imprint of sin and suffer both finitude and punishment. At the same time, the idea of the soul has a splendid side; it reflects humanity's deeply rooted conviction that in some way we are more than mortal, that we have a true self capable of tasting immortality and infinity, and that we are worthy of judgment by deity. Indeed, even to be worthy of punishment from divinity is better than the lot of a creature born only to die forever, or so religion has generally thought.

The theory of creation also involves a widespread awareness that something after creation must have gone wrong. Somehow humankind, despite or because of the priceless possession of souls, has lost the closeness to divinity the original creation implied. The explanation of this lapse, like the accounts of creation, varies considerably. It may be due to some accident—a misunderstanding on the part of our primal parents or cantankerousness on the part of one creature out of all creation. It may be due to a fierce rebellion by the creation against its maker. It may stem from ignorance of the true nature of things because of blind attachment to the things of this world or to pet ideas and concepts. It may, as in some Gnostic myths, be because humans have been enslaved by greater and more malevolent beings than ourselves. Each explanation suggests a different view of humanity and the kind of God who is susceptible to each mode of human separation from him.[3]

THE PATH TO SALVATION

Religion not only postulates that something has gone wrong since the creation of the world in original harmony with its divine source but also tells us the way back to the original union, for that is implied in the description of the separation. If the separation is due to ignorance, it offers us the hidden knowledge; if due to rebellion, it enlists us in the armies of the commander of the counterattack. The method and goal of the return vary.

The goal—a human order in absolute harmony with the ideal understanding of our origins—may be a supremely good society, cosmic consciousness, or the restitution of the right relations to God in love and service. The diverse ways back are typically initiated by God and are exemplified by a paradigmatic hero who is pioneer of the return. Through identification with him or her, or with his or her vision of society, one may become a real self. The hero may be a great teacher such as Confucius, the wayshower of an ideal society; or Laozi, the sage in harmony with nature and infinity; it may be the Buddha, Muhammad the emissary of God, or Jesus Christ the savior.

Whoever the teacher and whatever the way, the follower has to make a choice of priorities. It may seem easy or hard, but there must be a

---

[3] For a valuable discussion of how different theories of the origin and nature of evil correlate with different worldviews, see Paul Ricoeur, *The Symbolism of Evil* (New York: Harper & Row, Publishers, Inc., 1967).

discipline that requires the subordination of some values to others. It is not a course one must pursue out of one's own power, though, for as one achieves closer harmony with the way things really are, one finds oneself aided by powers even more deeply in union with the way things really are: a Buddha totally enlightened into horizonless awareness of reality; a savior such as Jesus Christ who is both God and human; even a wise sage such as Confucius who, though no more than fully human, saw with unparalleled clarity in the eyes of his followers the nature of an ideal human society based on the right human relationships.

Finally, the way of salvation teaches that the final end of human life is ultimate transformation, in the expression of Frederick Streng, who defined religion as "means toward ultimate transformation."[4] As we have observed in Chapter One, the way moves toward a transcendent state of being beyond all qualifications and conditions, meaning in effect that one is unbounded. There is the path toward ultimate transformation—the total reversal of all boundings by either society or one's own psychology—if one has the wisdom and skill to lay hold of it.

Religious teaching about the way back, salvation, and ultimate transformation is not limited to this present world and an afterlife only. Many religions, if not most, teach that the world itself can change too. Someday, the powers of evil within the world shall be defeated, and it will be turned into a paradise. This is the well-known teaching of many faiths of an end to time as we know it, a last judgment, a final resurrection of all the dead, and the making of a new heaven and earth or the inauguration of a paradisiacal era. If transformation is truly ultimate—that is, without any reservation, without any corner of self or universe left unchanged to what is totally good—then it must seem to affect the whole of the world. This is the case whether the world is changed outwardly and physically or only subjectively in the eyes of the mystic who sees it cleansed when, in Blake's phrase, the "doors of perception" are cleansed.

Transformation, and above all the sometimes contrasting role of religion to uphold the normative values of society, requires following certain standards of behavior in this life. The ethical teachings of a religion are not in isolation from its transformative goals but either create the necessary preconditions for inward spiritual advance—such as the *niyama* and *yama*, constraints and advice, that prelude serious yoga—or, like the Sermon on the Mount, suggest a perfectionist way of life that foreshadows here and now the Kingdom of Heaven.

In summary, then, an important part of religious doctrine is the manner in which it maps the return from separation to union with God or

---

[4] Frederick J. Streng, *Understanding Religious Life*, 2nd ed. (Encino, Calif.: Dickenson Publishing Co., 1976), pp. 7–9.

the absolute. The picture of return generally focuses on a symbolic individual who encapsulates and demonstrates it, such as the Buddha or the Christ, and associated with the individual are a pivotal time and event that open doors to return. The way to return combines the inner transformation and outward ethical aspects of religion; it requires both even as it enforces the quest for ecstasy and support of normative values in society. Ultimately, these are pulled together in the teachings of the religion about the end of time as we know it: eschatology, teachings about the final times, or apocalyptic teachings that emphasize things will get worse until the end, when God will intervene in a sudden, unexpected, and radical reversal of the way things seem to be, as in a Last Judgment breaking through in the midst of a cataclysmic battle. In the end of time, and the subsequent new and perfect creation, both perfect joy and a perfect social order coexist. All these are common religious doctrines and very important doctrines for the religion's view of the real self, transcendence, and ultimate reality.

DETERMINING TRUTH IN RELIGION

After looking, as we have, at many different styles of religious belief and many manifestations of religion, one may ask—whether in eagerness, indifference, or despair—if it is possible to determine what in all of it is true. Some people, in fact, may reject the word *true* altogether and only ask what in religion has *meaning*—what, in other words, would provide a workable symbol system for the individual concerned. I have had vehement discussions with students about whether truth in religion can be ascertained, or only meaning or value for the individual.

Nevertheless, let us keep the word *truth*; I cannot quite persuade myself that there could be real meaning or value in a religious experience or symbol one was not convinced was founded on some sort of truth. The means for determining what is true in religion are diverse, however, though not as varied as the beliefs themselves. Yet it is fair to note that different sorts of beliefs carry with them distinctive styles of verification. Belief in a sovereign creator God is likely to include an appeal to reason; belief in salvation and afterlife is likely to include appeals to personal experience and teachings accepted on authority. The following are some major approaches to determining truth in religion.

Reason

This approach is based on the presupposition that the mind can know truth through the honest and unbiased use of its capacities to work through logical process from pure premises to their consequences; and the

New York Public Library Picture Collection

Osiris, a dying and living Egyptian god of salvation. He was associated with agriculture, the pharaoh, and the realms of the dead; those who adhered to him shared in his immortality.

presupposition that fundamentally the universe is orderly and works by cause and effect. If these presuppositions are granted, it seems justifiable to assume that a logical process can parallel the way things are when it starts from accurate data and is procedurally flawless. It would then yield up real truth, even to knowledge of the God who is the source of all other truth.

The most famous example of an approach based on **reason** is that of Thomas Aquinas, the great philosopher and theologian of the thirteenth century, noted for his five proofs of the existence of God. Other philosophers, such as the Mahayana Buddhist Nagarjuna, of approximately the first century C.E., and David Hume (1711–1776) in Britain have used reasoning processes to show the limitations of reason, of cause-and-effect thinking, and of language itself. They would say that most reasoning, including traditional proofs of God, is really circular and proves no more than what is implicit in the way the original premises are put, which in turn is based on our human modes of perception. (Perhaps it is the mind, not nature itself, in which everything is intricately interrelated, that sets up the neat patterns of cause and effect from which we extrapolate a First Cause, or that isolates out of infinite variety phenomena we call evidence of purpose because they happen to parallel what we as humans can understand as purposeful.)

Reason as a means of determining truth in religion has the advantage of seeming to be as independent as possible from emotion or bias. Critics point out that this is not so much the case as practitioners of reason may assume; a façade of reason can mask decisions made on quite different grounds or be based on premises themselves assumed on nonrational bases. Furthermore, reason is said to be cold and even inhuman—a poor basis for determining something as warmly human as religious commitment. Reason is not especially in fashion today as a way to determine truth in religion. Many people are suspicious of it and prefer to follow the late twentieth-century emphasis on experience as the royal road to spirituality and personal growth. If you have experienced something, we tend to say, that is better than merely deducing it (or criticizing it) from cool reason alone. Perhaps we need to have a chastened rebirth of confidence in reason; although it can easily go awry, it does affirm a precious human capacity, the power of the mind to think.

Experience

This is the great alternative that stands against reason in the minds of many. Whether in conversion, mysticism, or simply gradual growth through worship and reflection to subjective religious surety, felt **experience** of religious reality convinces in its own way. It seems beyond doubt or at least adequate for the individual. Its advantages are that it is accessible to all regardless of intelligence or education, it has immediacy, it is something that involves the whole person, and above all it provides religious motivation at the same time that it gives conviction. There are

Religious News Service Photo

This picture of American Protestant baptism by immersion suggests the intense subjective experience that to many is a reliable guide to religious truth.

weighty objections, however, that can be made against depending on experience alone as a religious guide. One can never be sure whether or not some psychological explanation is possible. Furthermore, intense and convincing experience can be found in all religion; one does not find that it points to any particular truth. If one tried to determine what is religious truth from religious experience in general, rather than just one's own, one would quickly be very confused about everything except that there *are* such experiences. (One may even be confused by personal experiences; those of one person are often far from consistent, and in following them exclusively one can be swept far out to sea on tides of emotion and subjective imaginings.) Usually one's relogous culture does much to explain the content of religious experience (for the experience itself, say a sense of the numinous or transcendent, is not the same as the interpretation, even that which the experiencer immediately makes to himself—that it is an experience of God or Christ or a bodhisattva or of certain gods). It would perhaps be safest to say that although certainly religious experience is real and significant *as experience*, we need to think deeply about what the experience is saying and from whence it comes; there may be important guides to truth and meaning in it, but they may not always be those that appear on the surface.

Empiricism

Empiricism bases claims to truth on direct observation of external things, rather than on inward experience or reason. A number of possible empirical tests of religious truth have been advanced by religionists. Eighteenth- and nineteenth-century philosophers such as William Paley drew from alleged evidences of design in nature to support the existence of a Designer. Others bring in claims of prayers answered, lives changed, and the beneficent effects of religion on human history to support its truth. Still others show that data of the sort produced by psychical research—telepathy, cases suggesting reincarnation or survival of physical death, nonphysical movement of matter—tend to affirm the religious world at least by demonstrating invisible forces and realities. Some go further to say that the existence of miracles, the soul, and life after death can be affirmed in this way, and so validate much of traditional religion empirically. We cannot assess the many empirical arguments for religious truth here. We can point out, however, that in an age when science, in which empirical data and testing are of crucial importance, has such great prestige and use, it is natural that empirical arguments in religion should become increasingly used, even as they have always (in prescientific or nonscientific forms) been central to popular religious advocacy. Whether they have much of a future in philosophical religious thought will depend on whether religion comes to parallel the sciences in method and kind of knowledge sought or whether it is essentially perceived as something very different—perhaps more akin to the poet's way of "knowing"—for which such quasi-scientific proofs are peripheral.

Authority

For millions the real touchstone of religious determination of truth is an **authority**—scriptures, tradition, church, pope, guru, and so on. Arguments from authority, of course, are finally dependent on other arguments, those by which the authority is established. These are often arguments from reason, experience, and empiricism, the last often generalizing from ways the authority can be shown to be correct. To say something is true because the Bible or the pope says it is true is meaningful only within a context in which that authority is accepted. Arguments from authority not only deliver a content message by affirming the point in question, but also deliver a structural message by reinforcing belief in the authority.

Sociological Factors in Religious Preference

Sociological considerations do not precisely argue for truth but for meaning and value, although they may be virtually a form of an argument from authority as general consent. For many people sociological criteria are immensely important. The operative determinant for them in affirming religious statements is that the statements are affirmed by a group important to them—given groups, such as family or ethnic tradition; or peer groups, activity groups, and other groups they want to feel a part of. Usually when people use such grounds to decide on religious belief, ultimate truth is not an issue; it is either taken for granted or handled relativistically ("This is our way; it's all we know. We follow our way and others can follow theirs") or pragmatically ("This must be true because it works for us"). Sociology does not answer all the questions that a highly philosophical mind might raise, but it indicates one of the main things a religion ought to fulfill—a sense of group coherence.

Existential Choice

This approach is based on the premise that religious truth *cannot* be proved by means extraneous to the real nature of religion, which is commitment. Means such as reason, empiricism, sociology, and the like are really distractions that only lead to false sorts of religion since they set up something less than God, or the absolute, as the real object of worship, be it the human mind, scientific method, or society. True religion can only be seized by faith, meaning a choice *not* based on such secondary support. The approach of **existential choice** was classically stated by Soren Kierkegaard, mentioned in Chapter Two. He said that the evidence for and against the existence of God in the philosophical arguments are equally balanced; from the vantage of the human mind, as much can be said on one side as the other. Therefore, whether one believes in God or not is pure choice, and that is the way it is meant to be. One must decide and one gets what one decides for. One can choose no God or even a "God" who is merely a God of reason or of social convention and live a fairly comfortable life devoted to aesthetic gratification or even ethical goals. Deep down, however, one feels in them a kind of emptiness. One can also choose a truly religious life of faith and commitment to the ultimate God, which may be hard and separate from both the philosophers and society but which is in touch with the highest meaning. It is through choice that one comes to this truth, but it is not choice that makes it true; rather, religious truth is a special kind of truth accessible not to reason or the other means but only truly discoverable in a decision for that greater than oneself.

ARE RELIGIOUS BELIEFS IRREFUTABLE?

The advantage of the existential choice is that it cannot be refuted. If one believes something simply because one chooses to believe it, there is really nothing anyone else can say. Some would say, however, that all religious beliefs are really of this character; although supportive arguments from reason, experience, consent, and so forth can be brought in, religionists easily shift from one to the other, and finally it is not possible to prove any beliefs are *untrue* as long as they are held as religion. According to the rules of modern logic, however, a statement must be falsifiable (that is, one must be able to show how it could be proved wrong) or it cannot really be considered verified as a newly deduced truth, either; it is only a tautology (that is, something that says in different words what you started out with). An example is the affirmation "God is Creator." One can support it through arguments such as the cosmological, but it is hard to think of an equal argument that would prove God is *not* Creator if one is thinking in terms of God and creation at all. This is because the two terms really imply each other by definition. Nonetheless, as a devotional or even creedal statement, the sentence might have deep religious meaning for those in a circle of believers and even be incapable of *disproof* for them. For every group has ways of handling within its own symbols most of what happens in life. Suffering, joy, doubt, and all sorts of experiences are given different meanings by different religious or even nonreligious ways of handling life.[5] A mystical vision has one meaning to religion—though particulars may vary with religions, as Hindus have visions of Krishna and Roman Catholics of the Blessed Virgin Mary—but by nonreligious people can be dealt with as psychologically explicable projections. As the great philosopher David Hume said, miracles may happen, but there could never be *reasonable* grounds for believing in them since by definition they go against reason. It also seems to be the case that there is no religious phenomena for which reasonable (that is, nonreligious or at least nonsupernatural) explanations that convince many people cannot be adduced. (Of course for some religious philosophers, like Soren Kierkegaard, this is only to be expected since it is precisely what makes choice and faith genuine for those who elect the religious life.)

On the other hand, the trouble with relegating religion to just the language game of a particular circle is that circles of belief are not air-tight. A given circle of belief can explain everything except the existence, or rather the subjective experience, of others with other systems once the others are genuinely acknowledged to be there, and this must increasingly be the case in our pluralistic world. Thus, whatever circle we are in, of one religion or another or of nonreligion, there is increasingly a price to be paid intellectually and spiritually for the privilege of remaining in that circle. We cannot help but be more and more aware of the *concrete* possibility, for

[5] See Frank B. Dilley, "The Irrefutability of Belief Systems," *Journal of the American Academy of Religion*, XLIII, 2 (June 1975), 214–23.

ourselves, of other modes of life. By the same token, we must be increasingly aware of the *nonabsoluteness* of language games because we are compelled to recognize, in most of our dealings with other people whether they are within our religious circle or not, a common humanity that suggests there are, regardless of religion, common human languages of value, logic, and experience.

The philosophical theologian Charles Hartshorne, then, is able to argue that what a proof of God's existence (and, by implication, a proof of God's nonexistence although he and others would argue that is logically impossible) would do is to show the intellectual price that must be paid by rejecting the argument.[6] A supposed proof of God does not so much prove God as show what one gives up if one elects to live in a universe in which God is not. It shows the cost of living in a situation in which logic and language have *no* validity except that given them by the person or circle using them at the moment. What logical proofs of God (as universal being and so symbol of universal meaning) contend, then, is that whereas logic may only appear as *proof* to the user and his or her circle, it also has some universal meaning as it states what one is giving up by being outside of the circle or even by holding that there are no universals and that truth is *only* relative to circles. A person outside a religious circle may not find the meaning that believers do in an argument for a Creator God, but he or she *still* must live without a divine first cause and without whatever meaning a first cause gives.

In fact there have been counterarguments to the insistence of some philosophers that language, in the sense of meaning and especially religious meaning, only works within circles who accept the rules of the particular language game being played. The French philosopher Michel Foucault argues that it is precisely language that can unify human life.[7] Language poorly used, reduced to jargon, may give us a sense of things being disparate and disconnected, of meaning and experience being reduced to atomistic subgroups or social science or psychological categories that give a sense of experience being explained away in a manner that devalues them.

Nevertheless, just as it is possible for a master translator to translate great literature from German, Russian, or Chinese into English in a manner that enables the English reader to participate richly and with understanding (even if *something* may be lost) in the experience behind the original, so it should be possible to translate the experience of each religious "game" into a language revealing a meaning that is universal. This is the interpretative task of the history of religions; it can also be the task of **theology**.

[6] Charles Hartshorne, *A Natural Theology of Our Time* (LaSalle, Ill.: Open Court Publishing Co., 1967), p. 30.

[7] Michel Foucault, *The Order of Things* (New York: Vintage Books, 1973).

SUMMARY

Conceptual beliefs—what religions think and say about such great issues as God, the soul, or the afterlife—are not the whole of religion, but they constitute a very important part of spiritual life. They may be symbols of psychological processes or experiences; they may be recognized as only "pointing" concepts indicating realities beyond the power of words to express; they may mean different things to educated elite and ordinary members of a religion. But nonetheless religious concepts are generally regarded by adherents of the religion as true in a significant sense, and they must be taken seriously as truth claims by those seeking to understand the religion, and by those seeking truth wherever it may be found.

Religious concepts express truths in two ways: through their content, that is, what is said explicitly in the statement, and through the structure of the statement, that is, how it is said, including the context of the statement. For example, different structural messages might be given the same content according to whether they were said in a traditionalist, liberal, or fundamentalist style and context. (For the meaning of these terms, see the glossary in the back of the book.)

A basic religious concept, of course, is that of God or gods. God or a god may be defined as a conscious center of being, knowledge, and power superior to the human, upon which ordinarily humans must depend or have relations of prayer and offering for their well-being. Divinity is expressed in three ways: as impersonal absolute, in terms of personal monotheism, in terms of polytheism. The last sometimes goes together with belief in an impersonal absolute.

Religion deals with several main areas: creation, the origin of humans, the soul, the existence of evil, the path to salvation, and the ultimate transformation of the world. In each of these there are messages not only about the specific topic but also about the overall view of reality and human nature. Two different views, for example, are contained in the ideas that God made the world by dividing himself up into its many parts, and that God made the world as something outside of himself, like a craftsman making his handiwork.

Ways of determining truth in religion include reason, experience, empiricism, authority, and existential choice. There are also sociological reasons why people adhere to particular religions. Each of these ways has strengths and weaknesses that must be critically assessed.

Finally, the question must be addressed of whether religious truth can actually be determined convincingly or whether it can only remain a "game" whose arguments have meaning only within the circle of belief.

To a large extent this may be the case, but some philosophers and theologians argue that religious statements at least show what one is giving up if one does not accept them, and they also argue that if well enough put, religious statements, like great literature, can have universal power to communicate and convince.

AP/Wide World Photo

Pro-choice and pro-life demonstrators holding signs on the steps of the Supreme Court building in Washington.

Chapter

8

How Shall We Live?
Religion and Ethics

Chapter Objectives

- Define meanings of the terms *ethics* and *morality*.

- Talk about how ethics are grounded in a meta-ethics, or overall worldview.

- Distinguish between deontological and teleological, or consequential-ist, ethics. What does each say? How can each be criticized? Are there any ways in which they can be combined? Are there any other possible bases for ethics besides these two concepts?

- Analyze the roles of law and love in ethics. Are they necessarily at odds?

- Discuss similarities and differences in the ethics of the major religions. In what respects are they generally similar? Where do differences come about? Be sure to think in terms of concrete examples.

- Present and analyze the major issues and points of view in important contemporary arenas of ethical debate: animal rights; medical ethics, including abortion and euthanasia; the rights of women in religion; liberation theology issues; and others. You will probably need to do some outside reading concerning these and other issues, but the text should point you toward what the discussions are about.

TAKING IT TO THE STREETS

You have just attended a fine religious service in a beautiful temple or church. The music was wonderful, the words and rites inspiring, and you leave feeling very good. In fact, for you on this occasion, religion was a true scenario for the real self. You think you have become who you really are in relation to human society and Ultimate Reality. Whatever you do now will be based on that faith. Your actions will be consistent with your innermost nature, and with God or however you best understand the supreme source and context of your life.

Then, on the street, you see a homeless person trying to keep warm over a heating grate, or living in a packing box in an alley. He indicates he would like money for food. How do you respond?

1. You could refuse, saying to yourself—or aloud to the homeless person—that if he had real faith, God would take care of him and he would not be in this situation.

2. You could refuse, saying that if he joined the true religious body, that organization would be like a second family and support group, and would take care of his needs. Or in any case, since you give to religious and other organized charities to help the homeless, you don't need to do it on an individual basis.

3. You could refuse, saying that individual acts of charity only make people dependent and may be scams anyway; they don't get at the real problem. But out of your religious faith you vow to redouble your efforts to work through political and religious institutions to eliminate the root causes of homelessness.

4. You could refuse, saying you would like to give but you have only so much money and you have already promised to help another needy person nearer your home.

5. You could refuse to help on "tough love" grounds, but stay to talk with the person about self-help and getting a job. You might even offer to help him get a job, since your religion says you should help others.

6. You could give to him, finding that to be the easiest way to forget him and continue to enjoy your religious experience.

7. You could give to him as an expression of the religious experience, because your religion says that everyone is a child of God and deserves to be loved, and giving is an act of love whether the recipient deserves it or not.

Then, when you get home, you find members of your family embroiled in a hot and heavy argument about sexual morality. Is abortion ever justified? Is sex before—or outside of—marriage ever right? What about homosexuality?

And when you go to school or work the next day, there are more issues. Someone shows you a way you could cheat on an exam or a business deal. How do you respond?

Your school or company has to reduce staff because of budget cuts. How do you think they should decide who gets the axe and who stays? Seniority? Competence? Gender? Race? Or any of these grounds but called something else?

Issues like these confront us almost every day of our lives. They are clearly related to religion. If religion is a scenario for the real self, it should guide us in how we act in the practical issues of life as well as in worship. If religion deals, as it claims, with the Ultimate Reality underlying everything that is, it ought to have something to say about every kind of situation that arises in the real world.

ETHICS AND MORALITY

These issues are in the realm of ethics and morality. They have to do with what behavior is right, and on what basis one decides what is right.

The line between ethics and morality is somewhat fuzzy. But ethics is usually defined as a somewhat broader term, referring to the rules of conduct or the highest standards of a tradition or group (Jewish ethics, Christian ethics; medical ethics), especially regarding honesty or the legitimacy of particular procedures (as when someone in a profession says, "I could do that but it would be considered unethical"). Moreover, those branches of philosophy or theology that inquire into right behavior and the principles of logic underlying it are usually now called *ethics*. Ethics may represent an ideal rather than everyday practice. *Social ethics* refers to issues of what is ethical for society as a whole to do, as in such questions as how to deal with the causes of poverty, or whether war is ever justified.

Morals now tend to speak more to the normal standards of conduct expected by a society, or to personal codes of conduct (as when one says, "To me that's immoral"), especially in such highly personal areas as sexual behavior or truth telling. As these terms are commonly used, morals spell out rules of behavior, while ethics articulate the justifications for those rules.

But, especially in a religious context, morals may also refer to the standard teaching of a religious institution on right personal conduct, and one may use such expressions as *moral theology* or *moral philosophy*, the systematic study of what is right in these areas in light of the thinker's ultimate religious or philosophical views.

Thus the terms often overlap. We will here ordinarily use the term *ethics* since it is most commonly employed today in religious studies. Yet it should be understood that ethics are not just a religious matter. Quite serious and demanding ethical systems can be, and have been, propounded entirely on philosophical grounds, by ancients such as Plato and Aristotle or the Stoics and Epicureans, down to modern, nontraditional religious ethicists like Bertrand Russell or John Dewey. In Western civilization, in fact, some tension has been brought about by the fact that the predominant religious influences, Judaism and Christianity, have sources in a different world of thought—that of the ancient Hebrews—from the predominant philosophical tradition shaped by ancient Greek thought. This has been as much the case in ethics as anything else, and has led to issues that have to be sorted out between *divine command* ethics and *rational* ethics, or between the ethics of *absolute commitment* and the ethics of the *golden mean*.

But in any case, ethical decision making is a constant requirement of life. We make ethical decisions—not always good ones—even by not making them. Religion, when a part of one's life, can help one decide.

DOWN FROM ON HIGH

Any thought-out ethical system has to begin with **meta-ethics**, that is, an overarching worldview from which it derives. All religions, and secular philosophies too, have a view of God or Ultimate Reality and of how the universe came into being that connects with the ethical values of the society. If a personal God is held to be the creator of the world, that God is usually also thought of as the supreme lawgiver. If, as in Hinduism, the universe itself is simply a visible manifestation of God, the social order with its rules (*dharma*) will be built into the manifestation. Nonreligious philosophies, such as those of contemporary scientific humanists, may present ethical views consistent with what (in the view of that philosopher) science shows the real nature and value of human life to be.

Then there is the matter of how religious ethics embedded in meta-ethics are transmitted to the society. Here, as in any aspect of religion, one may look at the role of revelation, of sacred texts, of exemplary human beings (for example, saints and heroes of the faith) and of guidance exercised through religious institutions.

A further question for analysis is this: how then does the religion or philosophy *motivate* ethical behavior? It may appeal to peer example in a sacred community, or activate an inner sense of guilt. Forceful talk of after-death rewards and punishment (or punishment in this life) can be convincing as can the offer of personal spiritual advancement and a sense of participation in sacred history. Religion or philosophy may simply point to the authority of its sacred scriptures or institution, if that authority is widely and unquestioningly accepted.

In thinking about the actual social enactment of ethics, one should also consider what values are primarily theoretical, and what values are actually put into practice. As is well-known, not all ethical ideals are always strictly upheld by the societies that hold them. Some may count for more than others in practice. Many societies that wink at various forms of minor cheating would harshly condemn public nudity. Some have, in practice, different standards for men and women concerning marital faithfulness. Some ethical ideals (strict celibacy or marital faithfulness, nonconsumption of alcohol, relative simplicity of life) may be expected of religious professionals but are not, in practice, demanded so rigorously of the laity.

We also find that practical ethical expectations differ between social classes. (The prudish Victorian morality supposed to be characteristic of nineteenth-century England and America, for example, was actually most held to by the burgeoning middle class; the upper and lower classes generally were less demanding of themselves.) Much can be learned about the way a society works by examining such seeming contradictions, which all societies have. Discussion of real-life ethical practice in a society or setting is sometimes called descriptive ethics. From now on, however, we shall talk chiefly about theoretical ethics, that is, the systems of ideal ethics promulgated by religions and philosophers.

KINDS OF ETHICAL THOUGHT

Ethical views are, first of all, divided into two broad types known by two words, **deontological ethics** (ethics as "oughts," that is, coming from duties or obligations seen as givens, presumably by God or nature or reality itself) and **teleological ethics** (meaning dependent on the consequence, or end product, of the act).

Deontological ethics are derived from a previously-determined view of the nature of God or reality. They tend to hold that certain actions or behaviors are right or wrong in themselves, because they are or are not in accordance with the will of God, or **natural law**—that is, the way the universe is set up. They should be done regardless of the consequences in each particular case. If God is love, then as a servant of God one should always act in a loving way. If God has forbidden murder, then one should not do it, both because it is contrary to love and is further prohibited by divine command.

Some would extend that command to such controversial issues as war or capital punishment, saying that if murder is wrong, the state has no more right to take life than an individual, regardless of consequence; some would extend the case to abortion, saying that one also has no right to take unborn life. Many deontological ethicists—some religious, some not—also talk about natural law, that is, whether acts are or are not in accordance with nature. Thus, nature clearly intends humans—unlike, say, solitary animals like the leopard—to dwell in families and in larger communities, the clan, tribe, city, or nation. Thus, what upholds the welfare of these units, including obedience to the legitimate ordinances of legitimate authorities, is ethical.

For some, natural-law considerations can therefore legitimate killing, as in war or capital punishment, when authorized by legitimate authorities, though the individual has no right to kill, save in extreme cases of self-defense or in the defense of another who is helpless; justification in such cases is thought to derive from *natural rights*.

These are good examples of a tension between divine-command and rational ethics even within deontology. The question is whether we determine what behavior is consistent with the nature or will of Ultimate Reality just by the latter's revealed command, or whether we may also use reason to so determine.

The command approach would say that one must obey what God has commanded regardless of circumstance, such obedience being most commendable when the risk or cost is great and the reasons least apparent. An example would be a lonely pacifist refusing to fight, at the cost of humiliation, imprisonment, or even being shot as a traitor, even in a war that most consider just, simply because he believes that all fighting and all taking of human life is wrong and forbidden by the Bible's "Thou shalt not kill." Rational ethics would say that one can and should take circumstances into account and balance one obligation against another. Even when conjoined with religion, natural-law considerations, being determined by reason and observation in the first place, are usually in the rational camp.

To give another example, natural-law theorists might also say that the arrangement of the human sexual organs is such that certain forms of sex, such as procreation and expression of marital love, are natural, and other forms therefore, by definition, unnatural, and so contrary to natural-law morality. This position has been taken, especially but by no means exclusively, by conservative Roman Catholic moral theologians, who argue that since God made nature and natural law in the first place, following it is a part of religion. Needless to say, they have engendered much controversy about just what is natural, and to what extent humans need be bound by nature.

Deontological ethics have been criticized for making guidelines for behavior too rigorous, insisting that certain acts are always right, or always wrong, regardless of the particular situation. Natural-law theory has been criticized for taking too narrow a view of what nature "says" regardless of the fact that nature itself, and our scientific perceptions of it, are always evolving. Defenders of these positions say that we humans need some firm, unquestionable limits given by a higher authority. Or else, they argue, we are likely to find ways to justify anything we really want to do, however dubious. Human ethics must always acknowledge its contingency on something greater than the merely human, deontologists contend; otherwise they demean humans by denying our chief glory, that we are free, decision-making children of God; or, that we are manifestations of nature at its best.

Teleological, sometimes called **consequentialist**, ethical theory says that the consequences of an action are what is really important. The crucial thing is not whether the act comes out of divine command or natural law, but whether it produces good results. The rightness or wrongness of, say, capital punishment or abortion, should be judged not by an *a priori* judgment about murder, but by whether those acts of killing produce good *consequences* for the persons involved and for society as a whole.

An important subdivision of consequentialism is **utilitarianism**, developed by nineteenth-century British thinkers such as Jeremy Bentham and John Stuart Mill. It says that the ideal should be "the greatest good of the greatest number," what Bentham called his "hedonic calculus" (from *hedon*, a Greek word for pleasure or happiness). Ethical principles and social policies, according to utilitarianism, should be judged on this basis. While admittedly it is not always easy to make such judgments,[1] the utilitarian ideal has lain behind a large amount of the social reforms of the last century and a half. Its gleam can be seen behind such staples of contemporary American life as universal suffrage, civil rights, and social security. No longer can the idea that policies are acceptable if they explicitly benefit only a minority be advanced without strident argument.

Yet teleological ethics, and utilitarianism, can also be criticized. Critics will say that without some deontological principles, we cannot even rightly decide which consequences are good and which are not. Is preserving life always good without regard to the quality of that life? Whether we are talking about the beginning of human life (the abortion controversy) or the end (the right-to-die issue), the matter of quality cannot be avoided, and it cries out for clarification by some investigation into the *a priori* nature of human life and its creation.

"The greatest good of the greatest number" can also be subjected to deontological critiques. The case of slavery is sometimes given as a hypothetical case, although Bentham and Mill would certainly not have used

---

[1] Jeremy Bentham worked out an elaborate hedonic calculus by which one could calculate the relative amounts of pleasure and pain for oneself and others in particular actions, and J.S. Mill further refined utilitarianism by distinguishing between higher and lower pleasures. Bentham was one of the first of the modern ethicists to take seriously the suffering of animals as well as humans, and in large part utilitarianism was a response in terms of democratic values to the gross inequities of the early Industrial Revolution.

utilitarianism in its defense. Even if, in a given society, the quality of life of the majority could arguably be improved by their enslaving a minority of the population, could this justify the suffering and degradation that would impose on the slave minority? If not, this indicates some limitations to utilitarianism must be imposed by deontological considerations about human nature in general.[2] This is not a merely abstract exercise. In American society down to the present, this argument has distinct resonances for the position of women (though they are not a minority), children, and African American and other racial minorities.

Those concerned with the treatment of animals, as was Bentham and more recently Peter Singer in *Animal Liberation*,[3] have pointed to very disturbing parallels in the human use of animals, asking on what moral grounds they can be subjected to pain, frustration of natural instincts, and wholly unnatural living conditions solely for the supposed benefit of their human owners and masters, whether for labor, meat production, or medical experimentation. Marjorie Spiegel, in *The Dreaded Comparison*,[4] has demonstrated many similarities between the past treatment of African slaves and present treatment of animals, and in the rationalizations given for the justification of this use. In the animal-rights issue both ethical sources are profoundly challenged: deontology, inasmuch as the subordination of animals is frequently given divine-command justification, and teleology insofar as human and sometimes even animal benefits have been invoked by defenders of the current situation. If animal suffering is figured in, how do our customary uses of animals compute by Bentham's hedonic calculus? More pain or more pleasure?

Utilitarianism and teleological ethics, when honestly applied, have wrought much good and have corrected the tendencies of deontology toward excessive dogmatism, as the latter has consequentialism's capacity to fall into excessive pragmatism. No doubt the ideal is some combination of the two, or (as the animal-rights and other ecological issues show) some new philosophical source that places fresh emphasis on the inherent goodness of species and beings in themselves.

But combinations have not always proved easy to work out, and the conundrum suggests the complexity of ethical thought. For religionists, belief in life after death may also be factored in, not just in a crude rewards-and-punishment sense, but also in terms of the added dimension eternal

---

[2] Again, this position should not be attributed to the original English utilitarians themselves, but to an extreme hypothetical statement of the case. Slavery, if fairly assessed, could hardly have stood up to Bentham's hedonic calculus, for the intense suffering often endured by many slaves would have greatly overbalanced the relative comfort and mixed pleasures enjoyed by the few who probably benefited: the master and his family. It would have been quite difficult indeed to make any customary sort of slavery honestly equate to the greatest good of the greatest number.

[3] Peter Singer, *Animal Liberation*. London: Jonathon Cape, 1976.

[4] Marjorie Spiegel, *The Dreaded Comparison*. New York: Mirror Books, 1988.

existence gives human deeds and experiences, including the prospect of timeless coexistence with all one has done and thought. There is plenty of ethical work left for future human generations to do.

A further complexity lies in the issue of **intentionalism**. Does one judge the intentions of an ethical actor, or the consequences alone? Not seldom—as most of us know from our own experience—we intend good, but the results of our supposedly ethical actions turn out to be disastrous. Often, deontologists claim that consequentialists, though meaning well, assess less adequately than they the true patterns of reality and human nature, and botch the job by being excessively optimistic, or pessimistic, about what will work. Teleological ethicists will respond that deontology usually doesn't work much better, its abstractions being far too hidebound to fit the infinite variety of real human life. In sum, ethical thinking is crucially important, but is no place for someone who wants a 100 percent success record.

LAW AND LOVE

Another tension in religious ethics lies in the spectrum that runs between the extent to which ethical decisions should be governed by external rules imposed by one's faith, and to what extent ethical decisions can be entrusted to the actor's internal intuition, even assuming it to be guided by pure intention to do what is right. To put it graphically—though to do so is very much to oversimplify—to what degree are ethics a matter of law, and to what a matter of the compassionate love which religions generally present as the highest ideal?

And it is important to say at the outset that putting the issue this way is a gross oversimplification simply because the same religions *all* indicate that there is no *inherent* contradiction between love and law, though they may often *appear* to be in conflict. Love—selflessly doing good for others— is surely the supreme ideal, but knowing *how* to do it aright requires some direction from persons or an institution with long experience in human affairs. All religions, in other words, intend love as the ideal, and at the same time present laws or rules or specific teachings on how it is to be implemented in specific circumstances. These codes of behavior may or may not channel ethical love aright, but certainly that is the intent.

Thus, in Judaism, love of God, not law, is ultimate—"Hear, O Israel: The Lord our God, the Lord is one. Love the Lord your God with all your heart and with all your soul and with all your strength" (Deut. 6:4–5)—and only in this context applies the law: "These commandments that I give you today are to be upon your hearts" (Deut. 6:6). The Law of Moses, spelled out in the Pentateuch (the first five books of the Hebrew scriptures, especially Exodus, Leviticus, Numbers, and Deuteronomy), diligently tell one how to live a life based on the love of God. On social issues, the law generally means implementing justice, and caring for the stranger and unfortunate.[5]

In Christianity also, love is the supreme value. Texts from the letters of Paul say, "If I have not love, I gain nothing" and "Everything is permissible for me, but not everything is beneficial" (I Cor. 13:3; 6:12). Yet the New Testament also contains numerous injunctions, on the level of law for all intents and purposes, that presumably show how love is to be applied and what is beneficial: those against adultery even in the heart (Matt. 5:27–28), and those commending care for the elderly and widows and declaring that slaves should respect their masters (for example, I Timothy 5:1–3, 6:1).

Buddhism likewise teaches *karuna*, compassion, as the great virtue, equal in value only to wisdom, that is, true insight—the two go together, for one does not effectively have one without the other. Yet Buddhism also presents a number of precepts for living in accordance with compassion and attaining Nirvana. There are many for monks, and five basic ones are often undertaken by laypersons: not to take life, steal, engage in sexual misconduct, lie, or take intoxicants. Mahayana Buddhism teaches that bodhisattvas, persons near to buddhahood, may act in a way guided solely by wisdom and compassion even when that seems to contravene ordinary moral rules. Unencumbered by egotism, they can glance down at a situation of human or animal suffering, with true insight see the actual factors that led to it, and guided by pure love take the right steps, whatever the cost in redemptive suffering on their own part, to counteract it.

Most of us, however, are too impure in our perceptions and motivations to risk such ventures; it is overwhelmingly likely, says normative Buddhism, that we would do much better to follow conventional morality as our guide. Only a truly wise and selfless bodhisattva can be guided by love alone and not mess up.

And that's the problem. We need guidance as to how love is to be put into practice, both in means and ends. Religions and their rules force us to ask such questions as the following: Are some acts almost always contrary to love by their very nature, so much so that the exceptions are negligible and it is wisest to make it a rule never to do them? Are there others that are almost always a sure expression of ethical love? Does it make a difference whether we look at the acts deontologically or teleologically?

In practice, all the major religions, in their conventional expression, believe there is more wisdom—and safety—in following the rules than not. Some ethicists, however, have not been so sure. Probably the best-known modern exponent of a more radical position is Joseph Fletcher, who was a professor at an Episcopal seminary when he wrote his controversial book

---

[5] Judaism has sometimes been called a religion of law and Christianity a religion of love, but this represents a serious misunderstanding. Both obviously work through both of these concepts in their own ways.

Situation Ethics.[6] The basic theme of this work is that ethical decisions should be based on whatever the application of love is in a particular situation, not prior rules or laws. It is, in other words, consequentialism taken to an extreme degree.

Fletcher opens his book with a story: A friend of his had arrived in St. Louis just as a presidential campaign was ending, and took a taxi. The cabbie remarked that he, his father, and his grandfather had always been straight-ticket Republicans. "Ah," said Fletcher's friend, "then I take it you voted for Senator So-and-so." "No," replied the driver, "there are times when a man has to push his principles aside and do the right thing." Fletcher concluded that this St. Louis cab driver was his book's hero.

Situation Ethics aroused passionate debate.[7] The clerical author was accused of "the most unstable and absurd relativism" and worse, but he made a strong case in his reply that he was simply saying what has, in fact, long been the Christian stance on issues ranging from marriage (for example, it is in principle indissoluble, but there are situations open to divorce) to war (it is evil, but there are situations that permit "just" war).

Try to think of how the situation-ethics principle could be applied to difficult problems like abortion, suicide, and the right to die. And whether situationalism really makes these hard decisions any easier or better in practice.

SIMILARITIES AND DIFFERENCES IN RELIGIOUS ETHICAL TRADITIONS

We have seen that religions are similar in their juxtapositions of love and law. The major religions are also, in fact, broadly agreed on certain great principles of religious ethics. Such sources as the Ten Commandments, the Sermon on the Mount, the Five Precepts of Buddhism, the Koran (for example, the "Islamic Decalogue" in 17:22–39), and the Analects of Confucius point to the evil of killing, inflicting injury, lying, the violation of property, and the breaking of oaths. All are concerned about the poor and the powerless, calling for justice toward them and commending the giving of alms and tithes for the assistance of those without means.

Increasingly, especially in the great religions as they emerged in the era of religious founders (see Chapter Two), awareness of the worth and moral responsibility of the individual became more and more apparent. Doctrines such as karma, personal judgment leading to individual salvation or damnation, or the obligations of the Hebrew prophet or Confucian sage to stand alone if need be in denouncing evil emphasized—as did the

---

[6] Philadelphia: Westminster Press, 1965.

[7] Harvey Cox, ed., *The Situation Ethics Debate*. Philadelphia: Westminster, 1968.

role of the founders themselves—that ethical religion is a personal as well as a collective duty.

At the same time, it must be recognized there are significant differences in the ethics of the major religions. Generally, these are in the areas of application rather than of fundamental principle.

Thus, all recognize the essential wrongness of killing. One religion, Jainism, extends that principle to forbid strictly the killing of animal as well as human life; so to a large extent do the much more numerous Buddhist and Hindu faiths, though practice on this matter varies considerably among different social and religious classes, as does the concomitant practice of vegetarianism. Other religions, including Christianity, have generally condoned the killing of animals but have embraced minorities, such as Quakers and Mennonites, who have traditionally rejected any taking of human life and so have refused to take part in war and have opposed capital punishment.

In the same way, all religions have recognized that marriage and sexual activity require some regulation for the well-being of society as a whole and to prevent exploitation of individuals, but have differed on the parameters of what is acceptable or to be recommended. Some endorse polygamy; others do not. Some hold up celibacy as an ideal, at least for religious professionals; others present marriage and the procreation of children as incumbent upon all. Some have taken premarital or extramarital sex much more lightly than others. As we have already noted, this is also an area in which much discrepancy between theory and practice has occurred, with a double standard not seldom obtaining between men and women. It must be further observed that traditional sex and marriage policies in most religions have worked toward the subordination of women.

CONTEMPORARY ISSUES
IN RELIGIOUS ETHICS

Ethics is not merely concerned with theories or hypothetical issues, or with objective descriptions of the positions of various religions. It is, instead, the place where religion most frequently meets the world where it lives, engaging in issues that are often quite literally matters of life and death for real people. The ethics of medicine, and no less those of war and peace, clearly involve their real-life practitioners in stark decisions about who lives and who dies, much as they might wish it otherwise. Questions of who receives the use of scarce medical equipment when life-support systems may be withdrawn from a terminal patient, or whether a city should be bombed, can hardly be construed in any other way.

Frequently, issues concerning the quality of life are a little less profound for those involved, especially when they concern such matters as motherhood, intimate personal relations with others, or lifelong social roles that appear predetermined by race or gender. Questions like abortion, birth control, racial discrimination, roles for women—including religious understandings of male and female images of God—involve nothing less than the extent to which one's scenario for the real self is shaped by one's society and biology.

In this book we began with the idea that religion creates scenarios for the real self—which means that each religion presents a *paradigm*, or ideal image, of a real self, or real personhood. We have seen how these paradigms interact with the symbols, worship, sociology, and concepts of religion. Now we need to examine how paradigms of selfhood work themselves out in situations of ethical decisions. The matter is further complicated by the fact that developments in the "outer" world—the worlds of science, politics, literature, television, sports—also profoundly affect the way people think about themselves and their roles.

What are some changes in the paradigm of personhood, or self, going on now, and how will they influence ethics? Anything that affects how people think of their real selves will affect how they behave ethically. Here are some areas in which ethical activity is happening with special velocity today: medical ethics, particularly the abortion and right-to-die controversy; women and religion; and the liberation theology critique of the role religion should have in situations of oppression. We will examine them as examples of contemporary ethical discussion; other examples could, of course, have been chosen.

THE MEDICAL REVOLUTION

An area in which science is creating new paradigms of human personhood is medicine. Many old and new issues involving ethics and, ultimately, philosophical or spiritual ideas about what it means to be a human person cluster about the field of medicine today. Even old issues that were known and discussed as far back as ancient Greece, such as artificial birth control, abortion, voluntary euthanasia or the right to die, and experimentation on humans, are revamped today because of immense advances in medical research that have vastly expanded the possibilities as well as intensified the moral problems.

There are also new issues growing out of explosive new possibilities for biological engineering—shaping genetic transmission and physiological nature in ways that would have seemed like science fiction only a few years ago and that may still seem fantastic to those who have not kept up with the new research. Today such things as the following are definitely on the horizon: the alteration of cells, transfer of genes and so of heredity from

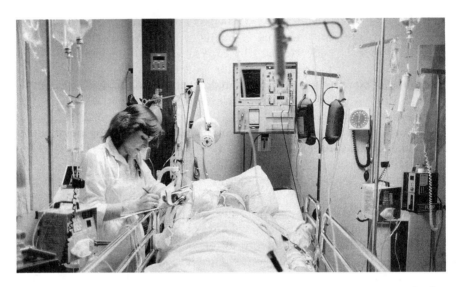

Ken Karp

A modern hospital room, the scene of many ethical decisions.

one person to another, genetic copies enabling the genes of one person to be indefinitely multiplied and implanted in many other organisms, cloning or nonsexual reproduction from a tissue specimen, predetermination of an infant's sex, controlling the aging process so most people may live many hundreds of years, and (much farther off) artificial creation of organic life and maybe even of humans.

This sort of biological engineering, which will seem to many like "playing God," causes questions to rush through the mind. What changes are desirable? What values must come into play? Who decides? Can scientists be trusted with such power, or can politicians or anyone else who is *not* a scientist?

More basic is the issue of what image of a human person, of what it means to be a self, would be operative as one decides such momentous matters. To be a person in the fullest psychological and spiritual sense—in traditional terms, to have a soul and be a child of God—is it necessary for one to have been a product of the genetic lottery in the traditional way? Would a genetic copy, a clone, or a "test-tube baby" be a person with a soul?

Actually, there has been genetic engineering by other means for a long time, often under the strictest religious sanctions. The caste system in India in effect maintained gene pools and so controlled heredity under Hindu religious sanctions. The social class systems of Europe and America, by which nobility or comparable elites were expected to mate and marry only within their class, received implicit or explicit sanction by Christian churches, as have most taboos against interracial or interreligious marriage. Even the institution of marriage itself is a socially and religiously sanctioned practice that in various complex ways controls human genetics with results far different from other conceivable arrangements for reproduction. The fact is, however, that class, caste, and marriage make the evolution of human biology a slow, half-conscious process that is the byproduct of social and spiritual agendas, whereas the new possibilities force immediate, conscious decisions upon us that shake our concepts of the relation of humanity and biology.

All the new prospects are not genetic. There are also emerging new ways of engineering human life after birth. The coming possibility of extensive organ transplants raises the issue of just what *is* a physiologically separate human. Suppose one could transplant or make artificially all organs, even the brain. We would have problems such as the ethicality of transplanting the brain of a dying genius into the body of a physically healthy but feeble-minded youth. Even now decisions of this sort must be made in regard to kidney transplants.

Transplanting even brains makes us begin to wonder where one life ends and another begins. In a world of procedures such as this, it might seem that human beings are not separate entities given a span of life by chance or God on this world but are configurations of an ongoing human biosphere that can be rearranged continually. (Of course, this is already more true than we often acknowledge on the psychological level; our minds and consciousnesses are the result of continual exchange— transplants, if one wishes—of ideas and moods between one another.)

So if bodies can be mixed up, do separate bodies really make separate persons? Or *is* there such a thing as a separate person? Is the new biology saying, as the new physics also seem to be indicating, that the universe is a single energy field taking many forms and that the mystics who have said that selfhood is an illusion were right all along? Or are these sciences looking at it from one angle only?

What would the world of new biology be like? Would this new earth of immensely enhanced physiological interchange, in which through genetic manipulation every child could be born a genius greater than Leonardo da Vinci or Albert Einstein, and perhaps even death could be made obsolete, be a utopia of wise and godlike immortals? Or would it reduce humanity to a beehive? Bees through instinct also perform remarkable feats of biological engineering. Even worse, would it provide the means for some set of totalitarians to take control of the human race and, quite literally, shape it irreversibly to serve their ends?

One is not reassured concerning this last possibility by still another prospect now coming into realization, the control of the pleasure and pain and learning centers in the brain by wired stimulators. It appears possible through mild electric charges at the right places in the brain to facilitate learning, modify memory, enhance intelligence, and curb aggressiveness, or effect the reverse of any of these. Again, such manipulation seems to offer vast opportunities for improving the human condition—or for making possible totalitarian control beyond the dreams of a Hitler or a Stalin, possibly bringing the latter in the guise of the former. Yet, as brain research touches the physics and chemistry of consciousness itself, its advocates rightly remind us that they simply offer opportunities for free control of what has so often been only illusory freedoms, so subject has mind itself been to vicissitudes of diet, disease, poor education, and repressive environment.

One thing seems certain; the future of religion will be very greatly affected indeed by these new images of personhood. And if religion does not come to terms with these issues, it will increasingly seem irrelevant.

It is just as important to realize that some decisions like these are being made now. Physicians and society must continually make life-and-death decisions and decisions between one life and another. Dramatic instances occur when only so many transplants or artificial kidney machines are available, and their allocation must be determined by a hospital "God committee." Questions such as abortion and human experimentation provide current foci for the kind of issues raised here. Society also decides the biological life and death of individuals when it decides how to allocate resources for preventive medicine, what medical facilities it provides or fails to provide for the underprivileged, and for what issues it will dispose of human life in war.

THE ABORTION CONTROVERSY

Since the 1960s and 1970s, one of the most bitter of all public ethics controversies swirled around abortion, the medical termination of a pregnancy by the removal or destruction of the unborn fetus. Lines are drawn between the *pro-life* faction, which sees nearly all abortion as nothing less than murder and favors laws narrowly restricting or prohibiting it; and the *pro-choice* side, which believes that in some cases the procedure can be morally justified. Pro-choice advocates therefore oppose most legislation against abortion, contending that the woman concerned is the only person who can morally make the decision. Let us look at the history and the issues.

In the United States until the 1860s, abortion was generally legal until the time of "quickening," that is, until the fetus began to move in the womb. The practice was then widely criminalized, largely under pressure from the rising medical profession. Laws against abortion were accepted without too much open dissent until the mid-twentieth century, when pressure mounted to once again legalize it. In the tumultuous 1960s, rising feminism and movements toward sexual and personal lifestyle freedom combined to convince many that whether or not to have an abortion should be an individual decision rather than a criminal matter. (It is no coincidence but characteristic of the times that, in the same period, sex of any sort between consenting adults was widely decriminalized and also made a matter of personal choice.) A number of states repealed anti-abortion laws. Finally, in 1973, the U.S. Supreme Court, in the famous *Roe* v. *Wade* case, declared laws banning abortion in the first two trimesters, that is, the first six months of pregnancy, to be generally unconstitutional. The Court said, "The right of privacy . . . is broad enough to encompass a woman's decision whether or not to terminate her pregnancy." But the right is not absolute, and in the last three months of development it can become a "compelling" interest of the state to protect the unborn life, and abortion may then be forbidden except when the life or health of the mother is at stake.

By now, however, religious groups were getting seriously involved. It is easy to see why. Abortion is an ethical issue with profound religious ramifications. It concerns the origin and meaning of human personhood, life and death, male and female roles, individual priorities, moral values—all to a very high degree and in a very provocative way. But churches and other religious organizations found themselves as deeply divided as the population at large.

Statements by religious groups range from those that hold abortion a denial of the "right to life" and so wrong in its very nature, to those that emphasize freedom of choice. It should be pointed out, though, that the range does not, in fact, cover all theoretical possibilities.

Groups on the pro-life side, such as Roman Catholics, Eastern Orthodox, and the more conservative Baptist and Lutheran denominations, have indeed condemned all abortion as murder, or at the most made concessions only in cases of rape, incest, or to save the life of the mother. They emphasize that some acts are simply inherently wrong, and so should be condemned as such by ethicists and forbidden by law, and that the taking of innocent human life—whether before birth or after birth—is one of them.

The more pro-choice religious bodies—even the most liberal, such as the Unitarian Universalists—do not, however, necessarily take an opposite position of condoning any abortion for any reason. They do not suggest that there is no moral problem with abortion on demand or abortion just for reasons of convenience. While some totally secular pro-abortionists may hold that an aborted fetus is nothing more than tissue, few religionists of any stripe would deny it is important to recognize it as a human being or a potential human being, and therefore to view the question of its life with appropriate gravity. But—note here they are at least partly consequentialist while the anti-abortionists are almost entirely deontological, starting with rules and "oughts"—pro-choice religionists believe other issues than the life of the fetus must be taken into account too: the physical and mental welfare of the mother, the prospect of the child's postnatal neglect or abuse, the kind of family (if any) there is. For them, the question of who decides?—church, state, doctor, or mother—is also important. Thus, though they may hold that the recriminalization of abortion is not the answer, liberal religionists recognize the moral complexity of the issue and urge that decisions about it in any particular case not be made lightly.[8]

What are the issues? Here are some, as summarized in Edward Batchelor, Jr., ed. *Abortion: The Moral Issues.*[9] I have added some queries and comments in brackets.

- Is abortion a religious issue at all? [We have shown, I think, that it touches on some of the gravest and most central issues usually associated with religion: the person, life and death, men and women, moral choice.]

- If so, how can the religious ethicist clarify the moral issues? [She or he can ask: What is life? When does it begin? When does human life become a separate person? How much does quality of life count when we have reason to think a baby will be deformed, neglected, abused, or contribute to the physical or mental pathology of the mother? What are the priorities? Who decides?]

- Is preserving and protecting innocent human life an absolute value? [If so, what about war? Modern war seems almost inevitably to entail the bombing or shelling of cities, in which babies and other innocents are slaughtered. If one is anti-abortion, should one also be a pacifist and opposed to capital punishment, since all evidence indicates that innocents are sometimes executed?]

- Are the rights of the mother or the embryo foremost?

- Is an unborn child a human being with full rights?

[8] For the statements of many churches and other significant religious groups, including Jewish and Muslim bodies and dissidents such as Catholics for a Free Choice, see J. Gordon Melton, *The Churches Speak on Abortion*. Detroit: Gale Research, 1989.

[9] Edward Batchelor, Jr., ed., *Abortion: The Moral Issues*. New York: Pilgrim Press, 1982. This book is a useful anthology of many perspectives, both Catholic and Protestant, on the question. For feminist perspectives, see Rosalind Pollack Petchesky, *Abortion and Woman's Choice*. New York and London: Longman, 1984; and Beverly Harrison, *Our Right to Choose: Toward a New Ethic on Abortion*. Boston: Beacon Press, 1983.

- If so, at which stage of its development? [The issue of *hominization*, or when an embryo became a human being in the full moral sense of the term, was one which concerned premodern as well as contemporary theologians. Many classical thinkers held such views as that it was not ensouled and so truly human until forty days after conception, or until after a full, though miniature, human body had formed. Modern thinking, as we have seen in the case of *Roe* v. *Wade*, has also made some distinction between stages of pregnancy, often in terms of trimesters, or periods of three months. For anti-abortionists ancient and modern, though, this periodization does not affect the moral case; to them, the unformed fetus must be seen as incipiently or potentially human, and so subject to moral treatment as a human.]

- What is the proper place and function of religious, judicial, and legislative institutions in public-policy decision making on this issue? [Again, the question is, who decides?]

Even one who holds that abortion is always morally wrong still must deal with the question of whether it should be a state or an individual decision. These are separate issues, for not everything that is immoral is necessarily an appropriate subject for legislation and police intervention. The example of overeating has sometimes been cited. Although most moralists hold that gluttony is a sin, it has rarely, if ever, been suggested that excessive consumption of food should be made a criminal offence, unless in the context of something like times of war or famine.

On the other hand, such parallels seem fatuous and demeaning of life to those for whom abortion is simply direct, premeditated murder, hardly on the same plane as having an extra piece of cake one doesn't need. They point out that in all societies the violent and unlegitimatized taking of life is plainly criminal. It may not be possible to enforce laws against it in every instance, and offenders may sometimes be able to plead extenuating circumstances. But criminal life taking is nonetheless a very serious denial of values most people hold sacred. Thus the state's visible, public, legal banning of it is a crucially important symbol of moral consensus, and the statutes are on the books.

Needless to say, the anti-abortionists' estimate of contemporary society, in which life as an unqualified value no longer appears to have consensus at least in the case of abortion, is not very high. The next step, they suggest, will be the "scientific" elimination of superfluous postnatal humans, as is now the fate of inconvenient prenatal persons.

Abortion is clearly a difficult and painful issue. It may be fair to say that no simple response to it is totally just to all the questions, points of view, and doubts that can be raised. It is probably no less right to suggest that discussion of the issue is immensely important today, not only because it is a major and divisive political question, but also because it raises extremely basic and crucial religious issues about human lives and souls.

THE RIGHT TO DIE

The next medical-ethics issue, involving euthanasia, or mercy killing, and the right to die, involves many of the same questions about the limits of human life and is, I am afraid, no less tangled.

We may take as an example the widely publicized case of Karen Quinlan.[10] In April of 1975, this young New Jersey woman of twenty-one, a few days after moving out of her parents' house in order to be on her own, consumed several alcoholic drinks in a bar along with friends to celebrate a friend's birthday. She had apparently also taken tranquilizers and/or barbiturates the same day, and had reportedly been dieting, maybe fasting, as well. All a bad combination. Suddenly she passed out, and never regained consciousness. She was taken home and then to a hospital. Her life was sustained, but without credible hope that she would recover mentally, talk, or ever be in more than a passive state.

She moved, showed various facial expressions, and even seemed sometimes to laugh or cry, but was never able to show any sign of clear intelligence or of being able to survive independently. Her family finally petitioned a court for permission to make Karen's father her guardian, with the expressed intent to withdraw life support from her, which the hospital would not do without legal consent. To Karen's loved ones, it was a matter of mercy, of the conclusion of a life that could never find further fulfillment, and of the right allocation of limited emotional and financial resources. The New Jersey attorney general opposed the petition, saying that such a course was "death at will" and would "open the way for euthanasia." That is, it would set a precedent for allowing others, whether family or the state, to decide whether such a patient shall live or die. Lawyers for the two attending physicians, who also opposed the petition, spoke of "Nazi atrocities" and implied that approval would move society in the direction of the Third Reich's euthanasia practices.

The petition for guardianship was denied by a lower court, but the New Jersey Supreme Court finally ruled in the family's favor. However, by then, the case was complicated for the Quinlans by ambiguous signals from the Roman Catholic church, of which they were devout members. Karen remained in a vegetative state for another ten years, then died of pneumonia in June, 1986. The family had at that time asked that no antibiotics or blood-pressure medication be given, that is, that no special measures be taken to keep this patient alive.

[10] Reported in Gregory F. Pence, *Classic Cases in Medical Ethics.* New York: McGraw-Hill, 1990, pp. 3–24. On the Quinlan case, see also Paul Ramsey, *Ethics at the Edge of Life.* New Haven: Yale University Press, 1978, pp. 268–99.

Were they right or wrong?

Many of us have had the sad opportunity to see a once lively and lovely friend or loved one brought to an apparently irreversible comatose state, with little or no flicker of consciousness, kept alive by various tubes and other "miracles" of modern medicine, perhaps—if and when aware—in pain or intense discomfort, and we have wondered if it would not be better just to "let her go" or "let him go."

Yet we, like the physicians involved, have also had to confront the awesomeness of any decision involving life or death, for oneself or another. When does one have the right—if ever—to unilaterally decide death for another? For a Karen Quinlan? For a grandmother obviously dying a hard and painful death of cancer? For a young friend suffering and despondent with AIDS? If one believes in a spiritual dimension to life, is pain, or even unconsciousness, necessarily the worst that can happen to one and death necessarily better? Who decides?

And when is or is not one really able to make that decision for oneself? For while patients may sometimes be totally unconscious or mentally incompetent, in many other cases it is not so easy to say—they may speak but not rationally, or drift in and out of rationality, and one may be at a loss just how to assess their poignant pleas to be allowed to die—or to be kept alive at all costs.

Often the issue can be put in terms of not directly letting a patient die by "pulling the plug," that is, withdrawing life-support systems including even nourishment, but of simply not taking *extraordinary measures* to sustain life beyond what could be seen as its natural termination. Here too, the ethicist must face hard questions. Is there any real difference? Should financial cost—since extraordinary measures are usually very expensive—be a factor in such a decision? What about the allocation of perhaps scarce medical talents and resources? Should a patient's likelihood of long-term survival in any case be part of the decision?

And again, who decides? In some cases, people have made prior legally recognized declarations, often called a *living will*, indicating just what medical care they want and do not want if they are unable to make a decision at the time. In other cases, the decision must fall to family and physicians, and the latter may well be heavily influenced by legislative guidelines and the prospect of malpractice suits.

And there is the other end of life. What about infants who are born seriously defective? Should they be kept alive by extraordinary measures, or allowed to slip away through "benign neglect?"[11]

Then there is the different—but comparable—case of Elizabeth Bouvia, terminally ill, who sought *voluntary death*, that is, suicide for

---

[11] On such difficult cases as deformed newborns, see Paul Ramsey, *Ethics at the Edge of Life*. pp 189–267; and on the ethical allocation of limited medical resources, see John F. Kilner, *Who Lives? Who Dies?* New Haven: Yale University Press, 1990.

medical reasons, in another recent widely publicized case.[12] This saga commenced in 1983. Elizabeth, then only twenty-five, had cerebral palsy and was almost totally paralyzed. Her life had been unhappy. She tried to starve herself to death. Her doctor determined to force-feed her, saying she would someday change her mind and be grateful to him. A local court was asked to enjoin him from doing this. But in December of 1983, it ruled in favor of the doctor and the hospital keeping the young woman alive even against her will. Later courts, however, upheld Elizabeth on the grounds that any patient has the right to refuse medical services. (Nonetheless, she did in fact appear to feel the point had been made and, after being allowed to decline nourishment, continued eating enough to sustain life. At the time of writing she was still alive.)

Undoubtedly, there are many unofficial suicides by seriously if not terminally ill patients who see no more point to their lives and just want to end the pain. Is this morally justified, whether done by a patient directly or with the help of a sympathetic physician? Joseph Fletcher wrote some time ago that there is no "real moral difference between self-administered euthanasia and the medically administered form when it is done at the patient's request," when the patient has become a "sedated, comatose, betubed object, manipulated and subconscious, if not subhuman."[13]

Those who favor euthanasia at a patient's request often cite the example of the Netherlands, where since 1985, the state has agreed not to prosecute physicians who administer euthanasia under guidelines adopted by the Dutch medical association.[14] These are:

1. Only a physician may implement requests for mercy killing.

2. The request must be made by a competent patient.

3. The patient's request must be free of doubt, well-documented, and repeated.

4. The attending physician must consult another physician before proceeding.

5. A determination must be made that no one pressured the patient toward the request.

Further, the patient must be in "unbearable pain," with no relief considered medically possible.

Within these parameters, in theory, even children could request to die and have the request implemented without their parents' consent,

[12] Pence, *Classic Cases in Medical Ethics*, pp. 25–44.
[13] Joseph Fletcher, *Morals and Medicine*. Boston: Beacon Press, 1961, pp. 85–86.
[14] Pence, *Classic Cases in Medical Ethics*, pp. 45–63.

since it was thought that parents might have extraneous motives in acting or not acting on their children's behalf, though at the time of writing no such case has actually occurred. The Dutch provisions do not, in fact, cover euthanasia requested for someone else judged incompetent; they deal only with self-requests made by competent patients.

Can these standards be morally justified? They were opposed in the Netherlands by certain conservative religious groups, which held that medically assisted suicide is only another form of suicide, which in turn is simply self-inflicted violent homicide. Only God or nature, opponents say, has the right to take life whether one's own or another's. (You will note a sharp conflict here between deontological ethics, which put the rules first, and consequentialist ethics, which are willing to bend the rules for the sake of a presumably overwhelmingly benign objective, the ending of hopeless "unbearable pain.")

Many Dutch citizens also recalled uneasily the Nazi occupation of their country in World War II, when it was the scene of some of the acts of involuntary euthanasia performed by that unholy regime. Altogether, the Nazis put to death "humanely" some ninety thousand people judged deformed, mentally defective, or otherwise useless—a figure that looks small only when set beside the six million Jews and other unwanted persons liquidated in the "final solution." In Holland as in the U.S., fear was expressed that opening the euthanasia door even a crack could lead in the end to public callousness toward all sorts of state-supervised "convenience," or public-policy deaths, perhaps ultimately even on the Nazi scale. (You will recall the same argument made about abortion.)

No doubt because of that memory, the Dutch provisions emphasized the patient's own voluntary request made in a condition of mental competence. Defenders of the policy say that this makes the Dutch practice absolutely different from the Third Reich's involuntary euthanasia and liquidation programs. Quite unlike the unspeakably dehumanized practices of the Nazis, defenders argue, the Dutch guidelines show extraordinarily acute sensitivity to suffering and to individual rights, including the right to die.

To confuse the two quite different policies, the Nazi and the contemporary Dutch, they would say, is to give way to totally irrational fears and emotions in a situation that calls instead for making hard, clear-headed distinctions and choices. These can only be made on a case-by-case basis, and that is what the policy permits.

Opponents of these practices contend that medically administered suicide and euthanasia are morally no different than murder, and say that no one has the right to prejudge the continuing worth of a human life, one's own or someone else's. Even a life in great pain, and seemingly close to natural death in any case, may be able to give and receive love, and experience spiritually important states. There are other values in human life than minimizing pain and maximizing comfort, even for one *in extremis*.

What do you think?

THE ROLE OF WOMEN IN RELIGION

There is a science fiction novel by Ursula LeGuin called *The Left Hand of Darkness*. It presents a world in which all the people are both male and female. They go through cycles in which they are first one sex, then the other, and the mentality, institutions, and customs of that society are permeated with the ramifications of this unearthly biology.

In our society, however, no fact is more basic than the division of humanity into people who are permanently female and people who are permanently male. This, together with the need to nurture children, affects everything from family structure to world politics and is profoundly reflected in the symbols and institutions of religion, from the Madonna or mother and child as a transcendent symbol to the almost exclusively male control of most religious institutions. Although occasionally religion may rise to the purport of Paul's dictum that "in Christ there is neither male nor female," it is also very conscious, even obsessively conscious, of the fact that humanity was created male and female and that there must be great meaning behind this division. Religious myths, symbols, and roles (and society as sanctioned by religion) are shot through with images implying set male and female patterns of life. It is fair to say that most traditional religion has been patriarchal in that it has made men the sources of authority and correct teaching in both church and family.

Today, the idea of distinctive male-female roles, and the validity of religious symbols and lines of authority based on distinctive sexual biology, are being challenged as never before. Women in particular, aware that traditional symbols and structures in religion and society have usually served to put them in a secondary role, pointedly query whether women should be ordained ministers and priests or whether God should exclusively be called Father. These challenges have had a profoundly disruptive effect because they raise issues and feelings that go very deep. For some people, religion should sanction the hierarchy of heaven and earth, with the father head of the family on earth as God is in heaven. For others, God is beyond gender, can transform all social structures, and liberates each person to be what she or he is as an individual self rather than one who just has to follow a predetermined sexual or social role.

If the latter attitude prevails, religion in the future will be affected by paradigms of personhood much less categorized by sexual roles than in the past. A person will be one of either sex who can do and be virtually anything—and this capacity will need to be reflected in roles in religious

AP/Wide World Photo

A woman Episcopal bishop, one of the increasing number of women ordained by a major American denomination.

institutions as well as in religious language and symbols. One of the greatest challenges Christianity and Judaism, together with other religions, will have to face in the next few centuries will not come from science, political revolution in the usual sense, or new vogues in philosophy or theology, but from the far-reaching implications of these changes in sexual images and roles. They touch deeply the structure and very language of these faiths, from God as Father on down. One could well ask how much change on such a deep level Judaism and Christianity could take without really becoming different religions. For some, such a transformation would be welcome; for others, tragic.

Not all who urge equality of men and women in religion, of course, insist that male-female roles should be flatly identical, as though there were *no* differences between the sexes except some physiological details. Instead, they feel that both have distinct and equally valuable contributions to make to worship and theology—which in itself does mark a radical enough change, since heretofore perhaps 90 percent of theology has been written and worship conducted by males and undoubtedly reflected mostly male experience. Perhaps that is why much orthodox, masculine religion favors the concepts of divine sovereignty and law. Teachings of feminine spiritual leaders, such as Mary Baker Eddy and Helena Blavatsky, favor ultimate unity and spiritual evolution on the analogy of, perhaps, the womb and nurture. In the same light, the image of a woman behind the altar, bringing forth bread and wine, might be congenial. I once attended an ordination ceremony in a tiny, modern Gnostic church in which the practice was for a husband and wife to be ordained as priests together and thereafter to celebrate the Gnostic Mass jointly and equally, each performing parts of the service that especially emphasized the sacred meaning of his or her sex.

LIBERATION THEOLOGY

Half a billion human beings are malnourished and hungry right now, on the brink of famine if not over it. Another billion and a half are in extreme poverty, no more than a day or a week away from the same state. They are illiterate or nearly so, have no access to medical treatment, no one to care for their elders or children if the worst happens. Millions more throughout the world, though perhaps somewhat better off materially, are despised and dehumanized on the basis of race, color, creed, or gender. And, deepest insult of all to any who care about human dignity, in the same cities, countries, and world, other human beings, whose brain cells and anatomy are no different, enjoy lives of abundance and have at their fingertips inordinate power over the lives of the other billions.

Also in the same world stands religion, which is supposed to proclaim freedom and liberation. Some might say that this refers only to spiritual liberation from sin, or freedom to go to heaven. But how can you talk only about spiritual liberation to a person who is sick, desperately poor, and whose children are dying of hunger-related diseases? Does theology—as "words about God"—include words about how God relates to such a situation? Does the Bible, which contains the Exodus story of the liberation of the children of Israel from slavery under Pharaoh in Egypt, offer any hope of contemporary liberation?

These were the appalling sights, and the questions, that some Christian thinkers faced in the 1960s. Concern for the poor and the social conditions behind poverty and human exploitation were not new, to be sure; there were the Christian fighters for the abolition of slavery in the nineteenth century, and Spanish and Portuguese Jesuits who were advocates on behalf of Native Americans and the miserable cargo of the first slave ships three centuries earlier. But it was the sixties group, then mostly Roman Catholics in Latin America, who inspired the movement known as *liberation theology*.

They were confronted by the extreme poverty of masses of people in Latin America, and by the inaction of corrupt governments, often supported by outside interests and a brutal military. They were, on the other hand, inspired by the new vision of the Church as the "People of God" proclaimed by Vatican II, the Catholic church's 1962–1965 Council. Vatican II was followed by conferences of Roman Catholic bishops, at Medellin, Columbia, in 1968, and in Puebla, Mexico, in 1979. These conclaves of the region's episcopate articulated a message—that the church was aware of the judgment of the Gospel on social evil, and was now on the side of the poor. It was proclaiming liberty to the captives, was prepared to lead them in Exodus, and to place before them a pillar of fire and manna on the way to freedom.

Common cause was soon made with others battling oppression. U.S. black theologians like James Cone, inspired by the image of Martin Luther King and the freedom marches, had already been describing the similar situation of blacks in the North American republic. Feminist theologians had already been using the language of liberation in relation to the age-old subjugation of women. Protestants in South Africa, Asian Christians, spokespersons for indigenous peoples in many parts of the world rightly perceived the common experience of all "second-class persons," and cross-fertilized their thought with liberation theology. But the transformed Roman Catholicism of Latin America was the heartland of the movement, and we shall refer primarily to it.[15]

Fundamentally, for liberationism, theology and ethics are inseparable. The ethical demand for justice must be reflected in theology. The latter must not retire into trying to justify the seeming injustice of God in the world, but display God's passion to remedy those evils.

Theology should be first to point out that many people in the world are very poor, and some are not. It ought then to adhere to Jesus' concern for the poor and his identification with them, and also his concern that they have the Gospel preached to them. It must, in characteristic terminology, show *solidarity* with the oppressed, and the church also must exercise a "preferential option for the poor."

---

[15] Here are a few basic and representative books. All are published by Orbis Books of Maryknoll, New York; so only the date is given here. Gustavo Gutierrez, *A Theology of Liberation* (1973) is the classic work. Arthur F. McGovern, *Liberation Theology and its Critics* (1989) is sympathetic but discusses criticism adequately. Leonardo Boff and Clodius Boff, *Introducing Liberation Theology* (1987) is by two brothers, both priests in Brazil, who have been very active in both the theory and work of liberationism; this is a good first book to read. Alfred T. Hennelly, ed., *Liberation Theology: A Documentary History* (1990) is essentially the documents of the ferocious controversies over liberation theology within Roman Catholicism in a Latin American context; it provides ample statements both pro and con for the reader to understand the issues and story clearly. James H. Cone, *A Black Theology of Liberation* (1970; 20th anniversary ed., 1990) is a good example of the application of liberationist thought in another situation.

One way liberationists did this was through the establishment of *base communities*, church centers where the ordinary people studied the Bible, discussed their problems, and found strength to take their lives in their own hands. A next step, from which many liberation theology writers did not shrink, was to identify reasons why some were poor while others were rich, and to advocate strategies for change. Here is where liberation theology has laid itself open to serious criticism, for in varying degrees, partisan liberationists have made use of Marxist analysis and concepts in this task.

This analysis was based on the same principles as those found in the Marxist position presented in Chapter Two, that economic inequality inevitably results from exploitation of the disadvantaged by the advantaged, and the capitalist economic system perpetuates that injustice. Alienation, or the inability of exploiter and exploited to relate to each other fully as caring human beings is the unhappy subjective product of this social pathology. Furthermore, religion too often is misused, and serves as a mere veil, or even "opiate," to smooth over the horrible evils of this situation.

Liberation theologians rarely went so far as to propose totalitarian political and economic programs, and of course they did not oppose religion as such (though they vehemently opposed its use to palliate oppression) in the manner of China or the former Communist regimes of Eastern Europe. Nonetheless, in the 1970s and 1980s there was no lack of liberation theological writing blaming Latin American and other Third World poverty on capitalism, with U.S. corporations and their behind-the-scenes support by the U.S. government frequently singled out. Those theologians commonly suggested the answer must lie in socialism or mixed economies of some sort. Though religion was the ultimate fire and light of the Exodus of which they dreamed and saw visions, politics and the interwinding of politics with economics was the way they perceived the problems and the solutions, and the concrete language of those perceptions was likely to be Marxist.

All this led to heavy conflict between liberation theologians and the Vatican, especially after the coming of Pope John Paul II to the throne of Peter in 1978. John Paul saw spiritual and social liberation as going together, and could not see the latter as an end itself or as something to be identified with the Promised Land. He did not believe that priests should be active in day-to-day politics, and he harbored a great deal of skepticism concerning Marxism's view of humanity or its likely practical consequences in human affairs. Undoubtedly, these views were rooted in the pontiff's own experience of living and struggling on behalf of the church and social justice—for example, the worker's Solidarity movement—in an ostensibly Marxist society, his native Poland.

The stunning, epoch-making events of 1989–1991, which saw the rapid demise of all but a very few Marxist societies and revealed the hatred of many of their subjects for them, inevitably led to the discrediting of that ideology—at least under that name—in much of the world. Hardly less significant for the spiritual future of Latin America may have been the very rapid growth of charismatic Protestantism around the same time. Liberation theology, in Latin America and elsewhere, may undergo very searching rethinking and rewriting in coming years. On the other hand, the end of the Cold War may be seen as liberating liberation theology from its debilitating association with the East-West ideological struggle, and free it to get on with its own grass-roots tasks.

By 1992, it was clear that the freedom so much boasted of by the victors in those four almost unparalleled revolutionary years would not, of itself, solve the grievous economic problems on both sides of the globe, not to mention those between North America and South America. Despite several false starts, and the example of improvement in parts of Asia, the abysmal poverty of much of Latin America and Africa remains appallingly deep. The African-American sociologist Orlando Patterson, in his award-winning book *Freedom*, has analyzed just how and why "freedom" came to be regarded as the central value of Western civilization, in the process pointing out that the concept actually embodies much ambivalence: there is the idealized freedom of civil liberties, and there is also the licentiousness, domination, and greed of all those for whom "freedom . . . meant the freedom to rule over others" . . . including frequently women, minorities, and slaves.[16]

So long as such inequities exist, and the paradoxes of freedom are unresolved, there will be a place for voices from the other side proclaiming liberty and summoning the oppressed to Exodus. The language and the pictures may change, as do all such things in human life. But the courage and vision of the twentieth century's liberation theologians will surely not be forgotten as Pharaohs come and go.

Today, numerous other arenas of ethical decision could be named. There is the newly appreciated area of ecological and environmental ethics. There are also very hard decisions that may have to be faced in the near future concerning world hunger and overpopulation. Perennial issues in personal, social, and political ethics remain as relevant as ever. So do the questions of poverty and homelessness with which we began this chapter. The awesome ethical questions of war and peace, and of diverse economic systems, are not likely to be resolved soon. The examples we have given, however, should be enough to help you understand the kinds of issues that ethicists face, the role that religion can play regarding them, and the way in which ethical thinking is done.

[16] Orlando Patterson, *Freedom*. New York: Basic Books, 1991.

SUMMARY

Virtually every day of one's life, one is faced with the need to make decisions involving ethics and morality. Although the line between them is often fuzzy, morality tends to deal with standards or practices in areas of personal life, while ethics deals with the philosophical reasons behind them, or with the practices of larger groups, such as professions or societies. Today, the intellectual analysis of proper human behavior is generally called ethics.

Ethical thought has been given two sources, deontology, or the "ought" approach—duty and obligation—probably derived from a greater power than the individual; and teleological, or consequentialist, which judges ethics by results. Both have been vigorously defended and criticized, and attempts have also been made to combine them or to bring in other considerations. Utilitarianism, the "greatest good to the greatest number," is a kind of consequentialism.

Most major religions in some way combine law and love—love or compassion as the supreme ideal, rules and norms showing how it is ordinarily to be implemented. Most religions also are fundamentally united in basic ethical values, such as opposing murder, theft, or sexual irregularity, and favoring honesty and justice. But differences can be found on some specifics of how these values are to be construed in practice.

Current areas of intensive ethical debate include abortion, euthanasia, and other aspects of medical ethics; the role of women; and the liberation of oppressed peoples. Others, not discussed in detail in the text, include ecology, war and peace, poverty and homelessness, and political and economic ethics.

Epilogue: Secularization and the Religious Future

What will the future of religion be, during your lifetime and that of your children? How will it change? And, overall, will it flourish or decline?

Behind all the issues concerning religion we have raised lies the greater issue that focuses on the world's *secularization*. Secularization literally means "becoming worldly," and the question is whether the power of religion is in fact decreasing in modern society. The sociologist Peter Berger has defined secularization as "the process by which sectors of society and culture are removed from the domination of religious institutions and symbols," together with its subjective effect, the "secularization of consciousness," which means thinking less about religion and basing fewer of our decisions in everyday life on religious considerations than did our forefathers.[1]

Some say religion is obviously on a downward trend, that the world is clearly less religious than, say in the Middle Ages or even the "good old days" of the nineteenth century. They cite the marked falling off of religious participation in places like Western Europe, and the long-term effect of science and social science as alternative sources of understanding and power.

Others say the observations on which such generalizations are made are deceptive, that the past was not as religious as popularly thought and

---

[1] Peter L. Berger, *The Sacred Canopy*, Garden City, N.Y.: Doubleday, 1959, p. 107.

that the present is not as unreligious as some think. Consider the continuing high level of church attendance in the United States, the power of Islam in contemporary affairs, and the significant relation of religion and politics in many parts of the world. But preachers, they say, always tend to idealize the past and its piety, the better to showcase the sins of the modern world.

An example of a scholar who says that religion is declining is the sociologist Bryan Wilson. He argues that the real underpinning of religion is faith in the supernatural, that is, everyday belief in miracles, divine intervention in the affairs of the world and the individual, heaven and hell, and the like. As people more and more put their practical trust in science and medicine, and standards of living are high compared to those of past ages, the power of religion will diminish, even though religious institutions may survive for some time, and some people may maintain a "split-level" mentality, holding simultaneously both regard for the supernatural and willingness to live in the world science is creating, with its computers and biological engineering. But, says Wilson, people's inner outlook ultimately follows what is going on in society. The tension of a split-level mentality about the world will eventually be resolved in favor of answers to the meaning and value questions—the questions about the "real self" and Ultimate Reality—that come out of the same science-oriented world-view, which dominates our ordinary life of computers and communications marvels, rather than an increasingly remote world of the "supernatural."[2]

Wilson's perspective is mainly in the tradition of Max Weber, who emphasized religion as a way of knowing and controlling the supernatural. Peter Berger's stems from Emile Durkheim, who stressed social cohesion as the focus of religion. (Both Weber and Durkheim are discussed in Chapter Two.) Berger sees in history a process, accelerated in modern times, of the breakup of a unity people once felt of the sacred, the world, and human society which supported individual life. Our lives have, through this "disenchantment of the world," become more and more fragmented, with religion at best just another specialized activity. Furthermore, fragmentation has afflicted the religious world itself in the form of pluralism, the existence side by side of numerous religious groups offering inconsistent competitive views; according to Berger this pluralistic situation, highly visible in modern man, weakens all religion by making all religious truth only a personal, privatized, relativistic matter. It is a question whether that sort of religion can have much future.[3]

[2] Bryan Wilson, *Contemporary Transformations of Religion* (London: Oxford University Press, 1976). See also Wilson's article, "The Return of the Sacred," *Journal for the Scientific Study of Religion*, 18, 3 (September 1979), 268–80.

[3] Berger, *The Sacred Canopy*.

Others are more optimistic. Berger himself, in fact, has argued that despite the ravages of disenchantment and pluralism, the experiential sources of religion have not dried up; people still have the needs, the experiences, and the vision upon which religion is founded.[4] Another sociologist, Andrew Greeley, has pointed out that actually it seems to be precisely in those places such as Holland, Ireland, and the United States where the religious scene is most competitive that religion has most flourished in modern times. For many modern people accustomed to a pluralistic, competitive world, *pluralism* in itself is no mark against all religion; rather, far from weakening faith, it seems to keep it alive and alert, summoning up loyalty to one's particular group.[5] The Weberian Talcott Parsons has contended that the fact that modernity has made religion only one part of life among many—one institution among such others as education, business, government, and so forth, rather than a unifying worldview overarching them all, as in past ages—need not necessarily weaken it within its own sphere. In a world of specialists, religious specialists may be as credible as any other. When pluralism makes religion a matter of individual choice, that may well serve to make it more important to a person who has deliberately chosen or affirmed his or her religion than when it was a more or less automatic part of tribal or peasant life.[6] It is not our purpose here to predict the future; readers will have to decide for themselves which prophets are most correct. As a prelude to such reflections, though, as we close this pilgrimage through the world of religious studies, let us think again of the course we have covered.

Numerous ways in which religion, the drive to be a real self in the context of infinite reality, has manifested itself have been examined in this book. The roots of this process, or of some of the phenomena connected with it, have been observed deep in the animal world and in our successive self-discoveries of our own nature. Its association with certain states of consciousness and its representation in symbols, rites, social groups, and intellectual concepts have been noted.

It is evident that religion has always been changing in outward manifestation. Its institutional structures, symbols, services, and words are never the same from one age to another, whether or not one feels that the essence of religion or of a particular religion remains constant beneath the changes. The currently changing aspects of human life presented in this chapter represent, among others, factors that undoubtedly will affect fu-

[4] Peter L. Berger, *A Rumor of Angels* (Garden City, N.Y.: Doubleday and Co., 1970).

[5] Andrew Greeley, *Religion in the Year 2000* (New York: Sheed and Ward, 1969), p. 97ff.

[6] Talcott Parsons, "Christianity in Modern Industrial Society," in Edward A. Tiryakin, ed., *Sociological Theories, Values, and Socio-Cultural Change* (New York: The Free Press, 1963).

Appendix:
Studying Religion

Here are suggested projects to help you study and understand, particularly through experience, some of the material in this book. They are presented in connection with selected chapters. For further help, see Donald E. Miller and Barry J. Seltser, *Writing and Research in Religious Subjects* (Prentice Hall, Englewood Cliffs, N.J., 1992).

Chapter Three: Meditation Experiment

Although various states of consciousness can be given religious value, one of the easiest and most beneficial to try out as an exercise in sampling religiously important states is the meditative. As an exercise to use in connection with academic study, however, it should be regarded as a psychological experiment, not a religious or spiritual practice. Don't do this experiment unless you feel very comfortable with it on all levels, and stop it if anything about it bothers you or feels wrong. But understanding something about meditation is important for understanding many of the world's religious traditions, since it is a key practice in them, one that is a royal road to realizing the kind of consciousness they would consider liberated or enlightened. Even more generally, intentionally entering a meditative state can help one grasp how practices like chanting or focusing can significantly alter feelings, perceptions, and the experience of space and time.

To try meditation, first find a quiet, uncluttered place where you are not likely to be disturbed and there is little to distract you. For your first efforts, twelve to fifteen minutes should probably be about the right amount of time to allow.

Sit cross-legged on a cushion on the floor or the bed, or if you prefer, in a fairly hard chair. Fold or rest the hands gently, close the eyes or focus them softly on a single point. Keep the spine and neck straight but not rigid. So far as posture is concerned, the important thing is to find the right balance between too much strain from rigidity and too much relaxation that will lead to corresponding mental sloppiness. Be free of pain and strain, but poised and alert.

On the mental level, the key is to stop the activity of the "monkey mind," as some Zen people call it, the stream of consciousness always running from one thing to another, in order to allow your mind a little quiet time just to be itself as pure consciousness. The way to do this, many teachers say, is to stop the onrushing activity of the mind by focusing on just one thing, sometimes called "one-pointed consciousness."

One focus of one-pointed concentration can be the breath. Either count the breaths from one to ten, as some Zen practitioners do, or just maintain "mindfulness" of breathing, following it in and out. You can also concentrate visually on a candle flame or some other object that will permit a calming yet focused gaze. Or you can have an audio focus, repeating a word or phrase very quietly over and over, or listening to a natural sound like falling rain.

Keep up the practice until the mind is very still, then hold the stillness without—so far as possible—thinking about anything for a time. Then gently bring yourself out of the meditation state.

During meditation, you will undoubtedly experience wandering thoughts. Everyone does. Don't worry about them. Just let them go, following them away like released balloons disappearing into the sky, till they are gone.

You may want to write up this experiment as a paper or report, or a journal item for your own future reference. If so, here is a brief outline that may be of help in organizing and touching on important points.

1. Give the time and place, and describe the setting. Tell how you felt that day, especially as you went into the experiment. How was your health? Were there any major problems you were contending with?

2. Tell what technique (counting breaths, visual focus, and the like) you used.

3. Describe concisely what happened from beginning to end, particularly shifts in mood, emotion, and self-awareness. Include reference

to internal or external distractions, and any especially vivid images that arose in your mind.

4. Analyze your experience of time and space. Did the twelve minutes, or whatever, seem especially short or long? What kind of awareness, if any, did you have of your spatial and physical environment, including your own body? (For some people this awareness falls away, for others it becomes especially acute.)

5. Give your overall reaction to the experiment. How did you feel about it afterward? Did it help you understand anything about religion?[1]

Chapter Four: Visiting and Analyzing a Religious Service

A very helpful exercise you might do is visit a religious service in a tradition that is unfamiliar to you, and write it up as a report. Here is an outline you could follow.

1. *Background Information.* Give the full name, exact address, and religious affiliation of the group; give the date and time of your visit; give the name and type of service attended.

2. *General Information.* Describe the outside and inside appearance of the building, giving special attention to particularly important symbols and distinctive architectural features. Then describe the way visitors are greeted, and the sort of people in this group—their apparent social class, lifestyle type, ethnic background, average age, gender, and approximate number present. Describe in the same way the leadership conducting the service.

3. *Account of Service.* Describe what happened in the service from beginning to end. Try to give some sense of the emotional tone and subjective spiritual meaning of the activity. For example, was the opening dramatic or casual? Was the congregational participation emotional or reserved? Was much of the service spontaneous? Did it seem to be ancient ritual or contemporary?

4. *Analysis.* Analyze the worship experience in terms of the three forms of religious expression: theoretical (teaching), practical (worship), and sociological. At least one-third of the paper should be this part.

   a. Theoretical. What, essentially, does this religion teach? As far as you could tell from this one experience, from the sermon, prac-

---

[1] For more on meditation by the author, including some accounts of student experiments with it, see Robert Ellwood, *Finding the Quiet Mind.* Wheaton, Ill.: Theosophical Publishing House, 1983.

tices, symbols, and so on, what seems to be the main message of this religion? You may need to distinguish between what was "officially" said in creeds or the like, and what really seemed to be most important to the people in the congregation as they took part.

b. Practical. What was the basic nature of the worship? Formal or informal, old or new, structured or spontaneous, intellectual or emotional, or something of all of these. What message about how this group conceives of the role of religion, and the best way for humans to build bridges to Ultimate Reality, did this worship communicate?

c. Sociological. What kind of group was it? As well as you could tell from this one experience, was it close-knit or diffuse? Was this group comprised of mostly people drawn to the religion by family or ethnic ties, or mostly committed converts of different backgrounds? What role did the priest or leader play? What message about religious experience was communicated by the nature of the group?

5. *Conclusion.* Would you say this worship was in any sense a scenario for the real self? For whom and in what sense?

Chapter Five: Reading a Novel

One possible project in conjunction with this chapter would be a paper analyzing a novel from a religious and literary point of view. Here is an outline you could probably use with almost any novel suitable for analysis in this way. I hope you find it helpful.

1. Give full bibliographical information about the novel: author, title, place of publication, publisher, date, and number of pages.

2. Give a little information about the author, particularly data about his or her background, personality, life experiences, beliefs, and commitments that would be of help in understanding why the author wrote this novel and the points of view—religious, political, psychological, and the like—that seem to be expressed in it. You may need to go to other sources for some of this information.

3. Summarize the story of the novel.

4. Analyze the plot. Describe the main events and how they came about. Which characters contributed what elements to the way the plot developed? How aware were they of what they were doing?

Note important plot symbols (if any) and comment on their probable meaning.

Then look at the plot in religious terms. Do the symbols have any relation to important religious symbols—cross, tree, tomb, or the like? Does the plot seem to follow any important religious scenario—Joseph Campbell's hero myth, fate or destiny in classical mythology, the Christian redemption by suffering and death, the Buddhist quest for enlightenment, or similar religious themes?

5. Look next at the characters. Describe them, with specific references, showing how they relate or fail to relate to one another and what they experience. Notice especially how they change. Is there religious symbolism or significance in any of this? Do they, like Dostoyevsky's characters, represent character types, good or bad or mixed, that can be understood in common religious terms?—as sinners of the flesh, of the passions, of the intellect, or of the spirit? as penitents or converts? Christ figures or Buddha figures? saints?

6. Summarize whatever fundamental messages or perspectives—on religion, human nature, society—appear to come through from the author.

7. A perhaps optional but possibly very fruitful task would be to look at moral and ethical decisions that are made by one or more of the characters in terms of the categories in Chapter Eight of this book. How are they made? On deontological or consequentialist grounds, or other grounds? What are the results of these decisions? And what about religious decisions, in terms of Chapter Eight? Are they made on the basis of reason, experience, empiricism, authority, sociological factors, or existential choice? How do they stack up against the idea that religious choices are really irrefutable?

8. Finally, look at the novel in terms of a definition of religion that seems appropriate: as scenario for the real self, experience of the holy, salvation, finding a meaningful community, or whatever. Discuss.

Chapter Six: Looking at a Religious Group

This project will be a study of a particular religious group looked at in terms of several kinds of sociological questions. It should be undertaken only after discussion with your instructor, and probably also only after a conference with the clergyman or other leadership of the group. It is not recommended that you undertake a study of a religious group in this way without the full knowledge and consent of the group as expressed through its leadership, and also that of your instructor. This is a big project, requiring several weeks of fairly intensive research. It could be undertaken as a team project by several people working together.

First, here are some things to do during the period of research.

1. Attend most meetings of the group, business as well as worship.

2. Keep notes of what happened at each, and also on attendance—number, age, gender, ethnic background, dress, attitude. Note whether key individuals come alone or with others, and the nature of participation.

3. Pick out those who you find to be leaders in the group, whether officially or unofficially. In meetings and discussions especially, look at how power is distributed and exercised. Observe the symbols of relative prestige of different people, as well as the behavioral clues as to how people are regarded in the group and how they regard it.

4. In worship settings, also look for the things called for in the project above for Chapter Four.

5. Read the important books and literature on the group, both those by the group or sympathetic to it (including its magazines, which can give very helpful insights) and those by outside researchers.

6. Set up several interviews with leaders, key people, and people representative of different classes—for example, age, gender, background, length of experience, basic attitude—in the group. In these interviews, ask them for:

   a. Their own personal life stories, and the stories of their relationships to the group.

   b. History of the group as they know it.

   c. Its teaching as they understand it, especially in terms of what in it is especially significant for them.

   d. What aspects of the worship or other spiritual practices (meditation methods, prayer methods, and so forth) are particularly important?

   e. What interpersonal relationships, or relations to leaders and pastors or spiritual teachers, are especially important (sociologically), and why?

   f. Something of how interviewees see the sociology of the group—how they perceive the kind of people in it, how leadership is exercised and decisions made, what tensions exist, and the group's relationship to the larger community.

Then, correlating all this information, do a paper on the group. It could be outlined as follows:

1. *Identification of Group.* Give its full name and location, and fundamental data: denominational affiliation, size, ethnic make-up, type of building and services, nature of surrounding community, and unusual features.

2. *Nature of Study.* At the outset, tell why you wanted to study this particular group, and what questions you had in mind, or ideas about it you wanted to test. Discuss fully your methodology and the progress of the study, including any problems you ran into. Give exact dates and places of your attendance, interviews, and so on. Tell everything necessary for the reader to know fully how the research was carried out.

3. *History.* As background, give the history of the group, and more briefly, of the denomination or tradition out of which it came. Be sure the history tells *why* the group has the doctrinal and social features it presents today. Include perceptions of its history by members.

4. *Theoretical Expression.* Give the group's doctrinal and narrative expression (for example, significant myths, stories, memories, conversion and healing accounts, and religious "folk wisdom" you heard). This may be based partly on reading, but it will be important to contrast and compare the group's formal statements of belief with what seems to emerge from services and interviews as really significant beliefs to members today. How are these related to the tradition? Analyze sources of authority in teaching, the role of charismatic teachers, and the role of sacred texts.

5. *Practical Expression.* Describe services, using queries similar to those outlined in the project for Chapter Four above.

6. *Sociological Expression.* Again, use queries for analysis similar to those outlined in the project for Chapter Four. Deal with the initiation of new members, leadership, relationship with the larger community, and tensions within the group. Be sure to use interview data—but cautiously, remembering that each person's statements are only one point of view.

7. *Individual Case Studies.* This may be optional, but if you have time and sufficient data, you could select a few individuals within the group and discuss them as case studies in terms of conversion, varying relationships over the years within the group, moving into positions of leadership, and finally, serving as models to others. Ask what

problems and tensions they had to overcome, and why the group was so important to them.

8. *Concluding Reflections.* Here, try to pull together all your observations and reflections, and try to characterize the overall experience of this religious group. In the case of this group, ask if the forms of religious expression seem to work together to create a convincing unified experience, or if there are disconcerting tensions between what these different forms of expression "say"? Is the group stable or unstable, or in between? What sort of future would you project for it? How does it relate to general religious trends in society?

Chapter Seven: Analyzing a Religious Argument

As an exercise for this chapter, write a paper in which you take an important religious concept and show how it might be treated by the different approaches to determining truth in religion. Concepts so tested could be the existence of God, the meaning of Christ's death on the cross, the meaning of the Buddha's enlightenment, the significance of the god Krishna, the importance of religious ritual, and many others. For every concept discussed, ask what each way of determining truth would have to say pro and con, then give each approach a chance to rebut the other.

For example, if the topic was the existence of God, do it like this:

1. Define what you mean, for the sake of this argument, by God and existence.

2. What are the arguments from the standpoint of reason for the existence of God?

3. What are the arguments from the standpoint of reason against the existence of God?

4. How would the pro side rebut the con side?

5. How would the con side rebut the pro side?

Then do the same, in this or other papers, with arguments pro and con from the standpoints of experience, empiricism, authority, sociological factors, and existential choice. (On the last, you will have to ask why anyone would choose to make an existential choice for or against belief in God, or whatever the concept is.)

At the end, you may determine which side has scored the most debating points if you wish—and if you can!

Chapter Eight: Analyzing an Ethical Problem

Write a paper that analyzes a specific case in which an ethical decision must be made. It can be a hypothetical case, one you have read or heard about in the media, or, if you are free to discuss it without violating anyone's confidentiality, a case you know of personally. Here are some possible examples. Fill in the specifics.

- Should an employee report misconduct by another employee of which he or she has knowledge, such as misusing company funds or sexual harassment?

- Should a lawyer suppress or misrepresent important information she or he has uncovered while researching a case in order to help his or her client, even though the suppression of this information will damage an innocent person?

- Should an abortion be performed, or euthanasia permitted, in a particular case?

After describing the case in sufficient detail, being sure to include every fact that could conceivably be relevant to an ethical judgment, give the arguments on both the pro and con sides. Be sure to include the relevant meta-ethical principles behind each: concepts of God and divine command, ideas of personhood, of what life really means, and what you mean by quality of life.

Then tell how a decision would be reached, and what the decision might be, using both deontological and consequentialist principles.

Then give your own judgment and defend it in terms of what principles and methods of deciding seem most important to you. Be sure you make clear why you consider them the most important, and how they work in terms of the specific facts of the case as you have presented it.

Bibliography

The following lists of books present a few suggestions for further reading in several of the areas touched on in this introduction to religious studies. This bibliography should not be thought of as more than a sampling. I am well aware that many pages could be filled with worthwhile titles in any one of these areas. In assembling this bibliography, the needs of undergraduates and other interested but beginning students have been kept uppermost in mind. Thus, I have tried to include not only such books as would be considered best or most significant by specialists but also books that do an especially good job of whetting a budding interest in an area or providing an introductory aperture to it or a useful general overview of its history and current state. Also, some books particularly important for the presentation used in the text of this book have been mentioned. Most of the books given in footnotes have not been repeated here, except for the most important; they are, however, also recommended. Many of these books themselves contain extensive bibliographies in their own fields, to which the reader is referred.

Chapter One

BELLAH, ROBERT. *Beyond Belief: Essays on Religion in a Post-Traditional World.* New York: Harper & Row, Publishers, Inc., 1970.
   A collection of essays by a first-rate modern sociologist of religion, it contains perceptive insights into the meaning of transcendence, religious experience, and civil religion today.

BERGER, PETER L. *The Sacred Canopy.* Garden City, N.Y.: Doubleday Company, Inc., 1969.
A standard presentation of the social construction of reality interpretation of religion's role in human life, with a deep reverence for the validity of religious reality.

BERGSON, HENRI. *The Two Sources of Morality and Religion.* New York: Henry Holt and Co., 1935.
A classic treatment of the ambivalent roots of religion as enforcer of the normative values of society and as producer of the new in prophetic utterance.

ELIADE, MIRCEA. *The Sacred and the Profane.* New York: Harcourt Brace Jovanovich, Inc., 1959.
A modern presentation of religion as centering around the experience of sacred time and sacred space.

LANGER, SUSANNE. *Philosophy in a New Key.* Cambridge, Mass.: Harvard University Press, 1957.
An interpretation of religion, art, and language centering on the importance of symbolism.

SHARPE, ERIC J. *Comparative Religion: A History.* LaSalle, Ill.: Open Court, 1986.
A well-regarded historical survey of the field.

STRENG, FREDERICK J. *Understanding Religious Life*, 3rd ed. Belmont, Calif.: Wadsworth, 1985.
An excellent introduction to religious studies, based on an interpretation of religion as means toward ultimate transformation.

TILLICH, PAUL. *What is Religion?* New York: Harper & Row, Publishers, Inc., 1969.
A great theologian's interpretation of religion as "directedness toward the Unconditional."

VAN DER LEEUW, GERARDUS. *Religion in Essence and Manifestation: A Study in Phenomenology.* New York: Harper & Row, Publishers, Inc., 1963 (first published 1933).
An important presentation of types of religious expression and personality, together with the phenomenological approach that endeavors to see things just as they appear.

WACH, JOACHIM. *Sociology of Religion.* Chicago, Ill.: University of Chicago Press, 1944.
A view of religion in society emphasizing the three forms of religious expression: theoretical, practical, and sociological.

WHITEHEAD, ALFRED NORTH. *Religion in the Making.* New York: The Macmillan Company, 1926.
A prominent philosopher's view of religion as "the art and theory of the internal life of man, so far as it depends on the man himself and on what is permanent in the nature of things."

Chapter Two

DURKHEIM, EMILE. *The Elementary Forms of the Religious Life.* New York: Collier Books, 1961 (first published in French, 1915).
A classic view of primitive religion as an expression of the "mystique" of a group.

ELIADE, MIRCEA. *History of Religious Ideas*, 3 vols., Chicago: University of Chicago Press, 1978–85.
The last major work of an important historian of religion and a valuable summary of religious history.

JASPERS, KARL. *The Origin and Goal of History*. London: Routledge & Kegan Paul, 1953 (first published in German, 1949).
A study presenting the concept of the axial age of transition from prehistoric to historic modes of human consciousness marked by the great religious founders.

LESSA, W. A., AND E. Z. VOGT, EDS. *Reader in Comparative Religion: An Anthropological Approach*. New York: Harper & Row, Publishers, Inc., 1965.
A valuable resource, especially for the material on religious origins, concepts, and roles in societies.

MACQUARRIE, JOHN. *Twentieth Century Religious Thought*. New York: Harper & Row, Publishers, Inc., 1963.
A very competent overview, surveying nineteenth- as well as twentieth-century theology and philosophy of religion.

NORBECK, EDWARD. *Religion in Primitive Society*. New York: Harper & Row, Publishers, Inc., 1961.
A good introduction that includes discussion of the origin of religion in anthropological thought and emphasizes religious concepts and religion's role in societies.

OTTO, RUDOLF. *The Idea of the Holy*. Trans. J.W. HARVEY. Oxford: Oxford University Press, 1923, reprints.
A classic work emphasizing religion as a "non-rational" response to "the Other."

TYLOR, EDWARD B. *Primitive Culture*, 2 vols. London: J. Murray, 1973 (several reprints).
The second volume of this pioneering anthropological classic deals with religion and presents the theory of religion's origin in animism, or belief in souls in persons and objects.

WILSON, EDWARD O. *On Human Nature*. Cambridge, Mass.: Harvard University Press, 1978.
A controversial but important book on the biological basis of human culture with a major chapter on religion. It argues that traits such as altruism and religion have biological origin based on their survival value for the species.

Chapter Three

ALLPORT, GORDON. *The Individual and His Religion*. New York: The Macmillan Company, 1950.
A standard text that is especially important for its treatment of stages of religious development.

CRAPPS, ROBERT W. *Introduction to Psychology of Religion*. Macon, Ga.: Mercer University Press, 1986.
An excellent introductory textbook.

FREUD, SIGMUND. *The Future of an Illusion*. Garden City, N.Y.: Doubleday, 1957, reprints.
A short essay that introduces the reader to basic Freudian perspectives on religion.

HOMANS, PETER. *Theology After Freud*. Indianapolis: Bobbs-Merrill, 1970.
An important study of how theologians and interpreters of culture like Niebuhr, Tillich, and others have written about religion in the light of Freudianism.

JAMES, WILLIAM. *Varieties of Religious Experience*. New York and London: Longmans, Green and Co., 1902 (reprinted several times).

A classic on the psychological interpretation of religion full of case studies in religious experience.

JUNG, C.G. *Modern Man in Search of a Soul*. New York: Harcourt, Brace, 1933, reprints.
An essential essay touching on many aspects of Jung's position on religion.

LEWIS, I. M. *Ecstatic Religion*. Harmondsworth, England: Penguin Books, 1971.
A valuable study of shamanism and ecstasy in religion, especially in their role among oppressed groups.

MALONEY, H. NEWTON, ED. *Current Perspectives in the Psychology of Religion*. Grand Rapids, Mich.: Eerdmans, 1977.
An excellent survey of important ideas by the important writers.

MASLOW, ABRAHAM S. *Religions, Values, and Peak Experiences*. Columbus: Ohio State University Press, 1964.
An influential statement of the view that psychology should start, in its view of human potentials, with the peak experiences—which have much in common with classic mystical and religious experiences.

ULANOV, ANN BELFORD AND BARRY ULANOV. *Religion and the Unconscious*. Philadelphia: Westminister, 1975.
A discussion of the interpretation of religion from many different psychoanalytic and psychological perspectives; a splendid introduction in depth to the contemporary schools and thinkers.

Chapter Four

CASSIRER, ERNST. *The Philosophy of Symbolic Forms*, 3 vols. New Haven, Conn.: Yale University Press, 1953–57 (first published in German, 1923–29).
A basic philosophical statement of the importance of symbol in communication and society.

ELIADE, MIRCEA. *Images and Symbols*. London: Harvil Press, 1961.
An interpretation of the subject by a distinguished historian of religion.

———. *Rites and Symbols of Initiation: The Mysteries of Birth and Rebirth*. New York: Harper & Row, Publishers, Inc., 1975.
The Interaction of ritual and symbol in perhaps the most important of all religious contexts: a wealth of vivid illustrative material.

FIRTH, RAYMOND. *Symbols: Public and Private*. Ithaca, N.Y.: Cornell University Press, 1973.
An important discussion by a leading anthropologist, with many concrete examples.

HUBERT, HENRI, AND MARCEL MAUSS. *Sacrifice: Its Nature and Function*. Chicago, Ill.: University of Chicago Press, 1964 (first published in French, 1899).
A classic study of one of the most important types of religious rite.

JUNG, CARL, ET AL. *Man and His Symbols*. Garden City, N.Y.: Doubleday & Company, Inc., 1964.
A lavishly illustrated introduction to the subject from the Jungian perspective.

LÉVI-STRAUSS, CLAUDE. *Structural Anthropology*. Garden City, N.Y.: Doubleday Anchor Books, 1967.
An essential introduction to the structuralist approach to myth, culture, and religion, showing how they are all made up of component parts in significant and balanced relationships to serve as "languages."

MIDDLETON, JOHN, ED. *Gods and Rituals*. Austin, Tex.: University of Texas Press, 1976.
A valuable collection of anthropological papers.

OLSON, ALAN M., ED. *Myth, Symbol, and Reality.* Notre Dame, Ind. Notre Dame University Press, 1980.
A good overview of recent theories on symbols.

TURNER, VICTOR. *The Ritual Process.* Chicago, Ill.: Aldine Publishing Co., 1969.
A stimulating interpretation of ritual and religious experience based on the idea of *liminality,* or going outside of the limits of structure.

Chapter Five

BRANDON, S.G.F. *Man and God in Art and Ritual.* New York: Scribner's, 1975.
A well-illustrated, comprehensive, worldwide survey for the general reader by a noted historian of religion.

BROWN, FRANK BURCH. *Transfiguration: Poetic Metaphor and the Language of Religious Belief.* Chapel Hill, N.C.: University of North Carolina Press, 1983.
A high-level study showing how poetry and religion can help interpret one another.

CROSSAN, JOHN DOMINIC. *The Dark Interval: Towards a Theology of Story.* Argus, Tex.: Argus Communications, 1975.
Story, especially parables, as a means of religious communication which undercuts conventional views of the world and so makes way for transcendence.

DAVIES, HORTON AND HUGH DAVIES. *Sacred Art in a Secular Century.* Collegeville, Minn.: Liturgical Press, 1978.
An excellent and accessible study of modern religious painting.

DILLENBERGER, JANE. *Image and Spirit in Sacred and Secular Art.* New York: Crossroad, 1990.
An important discussion, with special emphasis on the human and particularly the feminine image in Western religious art.

ELLISON, JEROME. *God on Broadway.* Richmond, Va.: John Knox Press, 1971.
Great modern American plays in religious analysis, including Archibald McLeish's *J.B.* (a modern retelling of Job) and Eugene O'Neill's, *The Great God Brown.*

GUNN, GILES. *The Interpretation of Otherness: Literature, Religion and the American Imagination.* New York: Oxford University Press, 1979.
A collection of essays by a major specialist in religion and literature.

LACEY, PAUL A. *The Inner War: Forms and Themes in Recent American Poetry.* Philadelphia: Fortress Press, 1972.
A perceptive analysis of important American twentieth-century poets from a religionist perspective.

LYNCH, WILLIAM F. *Christ and Apollo: The Dimensions of the Literary Imagination.* New York: Sheed & Ward, 1960.
A classic work, discussing such topics as tragedy and comedy in their spiritual dimensions, the use of analogy, and religious and literary meanings of time.

MOORE, ALBERT C. *Iconography of Religions: An Introduction.*
A very good worldwide study of painting and sculpture in all major religions.

NORMAN, EDWARD. *The House of God.* New York: Thames and Hudson, 1990.
A well-illustrated survey of the styles and history of Christian church architecture.

ROSS-BRYANT, LYNN. *Imagination and the Life of the Spirit: An Introduction to the Study of Religion and Literature,* Chico, Calif.: Scholars Press, 1981.
An excellent introductory text to this field.

SCOTT, NATHAN. *The Broken Center.* New Haven: Yale University Press, 1966.

A representative book by a leading religion and literature theorist; this one stresses modern literature as reflecting a crisis of values.

TeSelle, Sallie McFague. *Literature and the Christian Life*. New Haven: Yale University Press, 1966.

A valuable essay, emphasizing that novels are about "experiencing" ranges of possibilities and creating a human image, which in turn can relate to religion.

Van der Leeuw, Gerardus. *Sacred and Profane Beauty: The Holy in Art*. New York: Holt, Rinehart and Winston, 1963.

A classic survey of many arts and their meaning from a history-of-religions point of view.

Von Balthasar, Hans Urs. *Theo-Drama*. San Francisco: Ignatius Press, 1988.

A very substantial work on drama and religion by a prominent German Roman Catholic theologian.

Chapter Six

Ellwood, Robert S., and Harry B. Partin. *Religious and Spiritual Groups in Modern America*. Englewood Cliffs, N.J.: Prentice-Hall, Inc., 2nd ed., 1988.

Presents a number of contemporary groups of the cult or emergent-expansive type, with emphasis on the nature of experience within them.

Festinger, Leon, Henry W. Riecken, and Stanley Schacter. *When Prophecy Fails*. Minneapolis: University of Minnesota Press, 1956.

A fascinating study of social process in a UFO group.

Greeley, Andrew. *The Denominational Society*. Glenview, Ill.: Scott, Foresman and Company, 1973.

An introductory book on sociology of religion in America.

Johnstone, Ronald L. *Religion and Society in Interaction*. Englewood Cliffs, N.J.: Prentice-Hall, Inc., 1975.

A good introductory textbook on the sociology of religion.

Lewy, Guenter. *Religion and Revolution*. Oxford: Oxford University Press, 1974.

Seventeen case studies from ancient China and biblical Israel to Gandhi and the modern world which illuminate the role that religion can have in dreams and achievement of radical social change.

McGuire, Meredith B. *Religion: The Social Context*. Belmont, Calif.: Wadsworth Publishing Co., Inc., 1981.

Another excellent introductory textbook.

O'Dea, Thomas F. *Sociology and the Study of Religion: Theory, Research, Interpretation*. New York: Basic Books, 1970.

Case studies on American Catholicism and Mormonism, and discussion of theoretical topics by a leading sociologist of religion, make this book an excellent introduction to quality writing in the field.

Wach, Joachim. *Sociology of Religion*. Chicago, Ill.: University of Chicago Press, 1944.

A survey of religious forms of expression and of types of groups.

Weber, Max. *Sociology of Religion*. Boston: Beacon Press, 1963.

A collection of fundamental writings of one of the seminal figures of the field.

Wilson, Bryan, Ed. *Patterns of Sectarianism*. London: Heinemann, 1967.

An important presentation of material on sectarian movements of various types, indicating that they are not all the same in derivation or style.

Yinger, Milton. *The Scientific Study of Religion*. New York: The Macmillan Company, 1970.

A comprehensive statement of classic categories—church, sect, and so on—in the sociology of religion.

Chapter Seven

BARBOUR, IAN. *Religion in an Age of Science*. San Francisco: Harper & Row, 1990.
Splendid discussion of the heavyweight science and religion issues—the "big bang," creation, God, evolution, and others.

BRANDON, S. G. F. *The Judgment of the Dead: The Idea of Life After Death in the Major Religions*. New York: Charles Scribner's Sons, 1967.
A good example of the study of a major conceptual matter in a cross-religious context.

CARNELL, EDWARD JOHN. *The Case for Orthodox Theology*. Philadelphia, Pa.: The Westminster Press, 1959.
An example of conservative evangelical religious thought; this author means by *orthodox theology* that which limits the grounds of religious authority to the Bible.

DEWART, LESLIE. *The Foundations of Belief*. New York: Herder and Herder, Inc., 1969.
A philosophy of religion by a modern Roman Catholic. The basic idea is that essence is the relation of being to consciousness; God as pure essence or reality as such is the reality in relation to which any other reality is real.

HESCHEL, ABRAHAM JOSHUA. *God in Search of Man*. New York: Farrar, Straus & Cudahy, 1955.
A "philosophy of Judaism" by one of the most revered modern interpreters of the religion.

HICK, JOHN. *Death and Eternal Life*. New York: Harper & Row, Publishers, Inc., 1977.
A well-received, groundbreaking Christian discussion of life after death that draws on data from philosophy, world religions, and psychical research.

————. *Philosophy of Religion*. Englewood Cliffs, N.J.: Prentice-Hall, Inc., 1963.
A highly competent introduction to the field.

HUXLEY, ALDOUS. *The Perennial Philosophy*. New York: Harpers, 1944.
A powerful statement of the view that God as impersonal consciousness realized in mystical experience is the foundation of all existence.

MACKINTOSH, HUGH ROSS. *Types of Modern Theology: Schleiermacher to Barth*. London: Nisbet and Co., 1947.
An excellent introduction to the most talked about modern Protestant theologians.

ROSS, FLOYD, AND TYNETTE HILLS. *Questions that Matter Most Answered by the World's Religions*. Boston, Mass.: Beacon Press, 1954.
A simple and direct statement of what the great religions teach about the meaning and goal of human life; good as an introduction to a study of comparative religious concepts.

Chapter Eight

BEAUCHAMP, TOM L., AND SEYMOUR PERLIN, EDS. *Ethical Issues in Death and Dying*. Englewood Cliffs, N.J.: Prentice-Hall, 1978.
Practical papers on the religious and legal aspects of the topics.

BORCHERT, DONALD M. AND DAVID STEWARD. *Exploring Ethics*. New York: The Macmillan Company, 1986.

A good textbook, especially useful for surveys of important traditional ethical positions.

CARMODY, DENISE LARDNER. *Women and World Religions*. Nashville: Abingdon, 1979.

Important though frequently depressing information for feminist religious thought: a survey of the position of women in the major world religions.

CARMODY, JOHN. *Ecology and Religion*. New York: Paulist Press, 1983.

A survey of this important contemporary topic.

CHRIST, CAROL P., ED. *Diving Deep and Surfacing: Women Writers on the Spiritual Quest*. Boston: Beacon Press, 1980.

A fascinating and important collection of women's viewpoints of religion. See also other works written or coedited by this writer.

COBB, JOHN B. *Matters of Life and Death*. Louisville: Westminster/John Knox Press, 1991.

Innovative thinking by a major theologian on sexual and end-of-life ethical issues.

DALY, MARY. *Beyond God the Father*. Boston: Beacon Press, 1973.

A controversial pioneering book in feminist theology.

FRANKENA, WILLIAM K. *Ethics*, 2nd ed. Englewood Cliffs, N.J.: Prentice-Hall, 1973.

A standard textbook, very helpful for understanding basic categories and concepts.

ODEN, THOMAS C. *Should Treatment Be Terminated?* New York: Harper & Row, 1976.

A discussion of these difficult cases by a theologian and religious ethicist.

OUTKA, GENE H. AND PAUL RAMSEY, EDS. *Norm and Context in Christian Ethics*. New York: Scribner's, 1968.

A collection of papers on various important ethical topics by two prominent ethicists, showing diversities of theoretical approach.

PENCE, GREGORY E. *Classic Cases in Medical Ethics*. New York: McGraw-Hill, 1990.

An invaluable real-life casebook, with insightful discussion.

PLASKOW, JUDITH. *Standing Again at Sinai: Judaism from a Feminist Perspective*. San Francisco: Harper & Row, 1990.

A groundbreaking book on this subject.

SMITH, HARMON L. *Ethics and the New Medicine*. Nashville: Abingdon, 1970.

Chapters on abortion, artificial insemination, organ transplants, and care of the dying.

For books on liberation theology see Footnote 15 in Chapter Eight above.

GLOSSARY

Here are some words used in this book that may be new to you or whose use in religious studies may not be clear. If there are any others, be sure to look them up in a dictionary.

Actualizing Acts and attitudes which make a reality visible and felt.

Anthropomorphic Having human form.

Archetype A form which especially emphasizes the original, eternal, supreme significance of something. In religious studies which are influenced by Jungian thought, it may refer especially to the psychological *type* represented by a deity or other sacred figure: for example, the Great Mother, the Wise Old Man, the Hero, the Maiden, the "Shadow," or Satan.

Audio symbols Symbols in the form of sounds or words rather than something seen.

Authority In religion, acceptance of a particular source of knowledge as reliable beyond doubt because of divine guarantees.

Bhakti The devotional tradition in Hinduism, especially noted for its emotional love and fervor.

Cargo cults Religious movements, usually under the leadership of a native prophet, common in colonial areas. They believe that if the natives follow certain prescriptions, such as a dance or destroying their present possessions, they will be sent abundant new riches like those on the white man's ships.

Chanoyu The Japanese "tea ceremony" associated with the Zen Buddhist tradition; its way of doing simple, natural acts gracefully and mindfully is expressive of Zen spiritual values.

Civil religion Beliefs and practices presenting a country as a whole, such as the United States, as having a sacred meaning apart from the sacredness of individual religious institutions.

Conceptual verbal audio symbols Words having symbolic power in which the emphasis is on the meaning of the words and their associations, such as in story, myth, doctrine, and religious rhetoric.

Consequentialist ethics Another name for teleological ethics.

Content message What a statement says explicitly.

Conversion In religion, a major change in one's faith often effected by a powerful experience, long or short, in which the new symbols of transcendence come through strongly as true and vital.

Cosmogenic myth A myth of the origin of the universe.

Denomination A structurally independent institutional and sociological organization within a larger religious tradition, usually holding an interpretation of the religion distinctive in certain particulars and frequently having its main strength in a particular country or culture.

Deontological ethics The ethics of "ought," based on a prior sense of duty or obligation, usually seen as deriving from divine command, from right reason, and/or from what is made incumbent on humans by their nature or natural law.

Doctrine Expression of the beliefs of a religion in propositional verbal form, as statements of truth.

Emergent religion A new religious movement arising out of established religion, typically characterized by a charismatic leader, a simple definite belief and practice, and future orientation.

Empiricism Direct observation and experimentation in the external world as a means for determining truth.

Established religion The dominant institutional religion of a society.

Existentialist From existentialism, a philosophy popular just after World War II but having roots in the work of earlier thinkers such as Kierkegaard;

it emphasizes the need of each person to determine his or her own "existence" or real being (real self) through decision and action. In religious existentialism, this action is taken through a free decision for faith and corresponding action.

Existential choice Religious faith recognized as freely given commitment, on the grounds that religious truth is not discoverable by outside means but only in the context of commitment to faith. The existential choice itself is choosing faith as the fulfillment of one's existence on the basis of no "proof" which acts as a compulsion, but as a free decision.

Expansive emergent religion Religious movements which borrow from several sources, often combining new and familiar features.

Experience In religion, what has happened to one or what one has lived through, particularly "religious experience"—moments of great realization, awakening, and emotional power attributed to direct encounter with transcendent reality—used as a basis for determining truth in religion.

Focal symbols Symbols specific to a religion which focus and express its major meaning or an important aspect of it and/or which have come to identify it to adherents and often outsiders.

Founder The originator of a new major religion.

Fundamentalist style Way of putting religious statements which indicates they must be taken literally and consistently with each other within the religious system, regardless of tension with outside worldviews.

General symbols Symbols which have religious meaning, often the same kind of meaning, in several religions.

God or god A self-conscious center of being, knowledge, and power superior to humanity, upon which ordinary humans must depend and have relations of prayer and offerings for their well-being.

Great tradition The religious life of a religion's elite, oriented toward the values of literacy, historical awareness, and the culture's artistic and political traditions.

Guilt In religion, a sense of having done wrong by violating the laws or expectations of God or Ultimate Reality; a sense of guilt may be followed by repentance or serious renouncing of that wrongdoing and by conversion or rebirth.

Hero/savior myth A myth of a person who, through great ordeal, works to restore the right relations between humanity and Ultimate Reality by defeating forces of evil, effecting redemption, or clearing and showing the way.

Icon   In the Eastern Orthodox tradition of Christianity, a stylized portrait of a religious figure used as a focus of worship.

Impersonal absolute   The divine conceived of as a pure being and consciousness without particularized thoughts or personality.

Initiation   A rite of passage which marks a transition from one stage of life to another. In religion, rites of initiation from childhood to adulthood are very common, as are rites of initiation (or experiences of initiation) into states of specialty in the sacred, such as that of a shaman or priest. Initiatory scenarios vary, but often they are quite intense experiences, involving isolation of the candidate, an ordeal such as fasting or even scourging, a physical transformation such as circumcision or knocking out a tooth, and an opportunity for experiencing the divine in dream or vision. After initiation, one is incorporated into society again in the new role.

Intensive emergent religion   Religious movements which stress a strict, devout following of the prevailing religion.

Intentionalism   The doctrine that ethics should be judged by the doer's intentions as well as, or instead of, the consequences.

International religion   A religious movement or institution spread through many countries, like Christianity or Islam.

Kagura   Shinto sacred dance.

Layperson   An ordinary member of a religion with no special office.

Liberal style   Way of putting religious statements which indicates their meaning must be consistent with the best current scientific and philosophical thought; often emphasizes a nonliteral interpretation of them.

Liminality, Liminal state   Being outside the ordinary structures of society, as is a novice during initiation or a wanderer during most of life; also called *marginality*.

Little tradition   Folk or popular religion; the nonliterate religion of ordinary people oriented toward the present, the seasonal round, the local place.

Liturgy   The text of a structured, frequently conventional and traditional religious rite, such as the Roman Catholic Mass or Anglican worship. Many parts of this kind of worship are often sung. **Liturgical**: pertaining to worship of this kind.

Magic   In religious studies, this word is generally used to mean producing desired results or controlling events by manipulating supernatural forces or beings through symbols such as charms, spells, and rituals thought to have an irresistible power over them. Magic differs from religion by working for particular limited ends rather than expressing the full nature of transcendent reality; it stresses power over the supernatural rather than oneness with it or devotional service toward it; and it desires that power for particular goals rather than full salvation, liberation, or real selfhood. But in practice, the line between magic and religion is often blurry.

Mahayana The "northern" tradition of Buddhism, predominant in China, Korea, Japan, and neighboring areas; it has many Buddhas and bodhisattvas and emphasizes many paths to enlightenment, Nirvana here and now, and the "buddha nature" in all things.

Mantra In Hinduism and Buddhism, a short chanted formula held to have particular sacred power, as for evoking a particular deity.

Meditation Calming the mind through withdrawal of sensuous stimuli and focusing awareness on one thing or voidness; often used to induce religious states of consciousness or valued in itself as religious and a means of getting in touch with religious reality.

Meta-ethics The philosophical or religious worldview, the view of God, nature, or Ultimate Reality, that underlies an ethical system.

Monk and nun Men and women respectively who live a life wholly devoted to spirituality; to this end they may be celibate, embrace poverty, and live in communities of persons devoted to the same end. They dedicate much time to prayer and meditation, though they may also study, do manual labor, and administer monastic holdings. Some, like the sadhus of India, may be wanderers or hermits as well as members of communities.

Mystic One whose spiritual life emphasizes states of consciousness considered direct, unmediated experience of religious reality.

Mystical, Mysticism In religion and religious studies, mysticism is usually taken to mean an experience interpreted by the experiencer as direct, immediate contact with Ultimate Reality, usually in terms of a profound awareness of oneness with that reality. In their classical form, mystical experiences are not so much emotional—as conversion and various other religious experiences may sometimes be—as deep, quiet experiences of awareness and of unity with that of which one is aware; commonly the experience is said to be beyond words.[1]

Myth In religious studies, a story which expresses in narrative form important aspects of the religion's and the culture's view of the universe and the human place in it, in relation to God or the gods.

[1] See my book, *Mysticism and Religion* (Englewood Cliffs, N.J.: Prentice-Hall, Inc., 1980), especially Chapter Two, for a fuller explication of this definition.

National religion   A religion basically limited to one country.

Natural Law   Principles with ethical implications derived from nature by reason alone, based on what appears to be the given predisposition or purpose of a thing, such as that humans are meant to live in families and that sexuality is intended for procreation.

Nirvana   The Buddhist term for absolute unconditioned reality.

Nonconceptual verbal audio symbols   Words, such as chants, having symbolic power in which the emphasis is on the sound rather than the meaning.

Nonverbal audio symbols   Sounds such as music, bells, and the like which have symbolic power but are not verbal.

Numinous   A quality of mystery, terror, and fascination often ascribed to the sacred.

Peak experience   Abraham Maslow's term for a "self-validating" state of intensity and joy in which one is completely fulfilled in the present; often compared to mystical states in religion.

Personal monotheism   Belief in one God who is personal, that is, able to think particular thoughts, will particular ends, and favor particular things deliberately, as well as give and respond to love and service.

Pluralistic   Having more than one example, as a society in which it is evident there is more than one religion.

Polytheism   Belief in many gods; a different way of experiencing the transcendent than monotheism, polytheism stresses the different nature of the divine in different times, places, and situations.

Popularizer   One who labors to bring the central message of a religion, as he or she understands it, to the ordinary people.

Priest   A person who performs religious rites and services as a specialist; their effect does not depend on his or her fervor or psychic state but only on the office. Priesthood may be hereditary, and facility is acquired by training, not necessarily by shamanistic call and initiatory ordeal.

Private symbol   A symbol which has special meaning for a particular individual because of its association with his or her personal life.

Prophet   A religious speaker or writer who is believed to speak with the voice of God to denounce evils, predict future events, call for justice, and comfort the afflicted.

Public symbol   A symbol which has a generally accepted meaning for a community, usually through association with a major institution.

Reason The unbiased use of logical analysis based on objectives, unquestioned premises to establish truth.

Rebirth A spiritual experience which is interpreted as spiritually parallel to physical birth, in that the individual is seen as a "new person" before God or the gods, now in the right relationship with Ultimate Reality, whereas before he or she was not.

Reformer One who strives to make major changes of faith, practice, and organizational structure within an ongoing religious tradition.

Religion Human networks or collections of ideas, attitudes, acts, social patterns, and other symbols expressing the nature of transcendent reality and what humans are in relation to it, and intended to draw power from that reality and that relation.

Religious Expression, Three Forms of:

Theoretical Expression in words and ideas, as in religious doctrines, philosophies, myths, and lore.

Practical Expression in practices, such as worship, rite, prayer, meditation, pilgrimage, and costume.

Sociological Expression in groups, institutions, social relations (as between spiritual leader and follower), and relation of the religion to the larger social order.

Religious group A set of people whose interpersonal relations are a part of one another's religious experience and who enact some religious activity together.

Religious rhetoric Religious language, as in preaching or inspirational writing, intended to trigger responses of belief and experience in recipients.

Rite A religious performance, such as a sacrifice or worship service, usually done by and for a group and usually "orchestrating" symbols in several media—for example, words, music, symbols together—which enacts the transcendent reality of the religion, making it seem present or easily accessible.

Ritual The pattern of words and actions through which a rite is carried out.

Sacrament A specific, visible action and object believed to convey divine grace and power, such as baptism or holy communion in Christianity.

Sacred Dedicated to religious purposes, as a shrine; in religious studies, the sacred often refers to the whole network of elements which stands against the ordinary or "profane" to symbolize the transcendent, as in the concepts of sacred space and sacred time.

Secondary specific symbols   Symbols particular to a religion but less important than focal symbols, such as those representing a particular god, saint, or doctrine.

Shaman   A religious specialist in primitive religion who typically attains his or her vocation by divine call and arduous initiation, then with the aid of helping spirits heals, tells the future, and contacts gods and departed souls in rites involving trance.

Sign   An indicator which merely points to what it indicates but does not share in its nature.

Sociology   The study of human societies or social units large and small in terms of their structure, processes, and interaction with other social units, with a view to looking for general principles that govern them.

Soul   An immaterial substance often conceived by religions to be within the self, as its ultimate identity, its place of rapport with transcendent reality, and often as that which bears one's moral record and leaves the body to incarnate in another after death or to experience heaven or hell.

Spiritism   Belief in spirits good and bad; they are invisible, limited, and localized entities with some supernatural power.

State of consciousness   A particular separate, discrete activity or "feel" of mind, such as concentration, daydreaming, or sleep.

Structural message   What a statement says by the way it is put and the context.

Subjective   Having to do with one's inner feelings, attitudes, ideas, and state of consciousness or with the life of the mind and emotions; subjectivity can be expressed outwardly only through some symbol: behavior, gesture, rite, speech.

Subuniverses   Areas of life in which particular "rules" and attitudes prevail which do not occur outside that realm, such as play, work, worship, etc.

Sufi   Common name for a mystic in the Islamic tradition.

Supernaturalism   Belief in that which is "above nature"; although the term can refer to ghosts and anything else which does not conform to natural law, in religious philosophy supernature is much the same as the transcendent.

Symbol   That which properly both reminds one of something, such as the transcendent or a loved one, and evokes feelings and behavior appropriate to it. A symbol therefore is more than a sign. It does not just give information; it calls forth a response and, like the image of a deity, may even virtually become that which it symbolizes. Religious symbols are often polyvalent, that is, having more than one meaning at the same time.

Teleological ethics Ethics based on the principle that the result of an action is that by which it should be judged.

Theology The study of God.

Theriomorphic Having animal form.

Traditionalist style Way of putting religious statements that emphasizes their being part of a longstanding religious tradition with strong links to the society's culture and history, and in which many people participate out of deep-rooted family or ethnic ties.

Transcendence Being above ordinary human knowledge and ordinary perception and reality; in religion the transcendent is usually identified with Ultimate Reality, that which one cannot go beyond: God, the absolute, existence itself. Under it all else is partial and "conditioned," or limited by being in only one place, one time, and one mode of being, and by boundaries of knowledge and ability.

Utilitarianism The doctrine that ethics should be based on "the greatest good to the greatest number."

Yantras In Hinduism, abstract diagrams that can represent certain deities.

Zen An East Asian tradition of Buddhism emphasizing mindfulness and closeness to nature.

Index